PUNISHING
RACE

PUNISHING RACE

A Continuing American Dilemma

Michael Tonry

UNIVERSITY PRESS

2011

OXFORD

UNIVERSITY PRESS

Oxford University Press, Inc., publishes works that further
Oxford University's objective of excellence
in research, scholarship, and education.

Oxford   New York
Auckland   Cape Town   Dar es Salaam   Hong Kong   Karachi
Kuala Lumpur   Madrid   Melbourne   Mexico City   Nairobi
New Delhi   Shanghai   Taipei   Toronto

With offices in
Argentina   Austria   Brazil   Chile   Czech Republic   France   Greece
Guatemala   Hungary   Italy   Japan   Poland   Portugal   Singapore
South Korea   Switzerland   Thailand   Turkey   Ukraine   Vietnam

Published by Oxford University Press, Inc.
198 Madison Avenue, New York, New York 10016

www.oup.com

Oxford is a registered trademark of Oxford University Press

Library of Congress Cataloging-in-Publication Data
Tonry, Michael H.
Punishing race : a continuing American dilemma / Michael Tonry.
p. cm.
Includes bibliographical references and index.
ISBN 978-0-19-975137-2
1. Criminal justice, Administration of—United States.
2. Discrimination in criminal justice administration—United States.
3. Crime and race—United States.   I. Title.
HV9950.T667 2011
364.973089—dc22   2010015822

1   3   5   7   9   8   6   4   2

Printed in the United States of America
on acid-free paper

CONTENTS

PREFACE

This book is about racial injustice in the American criminal justice system generally and about racial disparities in imprisonment in particular. Racial injustices are, by definition, wrong. They do harm to individuals, and they do harm to America's ongoing mission to ameliorate the persisting effects of slavery, racial discrimination, and bigotry.

Those effects persist, and that is not surprising. The first important federal civil rights legislation was enacted less than a half century ago, in 1964. Explicit appeals to race in elections disappeared only a decade later. Barely forty years have passed since George Wallace, in an openly racist campaign, in 1968 received 13.5 percent of the presidential vote and won five southern states. In 1966 Georgians elected as their governor a man, Lester Maddox, who was most famous for vowing to stand in the door of his restaurant, axe handle in hand, to greet black people who dared try to eat there. Constitutionally barred from reelection, Maddox was elected lieutenant governor in 1970.

Long before open appeals to racism disappeared from American politics, conservative Republicans fashioned the "Southern Strategy," a deliberate attempt to focus on issues—initially states' rights and later crime, welfare fraud, busing, and affirmative action—that everyone understood were coded appeals to whites' antiblack animus, anxiety, and resentment. The roots of the Southern Strategy lay in the 1940s, but the term came into use only in the 1960s. Republican presidential candidate Barry Goldwater in 1964 was the first to implement the strategy in a national election. In retrospect few people deny that.

It would be easy to dismiss these people—many Americans under forty-five probably recognize few of their names—and the things they did as ancient history, but that misses a major point. Although it is true that few whites any longer believe in white supremacy or the racial inferiority of black people, and that mainstream political candidates no longer make open appeals to racism, it is also true that too many black Americans are poor, disadvantaged, undereducated, and underemployed. Those realities have everything to do with race.

When racial discrimination ceased to be legal, and later on, when white beliefs about black inferiority substantially disappeared, large percentages of black Americans were poor, ill educated, and either unemployed or locked into menial unskilled jobs. That was not surprising. Blacks were long excluded by bias and discrimination from much that was good in American life. And so, of course, they were less well-off than whites.

An optimist in 1964, however, would have predicted that by 2000 blacks would catch up. Descendants of European immigrants normally were fully assimilated into American life and distinguishable, if at all, only by their surnames two generations after their grandparents arrived. If black Americans had been given a fair playing field on which to compete they too should have been fully assimilated, and indistinguishable from other Americans except for the pigment in their skin, within two generations after the great victories of the civil rights movement.

That didn't happen. On every demographic measure of well-being—life expectancy, infant mortality, income, education, employment, home ownership—black people in America are substantially worse off than whites. The reasons for that are inextricably caught up in the politics of race, and the public policies they engendered. No serious informed person on the right or the left, for example, any longer questions that federal housing policies on red-lining and mortgage eligibility long made it impossible for many urban black people to buy homes. The effect was to corral black Americans in deteriorating urban ghettos. Few remember the welfare rules in the 1960s and 1970s that made women ineligible to receive benefits for themselves and their children if there was a "man in the house." The effect was to break up couples and establish a pattern that persists to this day of poor black single-parent female-headed households. And American drug and crime control policies since the mid-1970s, the subject of this book, have disabled poor young black men from successful participation in American life and thereby damaged not only them but also their children, their families, and their communities.

The supporting statistics are legion. The U.S. Department of Justice predicts that one in three black baby boys born in 2001 will spend part of his life as an inmate in a state or federal prison. At any time in the first decade of the twenty-first century one-third of young black men in their twenties were in jail or prison or on probation or parole. Imprisonment rates for black men have for a quarter century been five to seven times higher than those for white men.

The explanations for those patterns are complex, but they collapse into three generalizations. First, the characteristics of people, black or white (or Hispanic), who commit crimes, and who go to prison, are exactly the same: disadvantaged childhoods, child abuse, unstable home lives, bad educations, lack of employable skills, and drug and alcohol dependence. These things, however, are much more likely to afflict or to characterize black than white Americans. Second, legislators have devised policies (e.g., the War on Drugs, crack cocaine sentencing laws) and police have developed practices (e.g., racial profiling, emphasizing drug arrests in inner-city neighborhoods) that hit blacks much harder than whites. Third, policy makers in the past twenty years have enacted laws (e.g., three-strikes, truth-in-sentencing, and mandatory-minimum sentence laws) that require prison sentences of historically unprecedented lengths for crimes for which black Americans are disproportionately likely to be arrested and convicted.

The history of American race relations has everything to do with each of those generalizations. Black people in the 1960s had to begin individual efforts to improve their social and economic lives from points well behind the starting line. They then found that housing, employment, and other forms of discrimination persisted, as they do to this day. By the 1980s the politics of racial resentment had led to the weakening of policies such as school integration, affirmative action, and equal employment opportunity that were meant to help blacks overcome the legacies of racism and slavery. Many more blacks than

whites were and are handicapped by the social and economic characteristics that lead to crime.

Black Americans, however, use illegal drugs less often than whites do.
The best evidence is that blacks are no more—probably less—involved
in drug dealing. Black people are more involved in violent crime than
are whites, but less so than in earlier times. In relation to drug offending,
criminal justice policies cause disparities in imprisonment. In relation
to violent crime, criminal justice policies worsen them.

The question I examine in this book is, how come? How did it happen that a long series of criminal justice policies that do special damage
to black people were conceived, adopted, and carried out in a country
in which few whites any longer believe in white supremacy or black
inferiority?

The answers after several decades of political and cognitive denial
are becoming clear, largely because of work by a generation of young
scholars in their twenties and thirties who looked afresh at problems
that most older people in emperor's-new-clothes style could not or
would not see. The explanations operate at two levels.

At the first level are features of modern American culture. A large
and diverse literature on the psychology of American race relations
shows that many white Americans resent efforts made to help black
Americans overcome the legacy of racism, and that stereotypes of black
criminality support whites' attitudes toward crime, criminals, and drug
and crime control policies. Sociological and historical literatures on
racial stratification show that whites have, unthinkingly but consistently, initiated and supported policies that advantage whites and disadvantage blacks. Finally, recent work by historians and political scientists
shows how the Republican Southern Strategy, which was shaped by and
worsened those problems, led to the adoption of the policies that have
done so much damage to the life chances of poor black Americans.

At the second level are deeper features of American politics and
government. One is what historian Richard Hofstadter long ago called
the "paranoid streak in American politics," a recurring phenomenon
in which proponents of particular views see the other side as a vast
conspiracy and believe that only way forward is to fight to the political
death. A second is the influence of Evangelical Protestantism, which

sees crucial issues in moral terms of right and wrong and is likewise often closed to the possibility of compromise. The third is a structure of government, unique among developed Western countries, in which judges and prosecutors are elected officials and government policy making about crime is not insulated from influence by short-term emotions and politics. These three elements created a political climate that was long on vindictiveness and short on empathy, and governmental institutions that were quick to adopt policies of unprecedented severity.

Walt Kelly's cartoon character Pogo was best known for his observation "We have met the enemy and he is us." Extreme racial disparities exist in the American criminal justice system because of policies adopted mostly by white politicians who were motivated by personal ambition, cynicism, and ideology and who were indifferent to the effects of those policies on black Americans. Those policies and the disparities they caused unnecessarily damaged the lives of millions of black people and contributed substantially to the perpetuation of a black underclass long after it should have ceased to exist. The damage cannot be undone, but its effects can be ameliorated. Practices can be changed so that they do less harm in the future. The way forward is clear. What needs to be done is clear. What is unclear is whether Americans and the politicians they elect have or can find the will to do so.

This book tells that story. The first chapter is a summary of the whole. The second documents racial disparities in prison and the immediate reasons for them. The third discusses racial differences in drug use and trafficking: blacks use drugs less often than whites and sell them no more but are vastly more likely to be arrested and imprisoned for drug offenses. Chapter 4 examines the psychology, sociology, and politics of American race relations and shows how they shape contemporary crime and drug policies. The fifth chapter digs deeper into American history, culture, and government to show why a political climate existed in which policies and practices that do so much damage could have been adopted. The sixth shows how things can be changed to do less unnecessary harm to black Americans in the future.

I primarily discuss the effects of contemporary criminal justice policies and practices on black people. In relation to the criminal justice system, the situation of black people in America is different from those of members of other minority groups. Other groups—Native Americans and, in earlier periods, various Asian-American groups leap to mind—have suffered from discriminatory laws and government practices. Hispanics have suffered from public and private discrimination. None of those groups, however, have been the target of broad-based criminal justice policies, experienced extreme disparities in imprisonment, or bear the legacy of three centuries of slavery, Jim Crow, and legalized discrimination. American blacks are the only group that satisfies those criteria. And only the unique political and social status of American blacks precipitated the Republican Southern Strategy.

Other books can, should, and no doubt will be written that consider the criminal justice system experiences of members of other racial and ethnic groups, or of a number of groups. Other books can, should, and no doubt will be written about the distinctive experiences of black women or of women of other groups. Worthy subjects all, but these are different subjects from mine.

ACKNOWLEDGMENTS

Nonfiction books are written by individuals and reflect their writers' idiosyncrasies but they draw mostly on collective knowledge. A writer may ask a slightly different question, or shine a slightly different light, or turn up what seem to be a few new bits of information, but, for most, that is all. Isaac Newton, not a notably modest man, and one who for his time said new things, nonetheless said that in doing so he had stood on the shoulders of giants. We lesser folk can do no less. I could not have written this book had not wise men and women who came before me written other books and articles that tried to make sense of things that perplex me. Some may have been giants. There is little point in listing them here; they were writing for all the world, not just for me.

There is a point in identifying people who wrote and did things meant only for me. Jamie Fellner, Roxanne Lieb, Marc Mauer, Michael E. Smith, and Vesla Weaver read complete drafts of this book. All shared knowledge that is deeper than mine and tried to save me from error. Francis Cullen, Barry Feld, Richard Frase, Myron Orfield, Kevin Reitz, and James Unnever read and commented on various chapters at various times and tried to help me see more clearly. Matthew Melewski and Eric Taubel ferreted out data and helped compensate for my exiguous graphic skills. Adepeju Solarin and Su Smallen, on this as on innumerable other occasions, provided invaluable editorial and administrative support. Colleen Chambers, Reece Almond, and Michael Abts provided research assistance. The University of Minnesota Law School Library provides remarkably prompt, able, and good-spirited support to faculty. David Zopfi-Jordan, in particular, tracked down fugitive materials from around the corner and around the world with bewildering but gratifying speed and efficiency. I am grateful to all those kind and generous people. None of them, alas, bear any responsibility for the contents of this book. That burden is mine alone.

Portions of chapters 2, 3, 4, and 5, substantially revised and updated, are based on articles that appeared in *Crime and Justice: A Review of Research*, published by the University of Chicago Press, and *Criminology*, published by the American Society of Criminology. Insofar as they are reprinted, it is by permission.

PUNISHING
RACE

A Continuing American Dilemma

Four aspects of American crime control policies stand out: the world's highest imprisonment rate, the Western world's only use of capital punishment, the Western world's most severe punishments short of death, and the devastating effects of those policies on black Americans. Black men for a quarter century have been five to seven times more likely than white men to be in prison, are much more likely to receive decades-long sentences or life without the possibility of parole, and are much likelier to be on death row.

Stark disparities in imprisonment and entanglement in the criminal justice system result partly from racial differences in offending. To a lesser extent they result from practitioners' conscious biases and unconscious stereotypes. Mostly they result from the adoption in the 1980s and 1990s of drug and crime control policies that place much heavier burdens on black Americans than on whites.

The classic example was a 1986 federal law generally referred to as the "100-to-1 law." It punished sales of crack cocaine, mostly by blacks, as severely as sales a hundred times larger, mostly by whites, of powder cocaine. Sale of five grams of crack, a typical low-level street transaction, was punished as severely as sale of a half-kilogram of powder, an amount typical of high-level distributors. Not surprisingly federal prisons filled up with convicted black crack dealers. Many other statutes—most conspicuously mandatory minimum sentence and three-strikes-and-you're-out laws—enacted in the 1980s and 1990s worked in the same way. They targeted offenses for which blacks were especially likely to be arrested, and they worsened racial disparities in imprisonment.

Why did legislators and law enforcement officials adopt those policies, and why were they not changed when their racially skewed effects became known? There is little evidence that raw racism in its crudest forms was a significant factor. There is, however, substantial evidence that social and political processes only slightly less pernicious played and play a major role. Three—which might be thought of as the politics, sociology, and social psychology of race and crime—are especially important.

THE POLITICS OF RACE AND CRIME

The Republican "Southern Strategy" was a major precipitator of the severity of modern criminal justice policies and the unfair burdens they place on black Americans. The strategy's executors focused initially on crime and "states rights." Later the focus broadened to include welfare fraud, busing, and affirmative action. The aim was to appeal to the fears and biases of southern and working-class whites, and thereby weaken their traditional support for Democratic candidates. Crime was given a black face, most emblematically later on that of Willie Horton in the 1988 presidential election. The criminal behaviors focused on, most involving drugs and violence, and the types, especially crack cocaine and street violence, were things for which blacks were more often arrested than whites. More vigorous enforcement and longer prison sentences could be expected to hit blacks hard, and did.

The Republican Southern Strategy had its roots in the 1940s when white southern segregationists and conservative Republicans found common cause in opposition to the civil rights initiatives of Democratic presidents Franklin Delano Roosevelt and Harry S. Truman. The term, however, dates from the 1960s, when Republican political operatives decided to rebuild the party on a southern base. The strategy was premised on an extraordinary non sequitur: that black/white differences in the South are indistinguishable from ethnic differences at other times and places in American history. In the preface to *The Emerging Republican*

Majority, a book announcing and justifying the Southern Strategy, Kevin Phillips, its chief intellectual architect, wrote, "Few people realize the extent of ethnic influences in American politics. Historically, our party system has reflected layer upon layer of group oppositions: Irish against Yankee, Jewish against Catholic, French against English and so forth. Racial and ethnic polarization has neither stopped progress nor worked repression on the groups out of power" (1969, 22).

Those words were written in 1968, the year George Wallace ran as an openly racist candidate for president and Martin Luther King was assassinated. It was the end of the decade made famous by the civil rights movement, the March on Selma, and notorious killings of civil rights activists. It was the end of three centuries of white supremacy in the South. The proposition that racial polarization has "neither stopped progress nor worked repression on the groups out of power" is a mite saccharine.

Phillips's political rationale was that ethnic group conflict has always characterized American politics. "Southern politics," he observed, "like those of the rest of the nation, cleave along distinct ethnic (racial in this case) lines. Whereas in New York City, the Irish are lined up against the Jews, in the South it is principally a division between Negroes and whites" (1969, 287–88). That is why the Republican Party "decided to break with its formative antecedents and make an ideological bid for the anti–civil rights South" (33). The "formative antecedents" were the party's historic commitment to civil rights of black Americans, from Abraham Lincoln onward.

Phillips's conclusion was that manipulation of racial passions would enable Republicans to achieve political dominance in the South and strengthen their appeal to working-class whites elsewhere. As a result he favored aggressive federal enforcement of civil rights laws and decisions, not because it was the right thing to do, but because it would alienate white Democrats. Enforcement of "Negro voting rights in Dixie," he wrote, "is essential if southern conservatives are to be pressured into switching to the Republican Party—for Negroes are beginning to seize control of the national Democratic Party in some Black Belt areas" (1969, 464).

In the decades that followed, the executors of the Southern Strategy managed to promote and implement a "tough-on-crime" agenda that imposed no special burdens on their white constituency. Tough sentences for violent and drug crimes disproportionately affect black people. Racial profiling disproportionately—mostly—affects blacks. The war on drugs targeted drugs that blacks sell and places where they sell them.

Black people were locked up to attract white votes. When severe policies occasionally hit whites especially hard, as happened in relation to marijuana in the 1970s, the policies were quickly changed. In many parts of the United States, possession of and small-scale trafficking in marijuana were effectively decriminalized. When by contrast it became clear in the early 1990s that federal crack cocaine policies disproportionately affected blacks, nothing much happened. The U.S. Sentencing Commission (e.g., 1995) repeatedly urged Congress to repeal or diminish the sentencing differential between crack and powder cocaine contained in the federal 100-to-1 law. Attorney General Janet Reno initially endorsed the Commission's 1995 proposal to eliminate the differential and, backtracking, she and "drug czar" General Barry McCaffrey later called for it to be reduced to 10-to-1, but to no avail (Tonry 2004, chap. 1). Change occurred only in August 2010 when President Obama signed the Fair Sentencing Act of 2010. It modestly amended the 100-to-1 law but removed neither its fundamental unfairness nor its foreseeable disparate effects on black offenders. It became an 18-to-1 law. A mandatory minimum five-year prison sentence awaits any low-level dealer convicted of selling 28 grams of crack. A powder cocaine dealer must sell a half kilogram to face such a destiny.

THE SOCIOLOGY OF RACE AND CRIME

A second, subtler, harder-to-grasp explanation for unjustifiable racial disparities is that they help white Americans maintain social, economic, and political dominance over blacks. This is not a conspiracy theory. It is not a claim that whites over centuries consciously conspired to keep blacks on the bottom (though of course at times many did), but an observation that we human beings rationalize things that are in our interest. Many men long believed that women are too delicate for contact sports or heavy physical training; money spent on sport mostly benefited men. Many men long believed that women are not temperamentally suited for demanding work, or that motherhood and a serious professional career are irreconcilable; women until recently had little access to powerful or lucrative jobs. Many whites long believed that blacks and members of other minority groups are less intelligent or disciplined or responsible than whites; they needed less education and were unsuitable for many jobs. Well-known patterns of educational and employment discrimination resulted. In less contentious realms owners of existing homes usually have "principled reasons," not merely a perceived self-interest, to explain why they oppose the expansion of a nearby road or construction of a shopping center or placement of a homeless shelter. Beneficiaries of federal subsidies—agricultural price supports, venture capitalists' low tax rates, homeowners' mortgage interest deductions—defend them as wise public policies, and not simply because more money arrives or stays in their own pockets.

Something similarly self-interested underpins modern drug and crime control policies. A variety of cultural practices and legal institutions maintained traditional American patterns of racial dominance and hierarchy for more than three centuries, and contemporary drug and crime policies do it today. Until the Civil War, slavery assured white domination. After the war, social practices and conventions and legal forms of discrimination known as Jim Crow laws kept blacks in their "place." After the large-scale migration of millions from south to north to escape Jim Crow in the early twentieth century, the big-city ghettos and employment and housing discrimination kept blacks subordinate. And when deindustrialization and the flight of jobs to the suburbs left disadvantaged blacks marooned in urban ghettos, the modern wars on drugs and crime took over.

Bruce Western (2006), a Harvard sociologist, has shown that recent criminal justice policies have devastatingly diminished poor black men's chances of living satisfying lives. If policy makers' aim in setting drug and crime control policies had been to reduce poor black men's chances of earning a decent living, or becoming a good husband and father, or being socialized into positive social values, it is hard to see how they could have done it more effectively. A dose of prison can damage anyone, and usually does.

Douglas Massey, the author with Nancy Denton of *American Apartheid*, a widely praised account of housing discrimination, observed in his book *Categorically Unequal*, "Whether whites care to admit it or not, they have a selfish interest in maintaining the categorical mechanisms that perpetuate racial stratification. As a result, when pushed by the federal government to end overt discriminatory practices, they are likely to innovate new and more subtle ways to maintain their privileged position in society.... As discrimination moved underground, new mechanisms for exclusion were built into the criminal justice system for African Americans" (2007, 54, 251).

Massey is but one of many leading scholars who have come to the same conclusion. Glenn C. Loury, an economics professor at Brown University and one of the leading conservative speakers along with Robert Bork at Republican Party conferences in the 1980s, is another. The relation of the contemporary criminal justice system "to the history of racial degradation and subordination in our country (lynching, minstrelsy, segregation, ghettoization) is virtually self-evident," he wrote. "The racial subtext of our law and order political discourse over the last three decades has been palpable" (2007).

Recent work by legal scholars reaches the same conclusion. The civil rights lawyer Michelle Alexander (2010), for example, has argued that the imprisonment of large percentages of poor blacks, and the employment and other handicaps they experience after release, have created a new racial caste system. It operates to keep poor blacks and, through them, blacks as a group at the bottom. She argues that civil rights leaders have mis-served poor blacks by focusing their attention on broad-based civil rights issues rather than on justice issues that disproportionately affect black people.

THE SOCIAL PSYCHOLOGY OF RACE AND CRIME

The third explanation for why the prospect of extreme racial disparities did not impede policy makers, and why they continue to be tolerated, is that most people, including many black people, are influenced by widespread stereotypes about black criminality. A number of separate literatures are relevant. One concerns attitudes toward punishment. Whites generally have more punitive attitudes than do blacks and greater confidence in the justice system and its practitioners (e.g., Unnever, Cullen, and Jonson 2008; Peffley and Hurwitz 2010). Despite widely acknowledged racial profiling by the police, for example, whites are much less likely than blacks to believe that blacks are treated unfairly (Blow 2009, A15). A rapidly growing body of research on public attitudes and opinions shows that "negative racial stereotypes, anti-black affect, and collective racial resentments are all positively correlated with criminal justice policy punitiveness" (Bobo and Thompson 2010). Put more bluntly, people who support punitive crime policies are especially likely to harbor antiblack attitudes and resentments, and those policies do disproportionate damage to black people.

Another relevant set of interrelated literatures concerns widely held stereotypes of blacks as criminals. Studies by media scholars demonstrate that the mass media—news and entertainment both—regularly portray criminals as black and victims as white. Those stereotypes seep into people's thinking. A different literature shows that, when asked to envision a drug addict or a violent criminal, most white people assume the typical offender to be black.

A rapidly growing body of research on "colorism" shows that Americans—blacks and whites alike—assume that blacks with a dark skin tone are more likely to be criminals than blacks with a moderate or light skin tone. Blacks with the lightest skin are no more likely than whites to be stereotyped as criminals. Blacks with dark or moderate skin tone are punished more severely than whites. Blacks with the darkest skin are punished the most severely of all.

A related literature examines "Afro-American feature bias." In many people's minds stereotypically black facial features—dark skin, wide nose, full lips—are associated with criminality. When shown pictures of black and white men and asked to guess which are criminals, observers much more often choose those with Afrocentric features. Blacks (and some whites) with Afrocentric features are punished more severely than typical whites.

Yet another related literature examines "implicit bias." Millions of Americans have visited a Harvard University web page to take the Implicit Association Test. The IAT encompasses a number of questionnaires and computer games that seek out unconscious associations of race with good and bad things. Every population group except blacks unconsciously associates blacks with crime. In one game test takers are told to shoot fleeing armed felons and are then shown images of black and white people in different settings and carrying different objects. Test takers are much more likely to shoot black felons in ambiguous settings, and to shoot black felons holding objects other than guns. Similar association tests have been given to police officers and judges, with the same results. An entire issue of the *California Law Review* was devoted to research on implicit bias. The conclusion: "A substantial and actively accumulating body of research evidence establishes that implicit race bias is pervasive and is associated with bias against African Americans" (Greenwald and Krieger 2006, 966).

These literatures all document the existence of widely held unconscious stereotypes about black crime and black criminals. It is hard to imagine that police stopping people on the street, prosecutors deciding whether to file charges, judges setting sentences, and legislators considering bills are immune from the influence of these stereotypes.

Put all these things together—the Southern Strategy, stereotypes of black criminals, whites' greater support for harsh punishments and lesser belief in racial bias, the association of whites' racial resentments with support for punitive attitudes—and it is, alas, not surprising that Congress enacted the 100-to-1 law, and that it and state legislatures enacted many others like it. And it is not surprising that almost all such laws remain on the books.[1]

All of these findings are consistent with the ideas that whites can comfortably approve harsh policies that mostly affect nonwhites and that social distance and racial stereotypes make white empathy for blacks who are affected weak and uncommon. This is not a radical or far-fetched observation. In a book that generally denies the significance of racism and racial bias in the criminal justice system, the conservative writers Stephan and Abigail Thernstrom nonetheless acknowledge that "the capacity to feel empathy across racial lines is in short supply" (1997, 277).

MORALISM, JUDGMENTALISM, AND SEVERE PUNISHMENTS

Other facets of American history and culture compound problems of race in the justice system by creating pressures for harsh crime and drug control policies. Throughout American history political movements have emerged with properties that the historian Richard Hofstadter long ago characterized as the "paranoid streak in American politics." It is a recurring phenomenon in which political movements, sometimes on the left but most recently on the right, adopt black-and-white, right-versus-wrong, take-no-prisoners positions. The law-and-order movement, especially in its victims' movement component, often had these characteristics. Crime control policy was seen as a zero-sum game: you were either "for victims" or "for criminals." There was no middle ground.

A second complication is the influence of Evangelical Protestantism. Many of its adherents see crucial criminal justice issues in terms of moral right and moral wrong and are likewise closed to the possibility of compromise. If criminals and drug users are immoral, well, then they deserve neither empathy nor compassion. They have sinned, and they should be severely punished for it. That's that.

The third complication is the American structure of government, unique among developed Western countries, in which judges and prosecutors are elected or politically appointed and in which government policy making about crime is not insulated from influence by short-term emotions and politics. Some judges and prosecutors are sensitive to public opinions and passions because they believe they should be. Others pay attention because they believe doing so will help them win reelection, be promoted to higher office, or just be more popular in their community. In any case the effect is that practitioners' decisions often reflect citizens' anger and upset. That ratchet operates in only one direction: upward. Similar pressures operate on other public officials.

Taken together these three factors—the paranoid streak, religious moralism, and the politicization of the justice system—created a political climate that was long on vindictiveness and short on empathy, governmental institutions that were quick to adopt policies of unprecedented severity, and practitioners who were quick to apply them.

Later I develop these ideas and show why they should be taken seriously.[2] Assuming, however, that these arguments and research findings have some merit, much else falls into place. Rising crime rates in the 1970s and 1980s, compounded by anxieties associated with rapid social and economic changes, including the fruits of the civil rights movement, made Americans anxious and eager for simple solutions to complex problems. Politicians offered them. The Republican Southern Strategy allowed politicians to appeal to whites' racial anxieties and resentments without doing so openly. American moralism made drugs and street crime understandable problems to attack. White-collar and corporate crimes, by contrast, are harder to understand, and the lines between admirable entrepreneurism and criminal opportunism are harder to draw and prove. Drugs and street crime, however, can be portrayed in black-and-white terms: street crime is reprehensible and drug use is irresponsible, and they are behaviors for which black people are disproportionately arrested.

Attacking drugs and street crime with vigor and self-righteousness appealed to white and middle-class voters in part because those priorities posed little threat to people like them. This is why antidrug policies treat crack much more severely than powder cocaine and why alcohol—which plays a bigger role as a precipitant of crime and violence than crack or powder and generates greater aggregate social costs—is not a target of antidrug policies at all. Much larger percentages of whites than blacks consume alcohol, and public health rather than criminal justice approaches to it predominate.

Racially skewed policies allow the white majority to indulge a taste for moralism at other people's expense. If their own children had been sent to prison in large numbers and had their later prospects for living satisfying lives greatly reduced, white voters might have felt differently.

Ghetto black kids were a different matter. It is hard to identify or empathize with people you don't know and who live lives almost unrecognizably different from your own. The Republican Southern Strategy, with its law and order corollary, emphasized how different white voters were from poor blacks. It also destabilized poor black communities and delayed full black participation in American life by at least several generations.

It is much easier to be tough on crime or drugs when someone else's children will go to prison. That this is part of the problem is demonstrated by marijuana law enforcement in the 1970s. Young whites in the 1960s and early 1970s were more likely than young blacks to be arrested for drug offenses, especially involving marijuana. When President Nixon's war on drugs resulted in prison terms for many young middle-class whites a backlash set in. In many places minor marijuana offenses were effectively decriminalized. White teens' arrest rates plummeted, arrests of black teens took off, and ever since black teenagers have had higher arrest rates than whites (Blumstein and Wallman 2006).

THE EFFECTS ON BLACK AMERICANS

The litany of ways drug and crime control policies disproportionately affect black Americans is depressing, but so familiar as to surprise no one with even nodding acquaintance with the subject. Blacks in 2005 constituted 12.8 percent of the general population but nearly half of prison inmates and 42 percent of death row residents. About a third of young black men ages twenty to twenty-nine were in prison or jail or on probation or parole on an average day in 2005. The Bureau of Justice Statistics estimated in 2003 that 32 percent of black baby boys born in 2001 would spend some part of their lives in a state or federal prison. That is a substantial underestimate; it does not take account of confinement in local jails, which is much more common than time in prison. By 2004 a third of adult black men had a felony conviction and half had been convicted of a felony or a misdemeanor (Bonczar 2003; Bureau of Justice Statistics 2007a, tables 6.33.2005, 6.17.2006, 6.80.2007; Pager 2007, 157; Uggen, Manza, and Thompson 2006).

Stop for a minute and think about those numbers. Try to step back in your mind's eye to the early 1990s and picture yourself in a classroom full of black, bright-eyed first-grade boys at the beginning of a decade of national prosperity. Then return to the present, knowing that one of every three of those small boys grown up is today entangled in the arms of the criminal law. Ask yourself, "How that can possibly be?" We know the answer to that rhetorical question, but it invites another: "How could American policy makers have let that happen?"

What is most striking about these patterns of racial disparity is not that they exist, but that they are well-known, have long been well-known, and have changed little in recent decades. Few people except academics, law reformers, and offenders and their loved ones much notice or care. The racial disparities caused by the federal 100-to-1 law were foreseeable when the law was passed (Tonry 1995, 4–6) and were irrefutably documented long ago (McDonald and Carlson 1993). The same is true of racial profiling by the police and of the wars on crime and drugs: their effects on black Americans have long been well known.

Since at least 1980 American drug and crime control policies have undermined achievement of full unbiased participation of black Americans in the nation's social, economic, and political life. The following list of social, vocational, educational, and economic differences between blacks and whites is drawn from 2010 edition of *The Statistical Abstract of the United States*:

In 2007, 34.3 percent of black children lived in households below the poverty line, compared with 14.4 percent of white children.

In 2005, the mortality rate for black infants was 13.7 per 1,000 live births, compared with 5.7 per 1,000 for whites.

In 2007, per capita income for black Americans was $18,428, compared with $28,325 for whites.

In 2008, 10.1 percent of adult blacks were unemployed and 36.3 percent were not in the labor force, compared with 5.2 and 33.7 percent of whites.

In 2008, 19.6 percent of blacks twenty-five and older had college degrees, compared with 29.8 percent of whites.

In 2007, 46.7 percent of blacks owned their own home, compared
with 72.5 percent of whites (U.S. Department of Commerce
2010, tables 112, 224, 576, 688, 696, 956).

Those differences partly result from and are exacerbated by the nearly
seven-to-one racial difference in black and white imprisonment rates
that has been typical for the past quarter century, the staggering difference
in black and white men's lifetime chances of going to prison, and the
entanglement of a large minority of young black men in their twenties in
the justice system at a time of life when other young men and most
women are building careers and conventional lives (Western 2006).
Accumulating bodies of research show that going to prison makes getting a job much harder later on (Pager 2007), reduces average and lifetime earnings (Fagan and Freeman 1999; Raphael, Holzer, and Stoll
2006), and reduces the later well-being of prisoners' children (Murray
and Farrington 2008). A different literature shows that disadvantaged
minority communities are damaged, not helped, when large numbers of
their residents are sent to prison. Low levels of imprisonment at least
arguably prevent crime in a neighborhood through deterrence, incapacitation, and removal of antisocial role models. High levels cause crime
rates to increase and neighborhoods to deteriorate (Clear 2007, 2008).

With the advantage of hindsight it is clear that much of the damage
to black people and their communities could have been avoided if the
law-and-order movement, with its insensitivity to the interests of black
Americans, had not taken hold. Prominent proponents of the Republican
Southern Strategy, looking back, regret it. Kevin Phillips, the author of
The Emerging Republican Majority (1969), long ago recanted and condemned the deliberate use of "crime" and "violence" as racial code words.
Harry Dent, chairman of the Republican National Committee in the
1970s, a principal implementer, in 1980 expressed his regret for anything
he did "that stood in the way of the rights of black people" (Stout 2007,
B7). Had we known thirty years ago where the law-and-order movement
would lead, that in 2010 nearly 1 percent of Americans would be behind
bars and nearly a third of young black men would be supervised by the
criminal justice system, it is hard to imagine that many people would
have chosen our present as an acceptable future.

If imprisonment rates for jail and prison together had remained at 1970 levels (around 160 per 100,000) or at 1980 levels (around 210), American crime control policies would have bitten much less deeply into black American communities. Those rates would still be high by modern international standards. In 2009 the highest rates in countries with which Americans would ordinarily want to be compared were 150 to 170 per 100,000 (England, Spain, and New Zealand). Canada's imprisonment rate was 115 per 100,000; rates in Scandinavia and Italy were between 65 and 75; and in France, Germany, and Belgium were under 100 (International Centre for Prison Studies 2010). Except for murder, crime rates in the United States are not higher than in other wealthy developed countries, and prisoners convicted of murder make up only 11 percent of the total.

By contrast, American imprisonment rates in 1970 were nothing special; higher than in other developed democratic countries, but lower than in others. Returning to 1970 or 1980 levels would simply return the United States to the mainstream—where it ought always to have been.

Fewer than half of the black Americans in prison in 2010 would have been there had 1980 rates continued, and fewer than a quarter if 1970 levels had continued. Many fewer black men would have suffered the pains of imprisonment, the resulting stigma, reduced employment prospects, and the socialization into deviant values that prisons provide. There would have been many fewer broken black families, fewer negative role models for black boys, and more black men whose social and economic prospects made them attractive marriage partners. There would have been less deterioration in poor black communities. Over at least three decades when civil rights and welfare policies aimed at improving opportunities and living standards for black Americans, drug and crime policies steadily worsened them.

WHAT HAPPENED?

The massive imprisonment of black men in twenty-first-century America did not happen overnight; it happened in the decades since

1973. In 1960 blacks made up 36 percent of the prison population. The black imprisonment rate was 661 per 100,000. Part of that differential resulted from racial bias and part from the greater involvement of blacks in the kinds of crimes, mostly violent, that commonly resulted in prison sentences. The part associated with bias was indefensible.

The part associated with relatively higher rates of arrest for violent crimes raised more complicated issues. Social and economic deprivation experienced by black Americans, caused and worsened by racial discrimination, went a long way to explain greater involvement in crime. Then as now, however, much violent crime occurred within racial groups, not between them. Before the 1970s, American police forces often did not record many black-on-black crimes that came to their attention. The condescending rationale was that such crimes were not police business and were best handled within the black community. This means that police data systematically undercounted violent crimes by black offenders against black victims.

Some blacks were no doubt arrested when whites would not have been, and some blacks were no doubt not arrested when whites would have been. It is impossible now to know whether the black percentage of prison inmates was too high or too low. In any case, failure by the criminal justice system to respond to violence against black victims constituted a different sort of discrimination.

After 1960 the civil rights movement grew in scope and influence. The U.S. Supreme Court struck down laws permitting racial discrimination. The first major twentieth-century civil rights legislation was enacted. Increased social and economic opportunities for blacks should have reduced their relative overinvolvement in violent crime, and the imprisonment rate for black Americans should have declined.

That did not happen. The overall imprisonment rate increased from 161 per 100,000 population in 1970 to 780 in 2006. That increase, enormous though it is, dwarfs what happened to black Americans. The black imprisonment rate increased from 593 in 1970 to 2,661 per 100,000 in 2006. The percentage of prisoners who were black reached 50 percent in the mid-1980s, a level at which it remained for a decade and from which it has since fallen only slightly. Prison population numbers were higher in 2010.

DOING BETTER

Much of the damage done to disadvantaged black Americans and their loved ones in the name of crime control and drug law enforcement was, and is, avoidable. We can do better. Two approaches are corrective: radical reduction in the use of prison sentences and abandonment of policies and laws that do unnecessary damage. Two others are preventive: reduction of bias and stereotyping and creation of devices that make future adoption of policies that cause unjustifiable racial disparities less likely.

REDUCED USE OF IMPRISONMENT

Efforts to reduce the influence of bias and stereotyping in official decision making are being made throughout the United States and should continue to be made. Unfortunately even if they were completely successful they could have only modest effects. Prison disparities result primarily not from biased decisions but from two other causes. The police unfairly target minority offenders by use of racial profiling and drug arrest policies that focus on crack cocaine and disadvantaged minority areas of large cities. Sentencing policies call for extraordinarily long prison terms for offenses of which blacks are disproportionately often convicted.

The only way to reduce the massive damage current policies do to black Americans is to reduce the prison population substantially, as is illustrated in table 1.1, using data for 2006.[3] Part of the disparity is caused

TABLE 1.1   Hypothetical Reductions in Imprisonment, Effects of Racial Makeup

	Black Imprisonment Rate	Black:White Ratio	Reduction in Black Prisoners
In 2006	2,661 per 100,000	5.5:1	
Less 10% disparity	2,395 per 100,000	5.0:1	101,000
Halve 2006 population	1,330 per 100,000	5.5:1	505,400
Return to 1980 level	827 per 100,000	5.5:1	697,000

Source: Tonry and Melewski (2008, table 5).

by racial bias and stereotyping. Ten percent is a high estimate of their likely contribution. As the table shows, reducing the number of black prisoners by 10 percent and holding all else constant would reduce disparity but would reduce the number of black people in prison only by about 100,000.

If instead the prison population were cut by half across the board, racial disparities would remain the same but the black imprisonment rate would fall by half.[4] There would be 500,000 fewer black people in prison. If imprisonment rates were brought down to 1980 levels the black imprisonment rate would fall by more than two-thirds and there would be 700,000 fewer blacks in prison.

The implications of these alternative approaches are enormous. Of course every effort should be made to eliminate bias and stereotyping, but even their diminution will not significantly reduce racial disparities or the absolute number of black people in prison. Only radical reduction in the scale of imprisonment in America can make a big difference. Devices need to be created for reducing the lengths of current prison sentences and releasing hundreds of thousands of people serving unnecessarily long terms. Sentencing laws and guidelines need to be changed to reduce the use of imprisonment and to shorten prison sentences. New programs need to be created to divert many people from prison or jail into community correctional programs. New systems of parole, pardon, and commutation need to be developed. So do new programs of social welfare and support to ease ex-prisoners' transition back into the free community. None of these changes need be focused on black offenders or on black prisoners. Black imprisonment rates are so high partly for the reasons set out here, but also because American imprisonment rates are so high.

The prison population cannot be reduced overnight or in a year, but it can be reduced relatively quickly and in ways that do not substantially impair public safety. As chapter 6 explains, there are no good reasons to believe that the enormous numbers of people in prisons make the United States a significantly safer place.

There are two theoretical rationales for current drug and crime control policies. The first is that aggressive drug law enforcement and severe sentences for drug crimes reduce drug use by making drugs less available. The second is that severe sentencing policies significantly reduce crime rates by deterring and incapacitating offenders. The evidence supports neither theory.

The enormous increase in the size of the prison population over the past 30 years is to a significant extent the product of the police and sentencing policies associated with the war on drugs. The clear weight of the evidence, however, and the conclusions of most leading drug policy scholars concur: Arresting hundreds of thousands of inner-city street-level drug dealers and sending them to prison has had little or no effect on the availability of drugs in the United States. A single measure— street prices of drugs—shows this. Federal drug enforcement agencies for forty years have regularly purchased drugs from street-level dealers in order to monitor drug prices and availability. If massive arrests and severe penalties were making drugs less available, simple economic theory instructs that prices should be rising. Instead they have fallen steadily since the early 1980s.

Crack cocaine has been the primary target of drug law enforcement since the mid-1980s; crack prices especially should have increased. Instead data from the Office of National Drug Control Policy show that the street price of one gram of pure crack fell from about $650 in 1982 to about $200 in 1992 (both in 2007 constant dollars) and has continued to fall since then.[5] The principal reason for this is that street-level drug dealers who are arrested are quickly replaced. Other disadvantaged young people are willing to accept substantial risks for what—mistakenly—they believe to be prospects of better earnings than are otherwise available to them.

The evidence concerning deterrence and incapacitation is no more supportive.[6] The clear weight of the evidence for more than thirty years has shown that, compared with lesser punishments, harsh punishments have few if any additional deterrent effects, and that lengthy prison terms are at best an inefficient, inhumane, and overly expensive way to prevent crimes. No one doubts that society is safer having some criminal penalties rather than none, but that choice is not in issue. The practical question is whether increases in penalties, or having more rather than less severe penalties, measurably reduces the incidence of serious crimes. The answer is no.

DETERRENCE

There are three main places to look to find out whether increasing penalties, or having severe penalties, deters crime. First, countries have sought advice from expert advisory committees or national commissions. Time and again they have concluded that knowledge about the deterrent effects of penalties is insufficient to justify basing sentencing laws on assumptions about deterrence. Examples include the Canadian Sentencing Commission (1987), the Finnish National Research Institute for Legal Policy (Törnudd 1993), and several panels of the U.S. National Academy of Sciences (Blumstein, Cohen, and Nagin 1978; Reiss and Roth 1993). A typical example comes from the British Home Office when Margaret Thatcher was prime minister: "It is unrealistic to construct sentencing arrangements on the assumption that most offenders will weigh up the possibilities in advance and base their conduct on rational calculation" (Home Office 1990, 6).

Second, a sizable number of surveys of research on the deterrent effects of sanctions have been published. With only rare exceptions, they conclude either that there is no credible evidence that increased penalties reduce crime rates (e.g., von Hirsch et al. 1999; Tonry 2008b) or that existing evidence is insufficient to provide meaningful policy guidance (e.g., Nagin 1998). The Canadian scholars Anthony Doob and Cheryl Webster concluded, "There is no plausible body of evidence that supports policies based on this premise [that increased penalties reduce crime]" (2003, 146). The American scholars Travis Pratt and his colleagues concluded in more technical language that "the effects of 'severity' estimates and deterrence/sanctions composites, even when statistically significant, are too weak to be of substantive significance" (2006, 379).

Third, evaluations have been conducted of the deterrent effects of a wide range of newly enacted mandatory penalty laws. These include New York's Rockefeller Drug Laws, the first major modern mandatory minimum penalty law in the United States, and one of the toughest (Joint Committee on New York Drug Law Evaluation 1978), and mandatory minimum sentence laws in Massachusetts, Michigan, Florida, Pennsylvania, and Oregon (e.g., Beha 1977; Rossman et al. 1979; Loftin, Heumann, and McDowall 1983; Loftin and McDowall 1984; McDowall, Loftin, and Wiersema 1992). All concluded that the laws had no deterrent effects or had short-term effects that quickly disappeared. The vast majority of evaluations of California's three-strikes law conclude that it had no significant effects on crimes rates.

INCAPACITATION

The evidence concerning incapacitation is little stronger. No one questions that some crimes in the community are avoided because would-be offenders are locked up, but that is not the issue. There would be no crime in the community if everyone was in prison, and relatively little if all males aged fifteen to thirty-five were. Those are not options. The question is whether enough crimes are averted by current practices to justify having so many people in prison. The answer is no.

There are four good reasons to conclude that there are too many people in prison from an incapacitative perspective. First, crime is a young man's game. Most who commit crimes in their teenage years or early twenties will soon stop because they get tired of it or realize they have too much to lose: a wife or girlfriend, a family, a job.

Second, crime is seldom an old man's game. Very few remain criminally active after their mid-thirties. With only a few exceptions confinement of people older than thirty-five is irrelevant from a crime-prevention perspective and a waste of taxpayers' money.

Third, for many behaviors, locking up a single offender is unlikely to prevent crimes. The "replacement" problem concerning drug dealers is the clearest; drug markets provide sufficient incentives to wannabes that filling an open street corner is seldom difficult.

Fourth, among the quarter to a third of American prisoners in recent years who were convicted of drug crimes, many were convicted of street-level dealing or possession. Most of them do not present significant risks of other forms of criminality.

There is a fifth reason why incapacitative considerations cannot justify current imprisonment levels: many sentences are just too long. It is a requirement of justice that punishments be proportionate to the seriousness of crimes. This is not a merely academic point. Most lay people believe as strongly as most philosophers that people who commit comparable crimes should receive comparable punishments, and that people who commit less serious crimes should be punished less than people who commit more serious crimes. Most three-strikes and mandatory minimum sentence laws require disproportionately severe punishments of five, ten, twenty, thirty years, and life. Sellers of tiny amounts of drugs are often sentenced more severely than people convicted of burglaries, robberies, and sexual assaults. Three-strikes laws require prison terms for minor crimes that are longer than those served by most people convicted of rape, robbery, or murder.

Some people deserve to be sent to prison for serious crimes, but not for so long as many are now sent. Some people pose meaningful risks to public safety; it is not unreasonable to confine them. There are, however, few such people, and very few of them remain dangerous past their mid-thirties. A large percentage of American prisoners could be sent home without significantly threatening public safety.

Moreover accumulating evidence suggests that sending people to prison makes them more likely to commit new crimes than if they had been punished in some other way. The most recent authoritative survey of the evidence concludes: "Most studies of the impact of imprisonment on subsequent criminality find no effect or a criminogenic effect. . . . Existing research is not nearly sufficient for making firm evidence-based conclusions for either science or public policy" (Nagin, Cullen, and Jonson 2009, 121). Sending people to prison makes them more likely to commit crimes after they are released, not less. From a crime prevention perspective, little would be lost if prisons held many fewer inmates. The savings in money and human life chances would be substantial. The benefits for black Americans would be enormous.

Targeting the Causes of Racial Disparities

A wide range of contemporary criminal justice policies do unnecessary damage to black Americans. Some can be addressed by the police. Others require administrative or legislative changes.

RACIAL PROFILING

Under current American law, racial profiling is legal as long as the police offer another, pretextual reason for stopping someone. Kevin R. Johnson (2010) has shown, through a careful analysis of U.S. Supreme Court decisions over four decades, that the court has systematically dismantled constitutional procedural protections that in earlier times would have made racial profiling difficult to impossible. Under current law, police can stop people *because* they are black or Hispanic or are members of other ethnic groups, as long as the police provide some additional reason for doing so. This reason can be no more than a hunch or a statement that "my experience led me to believe...." Subjective considerations such as those are impossible for courts to second guess.

Racial profiling is per se unfair. It alienates many minority citizens and makes them distrust the police and the criminal justice system. It also puts black people at greater risk than whites of being arrested for reasons that would otherwise not come to the attention of the police. It should stop. When an arrest results from an unlawful search or seizure, the criminal charges are tossed out. Criminal charges resulting from arrests based on racial profiling should be dealt with in the same way. Police incentives would change substantially if after the fact every arrest arguably resulting from profiling were subject to the same degree of judicial scrutiny that warrants before the fact are supposed to receive.

DRUG ARRESTS

Drug arrests are the second source of disparity that is within the power of police executives to alter. Police targeting of inner-city drug markets has produced racial disparities between blacks and whites for drug arrests as high as six to one in some years. Retargeting to focus equally on white drug dealers would make an important symbolic statement about racial fairness, reduce racial disparities, and pursue the aims of drug law enforcement no less effectively. As a practical matter police efforts to target whites and blacks equally would reduce arrests overall. It takes much more time to apprehend whites selling drugs behind closed doors than to arrest black sellers in open-air street markets. Greatly increased emphasis on drug dealing by whites would most likely produce a political backlash that would lead to a reconsideration of drug enforcement policy, as happened with marijuana in the 1970s. In any case it is unlikely that arresting many more whites would be more effective in reducing drug sales, use, and prices than are current practices. Police who try seriously to reduce unfair arrest disparities will need to rethink their approach. The obvious move is to shift primary emphasis from law enforcement approaches to treatment and rehabilitation.

CRIMINAL RECORDS

The United States is unique among Western countries in giving very great weight to prior convictions in setting sentences for new crimes. In most countries, the effect of an offender having one or more prior convictions is to increase sentences for new crimes by a few months. In the United States, the "recidivist premium" often doubles or triples the sentence. Because black offenders are arrested more often and at younger ages than whites, they are more often affected by prior record increments. Richard Frase (2009) has shown that two-thirds of the difference in prison sentences received by blacks and whites in Minnesota result from racial differences in prior records. Ways need to be devised to change that. Exactly how is not so important. What is important is recognition that current practices and policies greatly worsen racial disparities in imprisonment, to no good end, and that means must be found to lessen the damage they do.

LENGTHY PRISON SENTENCES

Mandatory minimum, life without the possibility of parole, and truth-in-sentencing laws mostly affect drug and violent criminals, often require sentences measured in decades, and are a major contributor to racial disparities. They should be repealed and no new ones should be enacted. American jurisdictions need to establish principled new systems of sentencing guidelines coupled with new mechanisms for shortening unduly, disparately, or disproportionately long prison sentences. Parole release systems long performed that function, among others, but many have been abolished. They need to be reestablished. Parole boards that survived became much too cautious and in doing so increased both lengths of sentences served and prison populations. They need to rethink their policies. New sentencing guidelines will need to call for proportionate sentences measured mostly in months for many crimes, in single-digit years for most serious crimes, and in longer periods only for very serious crimes and very dangerous offenders.

Reduce Racial Bias and Stereotyping

Many states have created racial equity task forces in their court systems. Continuing education programs attempt to sensitize judges and court and correctional personnel about the ubiquity and perniciousness of unconscious stereotyping and attribution. Programs such as these are as important for the normative messages they send—about the injustice of racial stereotyping and the importance of treating people as equals—as for the improvements they produce in the quality of American justice. They need to continue and to be expanded.

Disparity Impact Assessments

Federal and state governments in the United States should require that racial disparity impact projections be prepared as a routine element of consideration of proposed sentencing legislation, and that operating agencies conduct racial disparity audits. Both should be relatively uncontroversial. Most legislatures now require that fiscal impact assessments accompany proposed legislation. Every American jurisdiction requires development of environmental impact projections before new buildings are built or existing ones are altered in sensitive environments. Racial disparity audits examine current practices to see, in the first instance, whether they affect members of different groups differently. When disparities are documented, the next question is whether they can be justified. Disparity impact projections are similar except that they focus on proposed changes in policy and practice in order to identify foreseeable disparities and determine whether they can be justified. If disparities cannot be justified, the proposals should be abandoned.

Proposals for major reductions in America's prison population, repeal of punitive legislation, and requirement of race and ethnicity impact assessments may strike some readers as audacious. But if racial disparities and the damage they have unarguably done to millions of individual black Americans and their families, and to black Americans as a group, are pressing social problems, then strong measures are called for.

Perhaps as the normative developments that underlay the civil rights movement wrestle with the beliefs and attitudes that have long maintained white dominance in America, a time will come when these proposals do not look audacious. They are simple proposals that aim to address profound injustices. Seen in that way, they are not audacious at all.

IMPRISONMENT

MANY FEATURES OF THE CRIMINAL JUSTICE SYSTEM DISPRO-portionately hurt black Americans—racial profiling, the War on Drugs, bias and stereotyping—but the worst damage is done by excessive imprisonment. Racial disparities in imprisonment and the enormous absolute number of black people behind bars are major impediments to the creation of an America in which race does not matter. So long as 32 percent of black baby boys can expect to spend time in prison and 33 percent of young black men are at any one time under the control of the criminal justice system, the America in which race does not matter will remain an impossible dream.

If large numbers of young black men continue to be disabled from becoming successful workers, fathers, and citizens, black people will continue to be less healthy, wealthy, and successful than other Americans. Undoing, ameliorating, and compensating for the damage current criminal justice policies cause is one goal. Diminishing future damage is the other. Chapter 6 discusses how those things can be done. This and the next chapter document the damage American drug and crime control policies do to black Americans and show how current patterns of disparity and overimprisonment came to be.

Scholars have long paid attention to interactions among race, crime, and criminal justice. W. E. B. Du Bois (1899/1988), the pioneering black intellectual, and Gunner Myrdal, author of *An American Dilemma* (1944), the classic account of race in American life, are two of the most famous. There have been many others. The stories Du Bois and Myrdal told were of racial bias, greater black than white involvement in crime, and higher black than white rates of imprisonment. Both attributed higher rates of black crime to racial discrimination, disadvantaged lives, and blocked opportunities.

Problems of excessive and disproportionate imprisonment of black Americans are of long standing and are not getting better. In a 1995 book, *Malign Neglect: Race, Crime, and Punishment in America*, I surveyed what was known about racial disparities and their causes. Here is how things then stood. For a century before the 1960s black people had been more likely to be held in prison than whites. Racial disparities began to rise in the 1960s and then shot up to all-time highs in the 1980s, during the Reagan administration: blacks by then accounted for half of American prisoners, though they were only 12 percent of the U.S. population. A black American was seven times more likely to be in prison on any given day than a white American. Part of the reason was that blacks were sometimes treated more harshly than whites. Sometimes this was because of racial bias. Other times it was because of the influence of unconscious biases, stereotypes, and lack of empathy.

A larger part of the explanation for the historical pattern, however, was that blacks were more likely than whites to be arrested for robbery, rape, aggravated assault, and homicide, offenses that have long resulted in prison sentences. Victims' descriptions of assailants and police data on victim-offender relationships in homicides indicated that the racial offending patterns shown in arrest data were not far off from reality, at least for serious crimes. Critically, however, there had been no significant shifts in racial patterns in arrests for decades, and increased involvement by black people in serious violent crime could not explain why imprisonment rates shot up after the 1960s. A primary cause of the increase in the 1980s was disproportionate arrest and imprisonment of black people for drug offenses.

Little in that paragraph needs to be changed to describe conditions in 2010, with three important exceptions. First, overall imprisonment rates were much higher in 2010 than in 1993, and with their increase the lifetime probability of imprisonment for black men and the percentage of young black men in prison increased substantially. Second, the absolute number of blacks in prison was substantially higher in 2010. Third, however, blacks' involvement in violent crimes had declined substantially. If prison were used primarily as a punishment for serious violent crimes, as it is in most other countries, racial disparities should have been falling for at least fifteen years.

The black fractions of the prison, jail, and death row populations did not change much between 1993 and 2010. Nor did the ratio of black to white imprisonment rates: black men remain six to seven times more likely than white men to be inmates. Police arrest policies for drug offenses continue to be primary causes of racial disparities. Racial profiling by the police plays a major role. Other important causes include mandatory minimum sentence and three-strikes laws that mandate decades-long and life sentences, and the elimination of parole release and other devices that enabled officials in earlier times to shorten unduly long sentences.

Harsh sentencing policies for drug and violent crimes are a major cause of the continuation of racial disparities. Until the early 1980s tough sentencing laws mainly established minimum sentences for violent and gun crimes, and the minimums were usually one or two years (Shane-DuBow, Brown, and Olsen 1985). Beginning in the 1980s laws were enacted requiring lengthy prison sentences for drug offenses, including low-level street sales of small amounts. For fifteen years, through the mid-1990s, state and federal legislators repeatedly enacted laws requiring longer sentences for drugs, guns, and violence. Perhaps because fingers and toes provide a handy frame of reference, mandatory sentence laws often specify numbers in multiples of five—5 years, 10, 20, and 30. Classic examples include the federal 100-to-1 law governing cocaine sentencing that was in effect from 1986 to 2010, the 18-to-1 law that replaced it, and California's three-strikes law requiring sentences ranging from twenty-five years to life for third felonies, no matter how minor.

Black Americans have borne the brunt of this tougher sentencing. Arrest rates for black people for drug crimes are far higher—three to four times higher—than for whites and bear no relationship to levels of black Americans' drug use or involvement in drug trafficking. Black Americans are less likely to use most drugs than are whites, and there is no credible evidence that they sell drugs more often. High arrest rates for drug crimes result from police policy decisions to focus on substances blacks more often sell and places where they sell them. High imprisonment rates for drug crimes result partly from skewed arrest patterns and partly from legislative decisions to specify the longest sentences for drug offenses for which blacks are more often arrested.

Black people are also disproportionately damaged by tougher sentencing policies for violent crimes. Partly this is because black people more often commit violent crimes and are arrested for them, even though their relative overinvolvement in violent crime has been declining. In absolute numbers violent crimes by black people have plummeted as part of the national decline in crime since 1991, and constitute smaller percentages of absolute numbers that are about half what they were twenty years ago. The murder rate in 1980, for example, was 10.2 per 100,000 inhabitants of the United States. In 2008 it was 5.4. The robbery rate in 1980 was 251.1 per 100,000. In 2008 it was 145.3.

Participation by black people in violent crimes has thus not only fallen, but has fallen proportionately more than for members of other groups. Prison disparities, however, have not fallen. Sentencing laws enacted in the 1980s and 1990s have worsened disparities because they call for prison terms that are vastly longer than in earlier times. If black people are relatively more often convicted of violent crimes than white people, longer sentences over time will increase the numbers and percentages of black people in prison. That is what has happened.

No serious person questions the appropriateness of punishing people who commit serious violent crimes. If black people more often commit violent crimes, more black people will be convicted for them, and be sentenced, and wind up in prison. So be it. That is a partial explanation for long-term racial disparities in imprisonment. The continuing American dilemma, however, is not that some disparity exists. Insofar as disparities result from bias or stereotyping, they are, of course, morally unjustifiable. Much violent crime is intraracial; higher rates of violent black offending mean higher rates of black victims of violence. That would justify some level of disparity. The real dilemma is the rapid increase in disparity in the 1970s and 1980s and its failure to decline significantly since then.

The rapid increase in racial disparities after the 1960s and their failure to decline since pose fundamental problems in social policy. Conditions of life facing many black Americans produce higher levels of involvement in crime. Contemporary crime policies perpetuate those conditions. Poor educations, limited employment opportunities, broken and unstable homes, and living in deteriorated neighborhoods are among the reasons why too many black people commit crimes and are sent to prison. People released from prison face special obstacles to improving their educations, finding decent work, establishing stable households, or moving to healthy neighborhoods. It is potentially an endless cycle, which started with centuries of racism and racial discrimination. That, after all, is why the conditions of life facing black Americans in the second half of the twentieth century, after the successes of the civil rights movement, were so much worse than those of whites.

We know why involvement in violent crime is greater among blacks than whites. More blacks than whites are afflicted by the factors that lead young people to become involved in crime. They are the same for members of all social groups: social and economic disadvantage, disorganized childhoods, educational deficits, child abuse, lack of employment skills, delinquent peers. Janet Lauritsen, for example, used data from the National Crime Victimization Survey (NCVS) to investigate the influence of individual, family, and community characteristics on victimization by nonlethal violence. The NCVS is a survey conducted by the U.S. Bureau of the Census since 1973 in which a large representative sample (40,000 to 60,000 households) of the U.S. population are questioned every six months about their experiences as crime victims. Lauritsen found that racial and ethnic differences disappeared when family and community factors were taken into account. Blacks (and Hispanics) had greater risks because they were more likely than whites to spend time away from home, live in single-parent households, live in disadvantaged communities, and have less stable living arrangements. She observed, "The sources of risk are similar for all adolescents, regardless of their race or ethnicity" (2003, 9).

A similar analysis of violent offending by McNulty and Bellair (2003) found the same thing. Differences in violent behavior disappeared when individual factors, family characteristics, social bonds, gang involvement, exposure to violence, and community characteristics were taken into account. Race does not explain higher rates of violence by black people; social and economic handicaps associated with being black in twenty-first-century America do.

The legacies of slavery, Jim Crow, and overt racial discrimination through the early 1970s have combined with employment, housing, and educational discrimination against black people even into our own time. Together they explain why many more young black than white people begin their lives in conditions that make involvement in crime, and in violent crime, more likely. For many young disadvantaged men, slightly older men with prison records provide the local role models and youth gangs provide peer acceptance. To people with no viable work prospects, or prospects paying only the minimum wage, drug dealing appears to promise material rewards available nowhere else. Laws that increase sentences for the crimes such young men commit, and are arrested for, inevitably exacerbate racial disparities.

The rest of this chapter documents the growth of racial disparities in the past three decades and the extraordinary degree to which disadvantaged black people have become enmeshed in the criminal justice system.

IMPRISONMENT RATES

Figure 2.1 shows black and white percentages of state and federal prisoners from 1950 to 2008. Blacks were about a third of prisoners in 1960 and under 40 percent in 1970. The black percentage rose continuously to the mid 40 percents through 1980, rising slowly thereafter until the early 1990s and reaching a plateau at about 50 percent. In most years between 1991 and 2002 there were in absolute numbers more black than white prisoners. If comparisons exclude Hispanics, in every recent year the absolute number of non-Hispanic black prisoners has exceeded the absolute number of non-Hispanic whites. In 2008, for example, 34 percent of sentenced state and federal prisoners were non-Hispanic whites; 38 percent were non-Hispanic blacks (Sabol, West, and Cooper 2009, table 5).

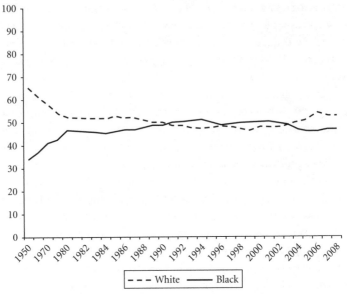

FIGURE 2.1 *Percentages of state and federal prisoners, by race, 1950–2008.*
Sources: for 1950–80, Cahalan (1986); for 1980–2008, Bureau of Justice Statistics (various years-a). Until the late 1990s race was broken down into three categories for all statistics: white, black, and other. In recent years the Bureau of Justice Statistics has added Hispanic as a racial category to various statistics, thus complicating linear representations of the data. In 1999 the Bureau added Hispanic as a racial category to combined state and federal prison statistics. The Hispanic category has been removed and redistributed for each year since 1999. For earlier years data without the Hispanic separation were used. The category "two or more races" has been redistributed evenly between blacks and whites.

Calculation of trend data has been complicated by a U.S. Bureau of Justice Statistics decision in the late 1990s to report separate figures for blacks, whites, and Hispanics. In earlier years Hispanics were included within racial categories and sometimes were also reported separately. The change had the misleading effect of reducing "black" imprisonment rates. Skin color and "racial" identity, however, have been more salient social characteristics in recent decades in the United States than has the difference between being Hispanic or non-Hispanic. Insofar as racial bias, stereotypes, and attributions have influenced officials' decisions, skin color is much more likely than an Hispanic surname or ancestry to influence decisions in individual cases. Accordingly in figure 2.1 (and most other figures) Bureau of Justice Statistics prison population data have been adjusted to take account of the estimated black and white fractions among Hispanics.[1] On the few occasions when "racial" data have not been adjusted to include Hispanics, I refer explicitly to non-Hispanic whites and non-Hispanic blacks.

The jail story is much the same. Figure 2.2 shows black and white percentages of local jail inmates from 1950 to 2008. About a third of jail inmates in 1950 and in 1960 were black and about 40 percent in 1970, a

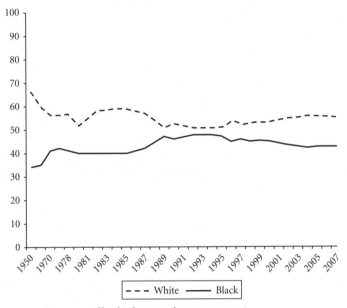

FIGURE 2.2 *Percentages of local jail inmates, by race, 1950–2008.*
Sources: for 1950–83, Cahalan (1986); Bureau of Justice Statistics (1984, 1990); for 1983–89, Bureau of Justice Statistics (various years-b); for 1990–95, Gilliard and Beck (1996); for 1996–2008, Bureau of Justice Statistics (various years-c). The Bureau of Justice Statistics began using a separate Hispanic category much earlier in reporting jail data than in reporting prisoner data. For every year starting in 1990 the Hispanic category has been removed and redistributed.

level around which the black percentage oscillated until the mid-1980s. For a decade after that, coinciding with the most aggressive years of the war on drugs, blacks were 45 to 48 percent of inmates, after which the percentage declined somewhat.

Because these two figures are expressed in black and white percentages they do not reflect the true magnitude of racial differences in imprisonment rates. It would be natural for someone new to the subject to compare the black percentage of the general population (12–13) to the black percentage of the combined jail and prison populations (46–50) and conclude that blacks are four times more likely to be confined than should be expected.

That would be incorrect, and misleading. Calculating the difference that way understates the extent of racial disparity. The correct way to calculate racial disparities in imprisonment is to compare the black imprisonment rate per 100,000 black people with the white imprisonment rate per 100,000 white people.

For the past two decades that comparison has shown that total imprisonment rates for blacks have been five to seven times those for whites. The differential is greater for men than for women. In 2000, for example, the total imprisonment rate for non-Hispanic black men for jail and prison combined was 3,457 per 100,000, and the rate for non-Hispanic white men was 449 per 100,000 (the corresponding rates for non-Hispanic black and white women were 205 and 34). The black male rate was seven times that for whites. The black female rate was six times higher. In 2008, the difference in male rates was about the same. The difference in female rates had fallen to three (Sabol, West, and Cooper 2009, table 6). Figure 2.3 shows aggregate black and white imprisonment rates for jails and federal and state prisons from 1950 to 2008. Black rates dwarf those of whites. The *increase* in the black rate between 1980 and 2006 (1,834 per 100,000) was 3.8 times the *total white rate* (483 per 100,000) in 2006. The magnitude of racial differences in combined imprisonment rates can be illustrated in another way. By 2006 the white rate of 483 per 100,000, after thirty-three years of increases beginning in 1973, failed to reach the black rate in 1950 (598).

The racial difference in aggregate imprisonment rates is huge. The extent to which increased imprisonment over recent decades

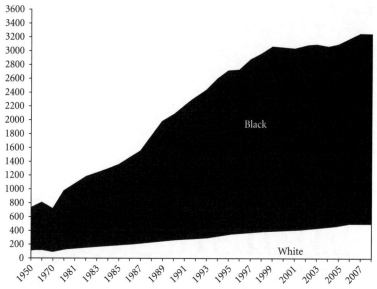

FIGURE 2.3 *Incarceration in state and federal prisons and local jails per 100,000, by race, 1950–2008.*

Sources: Bureau of Justice Statistics (1984, 1990, various years-a, various years-b, various years-c); Cahalan (1986); Gilliard and Beck (1996). This figure is based on data used in figures 2.1 and 2.2, then compared with the population statistics provided by the U.S. Bureau of the Census.

has destabilized America's black population can be shown in another way. The six- to sevenfold difference in imprisonment rates continued nearly unchanged for a quarter century. That means that the incremental increase for blacks each year has on average been seven times higher than the increase for whites.

Figure 2.4 shows this. It depicts year-to-year increases in total imprisonment rates for blacks and whites from 1990 to 2008 and the cumulative increases for the whole period. In eleven of the nineteen years shown the increase in black imprisonment rates exceeded 50 per 100,000. In four of those years the increase exceeded 100 per 100,000. Those *one-year increases* exceed the total imprisonment rates of Canada in many years and of many European countries at any time in the past forty years. In 2009 the imprisonment rates for the Scandinavian

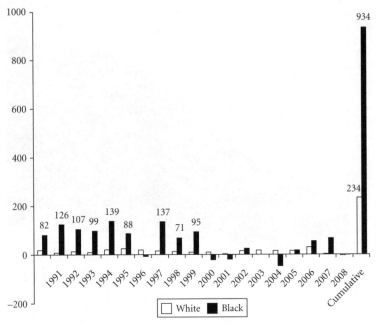

FIGURE 2.4 *Increases in the total imprisonment rate per 100,000, by race, 1990–2008. Sources: Same as for Fig. 2.3.*

countries ranged between 65 and 74 per 100,000 population. The rates for France, Germany, and Belgium fell between 88 and 96 per 100,000. The Canadian rate was just above 100 per 100,000 (International Centre for Prison Studies 2010).

In recent years the number of people serving life sentences has exploded. Seventy thousand people were serving life sentences in 1992. In 2008, after more than fifteen years of declining crime rates, nearly 141,000 people were. That is nearly 9 percent of the total state and federal prison population that year of 1,610,000. The imprisonment rate for state and federal prisons was 506 per 100,000. This means that the life sentence imprisonment rate for the United States was nearly 50 per 100,000, not much below the total rates for all prisoners, including people being held before trial, in the Scandinavian countries (Nellis and King 2009; Sabol, West, and Cooper 2009). Stop and think about that for a moment: America locks up for life almost as large a segment of its population as other developed countries lock up altogether.

Disparities affecting black people serving life sentences are even greater than prison disparities generally. As table 2.1 shows, 38 percent of sentenced federal and state prisoners in 2008 were non-Hispanic black, 34 percent were non-Hispanic white, and 20 percent were Hispanic. However, among people serving life sentences, 64.7 percent of those in federal prisons were non-Hispanic blacks and in all prisons 48.3 percent were. Among the 41,000 people serving sentences of life without the possibility of parole (LWOP) in federal or state prisons, the racial skewing is even greater: 56.4 percent were non-Hispanic blacks.

Table 2.2 shows similar patterns for juveniles. In most developed countries there are few or no people serving time in adult prisons for crimes they committed as children. In the United States, in 2008, nearly 7,000 people were serving life sentences for crimes committed as juveniles; 47.3 percent were non-Hispanic blacks. Of the nearly 1,800 serving LWOP sentences, 56.1 percent were non-Hispanic blacks. If Hispanics had been apportioned among black and white prisoners in this table and table 2.1, the black percentages and numbers would be even higher.

TABLE 2.1   Life Sentences in the United States, 2008, Black, White, Hispanic Percentages

Population	Black	White	Hispanic
Sentenced state and federal prisoners, total	38	34	20
Life sentences, federal	64.7	17.8	13.7
Life sentences, state and federal combined	48.3 ($N = 66,918$)	33.4 ($N = 47,032$)	14.4 ($N = 20,309$)
LWOPs, federal	66.8	15.6	14.7
LWOPs, state and federal combined	56.4 ($N = 23,181$)	33.5 ($N = 13,751$)	7.4 ($N = 3,052$)

Note: LWOP is the sentence of life without the possibility of parole.
Source: Nellis and King (2009, tables 3, 5).

TABLE 2.2   Life Sentences, 2008, Black, White, Hispanic Juvenile Percentages

Population	Black	White	Hispanic
Sentenced state and federal Prisoners, total	38	34	20
Life sentences, federal	53.9	22.9	17.1
Life sentences, state and federal combined	47.3 ($N = 3,219$)	22.7 ($N = 1,547$)	23.7 ($N = 1,615$)
LWOPs, federal	54.3	25.7	17.1
LWOPs, state and federal combined	56.1 ($N = 984$)	28.3 ($N = 497$)	11.7 ($N = 205$)

Note: LWOP is the sentence of life without the possibility of parole.
Source: Nellis and King (2009, tables 8, 9).

Death, finally, in this respect is not different. Racial disparities on death row parallel those for imprisonment generally. Figure 2.5 shows absolute numbers of blacks and whites on death row (including Hispanics). The black share has not changed significantly for twenty-five years, despite a steep decline in homicide rates, the huge increase in blacks serving LWOPs, and significant declines in the numbers of blacks arrested for homicide. On July 23, 2010, 41.6 percent of the residents of death row were non-Hispanic blacks (Death Penalty Information Center 2010).

The disproportionate presence of blacks in American prisons and jails has not changed substantially since 1980. The important questions are why black rates are so much higher than those for whites, and why they have remained so much higher.

There are at least five reasons. The three most important are that black Americans engage in violent crime at higher rates than whites do, that the War on Drugs has unfairly targeted black people, and that enormous increases in prison sentence lengths for violent and drug crimes have disproportionately affected black offenders. The other reasons, less important empirically but as important morally, are racial bias and the influence of unconscious bias and stereotypes. I defer discussion of the last of these to chapter 4 and mostly defer discussion of the effects of the War on Drugs to chapter 3.

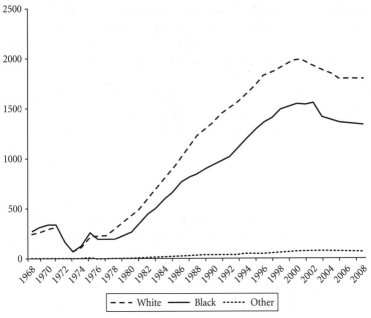

FIGURE 2.5 *Prisoners under sentence of death, by race, 1968–2008.*
Source: Snell (2009).

RACIAL DIFFERENCES IN CRIMINALITY

Thirty years ago possible explanations for why the prison population was nearly half black were contentious and hotly disputed. The belief was widespread that criminal justice officials were racially biased and too much influenced by racial stereotypes (e.g., American Friends Service Committee 1971). During the 1980s, however, a consensus view emerged that, though bias and stereotyping existed, they were not the primary causes of racial disparities. For serious violent crimes, racial differences in offending were a significant factor: blacks committed homicides, rapes, robberies, and serious assaults at higher rates than whites did. Much violent offending is intraracial, so failure to take black offenders' violent crimes seriously would constitute indifference to the experiences of black victims, and few people would want to do that. Racial disparities preponderantly based on differences in rates of violent offending are difficult to challenge on normative grounds.

There are two important caveats to the explanation that racial offending differences accounted for imprisonment differences. First, it applied mostly to serious violent offenses; for less serious offenses, offending explained much less of imprisonment disparities. For the most serious crimes, the crime itself appeared to be the primary factor explaining sentencing decisions, leaving comparatively little room for bias or stereotyping to operate. Less serious crimes allowed more room for discretionary decision making and the crime itself explained less. Second, for some crimes, arrest differences have no necessary link to offending differences; drug arrests are the most important example. Police can arrest inner-city street-level drug dealers almost at will, meaning that arrests are more a measure of police activity than of criminality. Disparities in arrests for drug offenses occur because police choose to arrest more black people.

The preceding paragraphs summarize analyses catalyzed by a landmark article by Alfred Blumstein (1982) that compared racial differences in arrests to racial differences in imprisonment, by offense and overall. It prompted additional, more refined analyses by others (e.g., Langan 1985; Tonry 1995). Blumstein's basic conclusions held up and were broadly confirmed by research on sentencing disparities. That work generally concluded that there are relatively few racial differences in sentence lengths for offenders sent to prison; differences are more likely concerning the decision whether to send someone to prison (typically concerning less serious offenses and offenders; Blumstein et al. 1983; Harrington and Spohn 2007; Spohn 2000, forthcoming).

In the next few paragraphs, I summarize Blumstein's original analysis, present the results of a replication of his analysis using 2004 data, and discuss other sources of information that might confirm or refute the conclusions he reached.

BLUMSTEIN'S ORIGINAL ANALYSIS

Blumstein (1982) compared racial percentages among people arrested for particular offenses to racial percentages among state prisoners sentenced following convictions for those offenses. Lots of questions can be raised as to whether arrests are a valid measure of offending (they might be, for example, systematically biased or erratically incomplete), whether jail inmates should have been taken into account, and whether arrest patterns should be compared with racial patterns in prison admissions rather than in prison populations. I return to some of those questions below.

Table 2.3 sets out Blumstein's original analysis and adds one additional column of information. The first two columns show black and white percentages among people serving prison sentences in 1979 for eleven offense categories and overall. The third and fourth columns show black and white percentages of people age eighteen and older arrested in 1979 for those offense categories and overall. The sixth column, which was not in Blumstein's analysis, compares the black percentages in the preceding columns and shows, for example, that black arrests for homicide "explain" all but 1.3 percent of the black percentage among people imprisoned for homicide. The unexplained variations among people imprisoned for robbery and aggravated assault are larger, but still small. For lesser assaults, auto theft, and burglary, the unexplained variation ranges from 16.6 to 29.8 percent, with the largest unexplained variation being for drug crime (36.7 percent).

Blumstein used a different analysis. His results are shown in the fifth column. He compared black imprisonment relative to black arrests to white imprisonment relative to white arrests. Whites were relatively underrepresented in prison compared with their presence among arrestees (e.g., 47.7 percent of homicide prisoners but 48.5 percent of homicide arrestees; 57.7 percent of burglary prisoners but 67.1 percent of burglary arrestees). He thus compared blacks' presence in prison given an arrest for a particular offense to whites' presence given an arrest for the same offense. Between-race calculations (column 5) produce higher rates of unexplained variation than do within-race calculations (column 6; 20.5 percent overall compared with 11.6), but the results using either calculation were inconsistent with the hypothesis that racial

TABLE 2.3 Comparison of Crime-Specific Percentages of Blacks in State Prison and among Persons Arrested, 1979

Crime	Prisoners		Arrests		% Black Prisoners Unexplained by Arrest, Relative to White Prisoners	% Black Prisoners Unexplained by Arrest
	White	Black	White	Black		
Murder and non-negligent manslaughter	47.7	52.3	48.4	51.6	2.8	1.3
Forcible rape	43.7	56.3	51.3	48.7	26.3	13.5
Robbery	38.8	61.2	42.9	57.1	15.6	6.7
Aggravated assault	57.7	42.3	59.0	41.0	5.2	3.1
Other violent	53.1	46.9	60.9	39.1	27.3	16.6
Burglary	57.7	42.3	67.1	32.9	33.1	22.2
Larceny/auto theft	50.7	49.3	65.4	34.6	45.6	29.8
Other property	64.4	35.6	65.4	34.6	4.3	2.8
Drugs	60.5	39.5	75.0	25.0	48.9	36.7
Public order	61.4	38.6	69.3	30.7	29.5	20.5
Other	71.7	28.3	66.3	33.7	-28.7	-19.1
Total	50.9	49.14	56.6	43.45	20.5	11.6

Source: Blumstein (1982).

bias and stereotyping explained the largest part of disparities in imprisonment rates for serious crimes.

There are two primary objections to Blumstein's analysis. First, arrests may be a biased basis for making comparisons. Second, prison population data result from a combination of how many people are sentenced to prison and for how long. Whites, for one hypothetical example, might be sentenced to prison less often than blacks for particular offenses, but for longer average times. That might be because prosecutors screened out most low-severity robberies involving whites but prosecuted those involving blacks. Simple comparisons of numbers of blacks and whites in prison following convictions for those offenses would obscure those differences.

Patrick Langan (1985) explored these objections. His aim was to get behind arrests by looking at data on assailants identified by victims and, to avoid the confounding interaction effects of prison admission rates and average sentence lengths, by looking at prison admission rates alone. He compared data from the National Crime Victimization Survey for 1973, 1979, and 1982 on victims' characterizations of their assailants' race with racially disaggregated data on prison admissions. Victimization data by definition cannot ask about homicides, and rape numbers in victimization data are too small to permit meaningful analyses, so Langan looked at robbery, aggravated assault, and three property crimes. For robbery, his findings paralleled Blumstein's. Possible racial bias in police arrests for serious crimes did not seem to be a major contributor to racial disparities: the racial patterns shown in victims' reports on the race of the people who robbed them were nearly identical to racial patterns in prison admissions. Like Blumstein, Langan concluded that about 80 percent of racial disparity in prison was explainable by reference to offending patterns and, overall, that "test results generally support the differential involvement [in crime] hypothesis" (678).

REPLICATION USING 2004 DATA

Matthew Melewski, then a University of Minnesota law student, and I replicated Blumstein's analysis using arrest and prison population data for 2004 (Tonry and Melewski 2008).

Table 2.4 shows the results. A much smaller part of racial disparities in imprisonment can be explained by arrest patterns in 2004 than Blumstein found for 1979. In Blumstein's between-race comparisons, arrests explained all but 2.8 percent of imprisonment disparities in homicide imprisonment; 11.6 percent remained unexplained in 2004. For robbery in 1979, 15.6 percent of imprisonment disparities went unexplained; in 2004, 37.2 percent. Overall Blumstein's 1979 analysis left 20.5 percent of imprisonment disparities unexplained; the 2004 analysis left 57.4 percent unexplained. That is a staggering difference. Had Blumstein in his 1982 article found unexplained disparities as large as we found for 2004, surely his conclusion would have been the opposite

TABLE 2.4   Comparison of Crime-Specific Percentages of Blacks in State Prison and among Persons Arrested, 2004

Crime	Prisoners		Arrests		% Black Prisoners Unexplained by Arrest, Relative to White Prisoners	% Black Prisoners Unexplained by Arrest
	White	Black	White	Black		
Murder and non-negligent manslaughter	48.9	51.1	52.0	48.0	11.6	6.0
Forcible rape	61.7	38.3	67.7	32.3	23.2	15.7
Robbery	37.6	62.4	49.0	51.0	37.2	18.2
Assault	53.3	46.7	73.5	26.5	58.8	43.2
Burglary	59.1	40.9	72.6	27.4	45.5	33.0
Larceny-theft	57.8	42.2	71.1	28.9	44.3	31.5
Motor vehicle theft	63.3	36.7	67.4	32.6	16.7	11.2
Drugs	45.5	54.5	66.2	33.8	57.4	38.0
Violent crime	52.1	47.9	63.9	36.1	38.4	24.6
Property crime	60.3	39.7	71.1	28.9	38.3	27.3
Total	53.2	46.8	65.0	35.0	38.9	25.3

Sources: Bureau of Justice Statistics (2006); Federal Bureau of Investigation (2005).

of what it was: such large unexplained variation creates a strong presumption of racial bias. Racial disparities in imprisonment in the United States are getting worse, much worse, not better.

This huge difference between our findings and Blumstein's does not mean that his core conclusion—that racial differences in offending were the primary cause of imprisonment disparities in 1979—was wrong. The analysis in table 2.4, however, shows that racial differences in offending are not the primary cause of imprisonment disparities in our time.

In trying to understand why the results are so different for 2004 we looked at racial trends in arrest patterns. Perhaps black percentages among people arrested for serious crimes rose rapidly after 1979, with black percentages in 2004 being anomalously low. That is not the

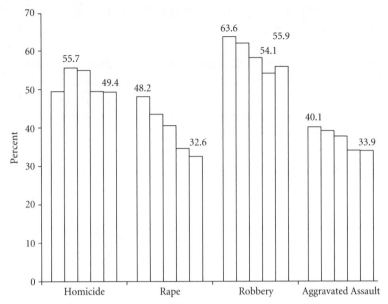

FIGURE 2.6 *Black percentages among the Uniform Crime Report violent index arrestees,*
1984–2008 (5-year averages).
Source: Federal Bureau of Investigation (various years).

explanation. The opposite is true: black Americans' involvement in
violence is declining. Figure 2.6 shows black percentages, averaged
over five-year periods, among people arrested for homicide, forcible
rape, robbery, and aggravated assault between 1984 and 2008. I use
five-year averages to eliminate year-to-year distortions and capture
the main underlying long-term trends. Although black Americans
continue to be overrepresented among arrestees, the degree of over-
representation has been falling for a quarter century. Fifty-six percent
of homicide arrestees in 1989–93 were black; 49 percent were in
2004–8. Forty-eight percent of rape arrestees in 1984–88 were black;
33 percent were in 2004–8. The declines are almost as steep for robbery and aggravated assault.

That's good news. Violent crime has been falling in the United
States since 1991–92. In absolute terms, black involvement in violent

crime has followed the general pattern. In relative terms, black involvement in violent crime has fallen substantially more than the overall averages.

Perhaps, we thought, the explanation for why imprisonment disparities are no longer closely linked to arrest disparities has something to do with changes in arrest data that operate to underreport black violence. To check this, using NCVS data we compared the percentages of black suspects among people arrested for robbery and aggravated assault with victims' descriptions of the racial characteristics of their assailants. Figure 2.7 shows the result: no significant

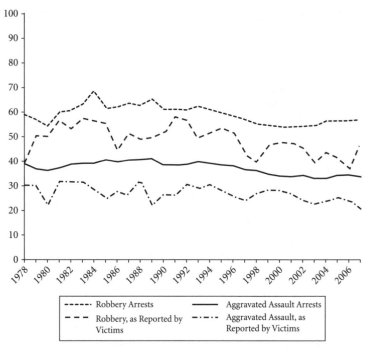

FIGURE 2.7 *Percentages of blacks among lone offenders as perceived by victims and percentages of black arrests, 1978–2007.*
Sources: Bureau of Justice Statistics (various years-d, various years-e,); Federal Bureau of Investigation, (various years).

change in a third of a century. The data on victim identification of assailants fluctuate more than the arrest data because both offenses (but especially robbery) are relatively rare events and numbers vary randomly from year to year. Black percentages among arrestees for both offenses have nonetheless consistently paralleled victims' characterizations but have been somewhat higher. The black percentages among people arrested are higher because some robberies and assaults involve more than one assailant. The NCVS data, by contrast, are based on victims' reports only about crimes involving a single assailant.

Comparison of racial percentages among people arrested and held in prison for serious crimes in Blumstein's analysis showed that crime and imprisonment were closely linked. Others' efforts to test his findings by looking at prison admissions rather than at prison populations, and by comparing victims' reports with police records, broadly confirmed Blumstein's main conclusion. Melewski's and my analysis twenty-five years later of 2004 data reached the opposite conclusion. Crime and imprisonment patterns are no longer closely linked.

Pulling things together to this point: black people are arrested for violent crimes at significantly higher rates than whites, but that difference has been declining over time. Victims' reports and police records show no difference over time in relations between violent victimization and police data on recorded crime. Racial disparities in imprisonment have, however, not appreciably declined since they reached historic highs during the Reagan administration in the 1980s. Blacks are to an enormous extent disproportionately affected by prison sentences generally, life sentences, LWOPs, and death sentences.

CRIMINAL JUSTICE SYSTEM EXPLANATIONS FOR DISPARITIES

Why are so many blacks in prison compared with whites despite both absolute and relative reductions in violent crimes committed by black people? Sentencing policies for violent and drug crimes and police drug law enforcement practices are a major part of the explanation. So is racial profiling by the police. Biased judges are not.

Sentencing Policies for Violent and Drug Crimes

Black Americans have borne the brunt of tougher sentencing policies. For drug crimes, as chapter 3 shows, police arrest blacks at rates that are way out of proportion to their drug use or involvement in drug trafficking. For understandable reasons of social disadvantage and limited life chances, blacks have long been more involved than whites in violent crime, but that difference is becoming less. Laws that increase sentences for drug and violent crimes inevitably exacerbate racial disparities.

The National Corrections Reporting Program of the Bureau of Justice Statistics, for example, reports new state prison commitments by conviction offense and race. In 2003, among whites 53.7 percent were committed for violent, drug, or gun crimes, compared with 69.4 percent of black offenders (in both cases including Hispanic same-race offenders). The racial skew is even greater when the focus is narrowed to robbery, drugs, and guns (52.1 percent of black prisoners, 32.3 percent of white). The effects of police policies concerning drug arrests explain much of the difference. Among black prisoners 37.5 percent were committed for drug crimes; among white prisoners, 25.5 percent were (Bureau of Justice Statistics 2010).

In chapter 6 I discuss current knowledge about the effects of the War on Drugs and about the deterrent and incapacitative effects of lengthy prison sentences. There have long been good reasons to doubt that longer sentences for drug crimes have any effect on levels of drug use, prices, or trafficking (e.g., J. Q. Wilson 1990; Dills, Miron, and Summers 2008; MacCoun and Martin 2009). And there are good reasons to doubt that increasing penalties for particular violent or drug crimes from three years to five, five years to ten, or ten years to twenty has any discernible effects on crime rates (e.g., Doob and Webster 2003; Tonry 2008b; Dills, Miron, and Summers 2008). Those things being true, to increase penalties for crimes with which blacks are charged, for whatever reason, is to increase racial disparities in prison for no good reason or for a poorly justified one.

Biased Sentencing

The sentencing literature documents relatively small racial differences in sentences for black and white offenders convicted of the same crime. Black defendants, all else being equal, are slightly more likely than whites to be sentenced to confinement, but, among those incarcerated, not to receive longer sentences (Spohn 2000, 2002, forthcoming). Blacks are less likely than whites to be diverted to nonincarcerative punishments, and more likely in states that have sentencing guidelines to receive sentences at the top rather than at the bottom of guideline ranges (Tonry 1996, chap. 2). Individual studies present divergent findings, often showing small disparities by race and ethnicity for men but not for women (or to different extents), for Hispanics but not for blacks, and for young offenders but not for older ones (or in each case vice versa; e.g., Walker, Spohn, and DeLone 2006; Harrington and Spohn 2007, 40–45). Overall, when statistical controls are used to take account of offense characteristics, prior criminal records, and personal characteristics, black defendants are on average sentenced somewhat but not substantially more severely than whites. Research discussed in chapter 4 shows that most people, black, white, and Hispanic, are influenced by subconscious stereotypes about black criminality, but the effects on decisions are probably not large in the aggregate. Those stereotypes no doubt sometimes influence judges' decisions. Overall, however, there is no credible evidence that biased decision making by judges is a major cause of sentencing disparities.

The sentencing literature, however, misses a major point. Researchers compare punishments received by black and white offenders for the same offense and attempt to control for other individual characteristics, notably differences in prior criminal records. Such comparisons overlook the larger reality that black defendants are much more likely than white to be convicted of drug and violent offenses for which American laws authorize or mandate sentences measured in decades and lifetimes. In 2008, for example, 79.8 percent of offenders sentenced in federal courts for crack cocaine offenses were black; 10.4 percent were white (U.S. Sentencing Commission 2009, table 34). That there were not major differences in the sentences black and white crack defendants received is much less consequential than that the prison sentences that crack offenders, mostly black, received were vastly longer than the sentences that powder cocaine offenders received for offenses involving comparable amounts of drugs. Judges may not impose substantially longer sentences on blacks than on whites when they are convicted of the same offense, but the federal 100-to-1 rule resulted in much longer sentences for black defendants and for many more blacks in prison. The 18-to-1 rule that replaced it in 2010 will reduce the difference but only slightly. Three-strikes laws, "dangerous offender" laws, and mandatory minimum sentences for violent and drug crimes work the same way. Vastly higher imprisonment rates for black Americans are attributable primarily not to bad and biased judges but to bad and biased laws.

Racial Profiling

No one doubts that racial profiling by the police takes place or that it results in many more arrests of black people than would otherwise occur. The fundamental questions concerning racial profiling are whether police stop blacks at higher rates than they do whites (yes, they do) and whether police have valid bases for stopping blacks much more often than whites (no, they do not). Answers to the second question are usually sought in evidence about the outcomes of the stops. If blacks are stopped at twice the rate of whites but drugs, guns, and other contraband are found in the same or a higher percentage of cases, that implicitly demonstrates that police had valid reasons more often to be suspicious of blacks. However, the reverse is true. Research on profiling generally concludes that police stop blacks disproportionately often on sidewalks and streets and generally find contraband at lower rates for blacks than for whites (e.g., Engel and Calnon 2004).

An especially comprehensive analysis of police stop-and-frisk practices documenting these patterns was released early in 2009. The data, on police practices in New York City for forty-two months ending in mid-2008, were compiled by the New York City Police Department under a federal district court order relating to a lawsuit on racial profiling. Also under court order, the data were turned over to the Center for Constitutional Rights (2009), which released an early analysis. There were nearly 1,600,000 police stops of citizens in those forty-two months. Ten percent of those stopped were non-Hispanic whites, though they made up 44 percent of the population. Half of those stopped were non-Hispanic blacks, though they made up only a quarter of the population. Hispanics constituted 28 percent of the population and 30 percent of those stopped.

Arrest rates were about the same for the three groups but for every other measure arrests of blacks were more intrusive and less productive. Once stopped, blacks were much more likely than whites to be frisked (28 percent of whites in 2006 and 41 percent in 2008, compared with 46 percent of blacks in 2006 and 56 percent in 2008). Only in 1 percent of cases were weapons found, but at higher rates among whites than among blacks and Hispanics. Overall and in each year separately, whites were more likely than blacks and Hispanics to be in possession of drugs or other contraband. Finally, police used force against the people they stopped in nearly a quarter of cases. Over the four years 15 to 19 percent of whites stopped were the victims of police use of force and 21 to 26 percent of blacks and Hispanics.

This massive data set on the operations of the largest police department in the United States thus strongly corroborates the findings of scholarly research. Blacks are stopped much more often than whites, relative to the composition of New York City's population, and are much more likely when stopped to be frisked and to have force used against them. They are, however, less likely to be in possession of guns or other contraband and are no more likely to be arrested. That last point warrants elaboration lest an important reality be ignored. Because so many more blacks than whites are stopped, the same or a somewhat lower arrest rate produces vastly larger numbers of black than white people taken into police custody (Center for Constitutional Rights 2009).

The effects of bias and stereotyping are likely to be different at police and sentencing stages of the criminal justice system. Stops of blacks often result in more arrests, however, partly because blacks are more likely to resent the stop and to resist or act disrespectfully or impatiently, partly because blacks are more likely to have outstanding arrest warrants or to be in violation of parole or probation conditions, and partly because some police are racially biased. Police profiling practices thus lead to higher levels of black arrests, and therefore convictions and prisoners, than would otherwise happen. These practices are particularly likely to worsen racial disparities for drug and firearms offenses as those are the two kinds of illegal contraband police stops are most likely to yield.

The situation with court officials is different. On the basis of personal interactions over decades with judges in many American jurisdictions, I do not believe invidious racial bias and gross stereotypes substantially affect sentencing decisions. This is a subject judges worry about, are taught about at judicial conferences, and discuss often among themselves and with others. Sentencing research showing that there are few racial differences in sentence lengths is consistent with this belief. Research showing that black offenders are slightly more likely than whites to receive prison terms are not strongly inconsistent with it. Black defendants, especially young ones, often have more extensive criminal records than whites, and judges take criminal records into account when deciding which defendants deserve another chance. Similarly black defendants on average have less stable home lives, less conventional employment records, and fewer educational attainments than whites, and judges take such things into account in deciding which defendants are more likely to succeed in community sentences and programs and which are more likely to reoffend.

Black Americans suffer from imprisonment rates five to seven times higher than whites primarily for two reasons. First, American sentencing laws and policies specify punishments that are both absolutely and relatively severe for violent, drug, and gun crimes, for which blacks are more likely than whites to be arrested and prosecuted. The effects of racial profiling exacerbate those differences. Second, as the following chapter shows, police arrest policies for drugs target a type of drug trafficking (street-level transactions in inner-city areas) in which blacks are disproportionately involved even though overall they are less likely than whites to use drugs and no more likely to sell drugs.

3

DRUGS

No honest observer can deny that racial disparities in imprisonment are substantially attributable to the War on Drugs. People disagree about whether its disparate effects on blacks and whites are justifiable. Reagan administration attorney general Edwin Meese argued that drug laws are inherently neutral and that disparities exist only because more black people choose to violate them. Critics, I among them, reply that policy makers understood that human behavior is predictable, that inner-city young people could be expected to be involved in drug sales, and that undue damage would be done to black people, individually and collectively. More succinctly, policy makers adopted policies they knew would especially damage black people. This is a morally important disagreement.

Those who agree with Meese say that policy makers made rational decisions aimed at reducing drug use and its damaging effects, and that black people who wind up in prison choose to disobey the law by distributing drugs. They have only themselves to blame. It is too bad that so many young black people decide to sell drugs, but so be it.

Those who agree with me say that the dismal realities and limited opportunities of urban ghetto life make it not at all surprising that many disadvantaged young blacks are enticed into drug use and selling. They also point out that so many young black people are convicted of crimes because police especially target drugs that black people sell and places where they sell them. Policy makers ignored the predictable unhappy consequences of their decisions for the individuals directly affected, and their families and communities, and for the interests of black Americans generally.

It is clear beyond peradventure of doubt that the War on Drugs produced massive racial disparities in arrest, conviction, and imprisonment. In 2008 the arrest rate of blacks for drug crimes was 3.5 times higher than that for whites. In 2006, the last year for which national data from state courts are available, 49 percent of defendants in urban courts charged with drug crimes were non-Hispanic blacks and 26 percent were non-Hispanic whites. For trafficking the racial imbalance is greater: 59 percent black, 16 percent white (Cohen and Kyckelhahn 2010, table A2). In 2003 37.5 percent of black people committed to state prisons had been convicted of drug crimes; among whites newly committed to prison, 25.5 percent were (Bureau of Justice Statistics 2010). In 2006, 45 percent (117,600) of those held in state prisons for drug offenses were non-Hispanic blacks and 27 percent (72,100) were non-Hispanic whites (Sabol, West, and Cooper 2009, table A15).

These differences do not occur because black Americans are more involved with drugs than whites. Black Americans do not use drugs as much or as often as white Americans. Drug selling is at least as frequent among whites as among blacks. Racial disparities are a product of how the drug wars have been fought.

These patterns are the products of two unwise strategic decisions and two tactical mistakes. The strategic decisions were to focus on the supply of drugs rather than on demand for them and to approach drug abuse as a moral problem rather than a public health problem. The tactical mistakes were police decisions to emphasize arrests of street-level dealers and legislative decisions to mandate breathtakingly long prison sentences for many drug crimes.

The decision to focus on supply rather than on demand meant that law enforcement approaches were given priority over treatment and drug abuse prevention, even though the latter are more effective and more cost-effective ways to reduce drug use and dependence. The decision to treat drug abuse as a moral rather than a public health problem contrasts starkly with alcohol abuse policies. Alcohol has not been criminalized, even though many more people are dependent on alcohol than on other drugs and even though the medical costs, years of lost life, and social damage associated with alcohol dependence are far higher than for any other drug. Much alcohol policy, however, is predicated on medical ideas about harm reduction and about genetic predispositions to dependence (Cook 2007). By contrast, for other drugs self-righteous and judgmental approaches were adopted rather than empathetic and problem-solving ones. This led to views of drug use and selling as moral matters of right and wrong. It also led to the characterization of drug dealers as evil predators rather than as the troubled, disadvantaged young people many were and are.

The decision to emphasize arrests of street-level dealers inexorably led to a focus on minority drug sellers in the inner cities. That is where drug deals are most visible and where dealers are easiest to arrest. The emphasis on lengthy prison sentences meant that drug dealers sentenced to prison stayed there a long time. Almost everyone who works on drug policy issues agrees, however, that street-level arrests and subsequent imprisonments have no significant effects on the availability of drugs. The gains to be realized from drug selling appear so great, and the benefits from legitimate employment available to poorly educated ghetto youth so small, that plenty are ready to step into selling roles opened up by their predecessors' arrests.

This is a pathetic dynamic. Ethnographic and economic analyses make it clear that aspiring low-level drug sellers generally make a big mistake: they overestimate their likely gains and underestimate their risks. Reuter, MacCoun, and Murphy (1990) estimate that an average daily drug retailer in Washington, D.C., in 1988 sold a median of $3,600 worth of drugs each month. Each was estimated to have spent sixty-six hours per month selling and to earn $7 per hour when they worked in the legal labor market. Hourly net earnings from drug sales were not significantly better, but vastly more dangerous to obtain (Caulkins and Reuter 1998). Levitt and Venkatesh (2000) worked with financial records of a drug-selling gang in Chicago in the mid-1990s. They estimated that most of those selling crack earned roughly the legal minimum wage.

An endless circle results: young people take risks they underestimate in pursuit of gains they overestimate. When arrested and convicted they receive lengthy prison terms that have no effects on others' willingness to take the same ill-considered risks. Other young people take their places and accept risks they underestimate in pursuit of gains they over-estimate. It goes on and on.

Because of those fundamental mistakes American prisons over the past three decades have held, and continue to hold, many hundreds of thousands of drug offenders whose confinement, and broken lives, have had little or no effect on the availability of drugs. And well over half of them have been black.

This chapter documents the criminal justice system effects of the War on Drugs on black Americans over the past thirty years, a period during which the number of inmates in state prisons convicted of drug crimes increased by seventeen times—from about 16,000 in 1979 to 266,000 in 2006—and racial disparities for drug crimes became much, much worse (Sabol, West, and Cooper 2009, table 8). Alfred Blumstein's 1982 analysis of the 1979 state prison population, which I discussed in chapter 2, compared racial percentages of people in prison after convictions for particular offenses with their percentages among people arrested for those offenses. For serious violent crimes, racial patterns among people arrested closely resembled racial pat-terns among people in prison for the same offenses. Arrests explained all but 2.8 percent of racial variation for homicide and 5.2 percent for aggravated assault (see table 2.3). Arrest patterns for drug offenses explained the smallest percentage of racial disparity in imprisonment (48.9 percent unexplained) of any offense. However, in 1979 only 5.7 percent of prisoners (16,000) had been convicted of drug crimes. Drug offenders were not and could not have been a major source of racial disparity.

Matthew Melewski and I replicated Blumstein's earlier analysis using 2004 prison data (Tonry and Melewski 2008). Arrest patterns for drug offenses explained the smallest percentages of imprisonment disparities of any offense (38.9 percent unexplained), just as it had for Blumstein twenty-five years earlier (see table 2.4). However, by 2004 vastly more people were affected. Twenty percent of state prisoners (249,400) had been convicted of drug crimes.

To be imprisoned people first must be arrested. Figures 3.1 and 3.2 show changes over time in racial patterns of arrests for drug crimes.

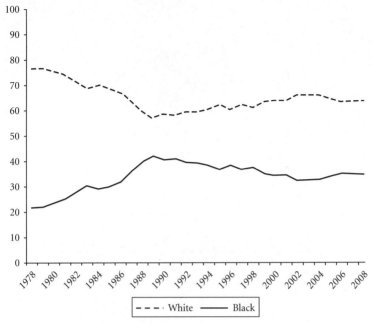

FIGURE 3.1 *Total arrests for drug offenses, by race, 1978–2008.*
Sources: Bureau of Justice Statistics (various years-d); Federal Bureau of Investigation (various years).

Two patterns attributable to the War on Drugs stand out: arrest rates for black Americans are vastly higher than those for white Americans, and the stark differences began to emerge thirty years ago.

Figure 3.1 shows black and white percentages among people arrested for drug crimes between 1978 and 2008 (including Hispanics). As recently as 1978, during the Carter administration, approximately 80 percent of adult drug arrestees were white. That, however, was before the Reagan administration's War on Drugs was launched. By 1989 the black share exceeded 40 percent, and in the years since it has fluctuated between 32 and 40 percent.

Figure 3.2 shows black and white arrest rates per 100,000 from 1978 to 2008. The black rate in 1978 was approximately twice the white rate. By the mid-1980s the black rate was three times higher. Startlingly, in

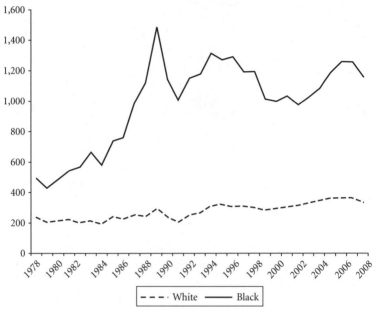

FIGURE 3.2 *Total arrests for drug offenses, by race, 1978–2008.*
Sources: Bureau of Justice Statistics (various years-d).

the late 1980s the black arrest rate for drug crimes was nearly six times the white rate. Since then the arrest rate disparity has usually been at Reagan administration levels, with the black rate between three and four times higher.

Why are blacks so much more often arrested and imprisoned for drug crimes? There are four possible answers: blacks use drugs at higher rates than whites, blacks sell drugs at higher rates than whites, police arrest blacks for drug offenses in numbers disproportionate to their involvement in drug dealing, and black drug offenders receive harsher sentences than white offenders. The first two explanations do not withstand scrutiny: blacks neither use nor sell drugs at higher rates than whites. The second two explain what has been happening: police focus substantially greater attention on drug sales by blacks, and once blacks are arrested they are dealt with more severely.

BLACKS DO NOT USE DRUGS AT HIGHER RATES THAN WHITES

The explanation for high black rates of drug arrests is not that more blacks than whites use drugs. National surveys carried out for the federal government have tracked self-reported drug use since the 1970s. The National Survey on Drug Use and Health is an annual representative survey among persons 12 years and older. Table 3.1 shows percentages

TABLE 3.1   Percentage Aged 12 and Over Using Illicit Drugs and Alcohol, by Race, 2007–8

Drug	2007		2008	
	White	Black	White	Black
Alcohol				
Ever used	87.0	74.7	86.5	74.8
Within past year	70.4	54.5	70.4	56.9
Within past month	56.1	39.3	56.2	41.9
All Illicit Drugs*				
Ever used	50.3	43.1	50.7	46.1
Within past year	14.9	16.0	14.4	16.9
Within past month	8.2	9.5	8.2	10.1
Marijuana				
Ever used	45.2	38.0	45.1	41.1
Within past year	10.5	12.2	10.4	13.5
Within past month	6.0	7.2	6.2	8.3
Cocaine**				
Ever used	16.4	10.0	16.5	11.2
Within past year	2.5	2.0	2.2	2.0
Within past month	0.9	0.8	0.7	0.9
Crack				
Ever used	3.4	5.3	3.4	5.1
Within past year	0.6	1.3	0.4	0.9
Within past month	0.2	0.5	0.1	0.4
Hallucinogens				
Ever used	16.4	6.6	16.8	8.8
Within past year	1.6	1.3	1.6	1.3
Within past month	0.3	0.6	0.4	0.4

(*continued*)

TABLE 3.1   Continued

Drug	2007		2008	
	White	Black	White	Black
Inhalants				
Ever used	10.7	3.7	10.3	4.1
Within past year	0.9	0.5	0.8	0.4
Within past month	0.2	0.2	0.3	0.1

Source: Office of Applied Studies (2010, tables 2.37B, 1.19B, 1.24B, 1.29B, 1.34B, 1.44B, and 1.39B).
* Illicit drugs include marijuana or hashish, cocaine (including crack), heroin, hallucinogens, inhalants, or prescription-type psychotherapeutics used nonmedically.
** Includes crack cocaine.

of blacks and whites who reported in 2007 and 2008 using alcohol, any other drugs, and five specific illicit substances ever, in the past year, and in the past month.

For everything but crack, the percentages of whites reporting that they had ever used particular substances were higher than the black percentages. For hallucinogens and inhalants, the white percentages were two to three times higher. For cocaine, the white percentages were 50 percent higher. For alcohol, the white percentages were 15 percent higher; for marijuana they were 10 percent higher. Only for crack, for which use levels are far lower than for powder cocaine, were the black percentages higher.

Larger percentages of whites reported using alcohol, cocaine, hallucinogens, and inhalants in the preceding year, and the differences are large. In 2007 alcohol was used by 70.4 percent of whites and 54.5 percent of blacks, cocaine by 2.5 percent of whites and 2.0 percent of blacks, hallucinogens by 1.6 percent of whites and 1.3 percent of blacks. Only for marijuana (12.2 percent versus 10.5) and crack (1.3 percent versus 0.6) were black levels higher. Crack, however, is chemically indistinguishable from powder cocaine, and as to cocaine generally, relatively more whites are users. Only for crack (considered alone) do blacks report significantly higher use levels than whites, but in absolute terms the levels of use are low. In 2008 there were six times more white (243 million) than black (39 million) Americans. The absolute numbers of whites using any dangerous substance are four to ten times higher depending on the substance.

Even though lower percentages of whites than blacks, for example, report having used crack ever in their lives or in the preceding year or month, the absolute numbers of white crack users are far higher. In 2007, nearly 5.8 million whites were estimated ever to have used crack, compared with 1.5 million blacks. Among whites, 938,000 were estimated to have used crack in the preceding year compared with 385,000 blacks. The use estimates for the preceding month were 399,000 for whites and 155,000 for blacks (Office of Applied Studies 2010, table 1.34A). One conclusion is clear: blacks are not arrested or imprisoned so much more often than whites for drug crimes because black people use drugs much more extensively than whites. They don't.

BLACKS DO NOT SELL DRUGS MORE OFTEN THAN WHITES

The second possible reason why blacks might more often be arrested for drug crimes is that they are much more extensively involved in drug trafficking. Several sources suggest that this is not true. The best are the national drug use surveys based on representative samples of the U.S. population. Figure 3.3 shows self-reported drug selling by twelve- to seventeen-year-old blacks and whites for the years 2001 to 2008. Three to 4 percent of each group typically reported selling drugs at least once during the preceding year, and 1 percent of each group reported selling drugs ten or more times. The black and white rates are nearly identical. However, on average for the entire period and for most years, self-reported rates of drug selling by whites were slightly higher than rates for blacks.

Other sources confirm the assertion that black Americans are not more actively involved in selling drugs than whites. The National Longitudinal Survey of Youth, a long-term survey of a representative sample of American young people, found that 13 percent of black youth reported ever selling drugs, compared with 17 percent of white youth. Among twelve- to seventeen-year-olds, the proportions who reported

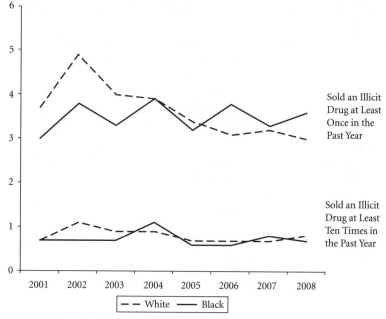

FIGURE 3.3 *Illicit drug sales among youths ages 12–17, by race, 2001–8.*
Source: Office of Applied Studies (various years).

selling drugs were the same for black, white, and Hispanic young people
(H. Snyder and Sicklund 2006).

Representative national surveys undercount transient and homeless
populations and do not count institutionalized populations (in prisons,
jails, mental institutions) at all. The effect is that measures that distinguish black and white rates may undercount black rates because relatively
more blacks than whites have no permanent address or are confined in
institutions. These problems, however, are much less significant for
twelve- to seventeen-year-olds, most of whom live with a parent or care-
taker and few of whom are confined in institutions. However, even if
these sampling problems to some degree affect the data in figure 3.3, they
are unlikely significantly to change the drug trafficking patterns shown;
increasing black rates by 25 percent, for example, would not materially

alter the black-white comparisons. It would make the black rates slightly higher than the white rates rather than slightly lower.

The reason why so many more blacks than whites are arrested and for drug crimes is well-known and long recognized. They are much easier to arrest. Much white drug trafficking occurs behind closed doors and in private. Much black drug dealing occurs in public or semipublic, on the streets, and in open-air drug markets. And much black drug dealing occurs between strangers.

Figures 3.4 and 3.5 present self-report data from the national drug use and health surveys for 2001–8 on where and from whom twelve- to seventeen-year-olds most recently purchased marijuana. As figure 3.4 shows, in each year 87 to 88 percent of whites made their purchases from friends, relatives, and family members. By contrast blacks purchased

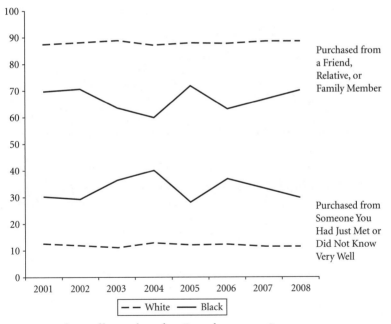

FIGURE 3.4 *Source of last purchase of marijuana, by race, 2001–8.*
Source: Office of Applied Studies (various years).

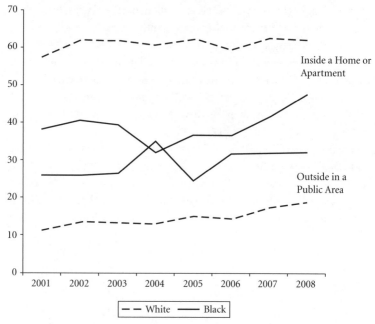

FIGURE 3.5 *Location of last purchase of marijuana, by race, 2001–8.*
Source: Office of Applied Studies (various years). Categories do not add to 100 percent of purchases. Some response categories were excluded.

marijuana from people they had just met or did not know well 30 to 40 percent of the time.

The importance of that difference should not be underestimated. Purchasing drugs is a much riskier activity for young black people than for young whites. Only one in ten whites bought marijuana from someone they did not already know. The chances that they were purchasing from an undercover police officer who might arrest them were low. Conversely the chances that sellers to white buyers were selling to an undercover police officer were also low. For blacks, the transactions were far riskier for buyers and sellers alike, especially for the black seller: a much larger proportion of sales are to strangers.

Drug transactions involving strangers rather than friends or acquaintances are much less likely to occur in comparatively safe private places such as dormitories and private homes. Transactions involving strangers are much likelier to occur in riskier settings out of doors or in public spaces. Figure 3.5 presents data on where marijuana is purchased. Depending on the year, 57 to 62 percent of purchases by whites occurred inside a home, apartment, or dorm, and only 11 to 14 percent outdoors in public spaces such as parking lots or street corners. For black purchasers the pattern was reversed. Forty percent or fewer of purchases occurred in private indoor spaces; 26 to 35 percent were made outdoors in public spaces.

The surveys show that black people buy and sell drugs in riskier transactions and in more vulnerable circumstances than whites. Evidence from studies supported by the federal Office of National Drug Control Policy (ONDCP), the office of the drug czar, points in the same direction. People arrested for serious crimes in ten cities were asked to consent to a short interview and to provide a urine sample to be tested for indications of recent drug use. More than 80 percent agreed to the interview and 86 percent of those provided the urine sample. From 49 to 87 percent of the interviewed arrestees in the ten cities tested positive for some drug, though the drugs of preference varied widely.

Arrestees were asked where they obtain drugs and from what kinds of sources. People who used crack cocaine (the only drug blacks use at higher rates than whites, and for which the vast majority of arrested sellers are black) were much more likely than other users to purchase drugs outdoors and the least likely to purchase in a house or apartment. Crack is "often exchanged in an open air or more public market; in 9 of 10 sites at least 40 percent of arrestees report that their crack purchases were made in outdoor settings and in some sites (Atlanta, Washington, D.C., New York, and Chicago) that proportion is even higher (63–87 percent report outdoor sales)" (ONDCP 2009, viii).

Table 3.2 shows data on the locations of purchases of marijuana, crack cocaine, and powder cocaine in the ten cities. Except by a narrow margin in Portland, Oregon, purchase of crack in public places is much more likely than public purchase of marijuana and powder cocaine. The transactions in which blacks are disproportionately involved are the most vulnerable to police surveillance and apprehension.

TABLE 3.2   Outside Location of Last Purchase of Marijuana, Crack, or Powder,
ADAM II Arrestees, in Percentages

Site	Marijuana	Crack	Powder
Atlanta	45.3	63.9	30.0
Charlotte	32.8	46.6	29.2
Chicago	60.7	67.1	39.4
Denver	42.7	53.9	48.3
Indianapolis	32.4	44.8	40.2
Minneapolis	57.6	59.4	32.3
New York	70.4	75.0	55.1
Portland, OR	34.9	63.8	64.1
Sacramento	40.9	43.0	23.9
Washington	60.9	77.9	unavailable

Source: Office of National Drug Control Policy (2009, appendix C).

The data I have discussed so far come mostly from national surveys. Other substantial literatures have accumulated on racial patterns in arrests (with particular emphasis on profiling). They document race-based police practices. Police invest more time and energy on street-level drug dealing than on white and middle-class dealing behind closed doors. Even among open-air street dealers police emphasize arrests of minority dealers in crack over white dealers in other illicit drugs.

The most extensive and fine-grained studies of street-level drug markets and police arrest policies were carried out in Seattle. Overall only 8.4 percent of Seattle's residents in 2000 were black, but in a twenty-eight-month period during 1999–2001, 51.1 percent of those arrested for drug offenses were black (Beckett et al. 2005, 424). A majority of people who shared, sold, or transferred drugs were white, but 64 percent of people arrested for trafficking offenses were black. Among outdoor drug transactions, a third involved crack, a third involved heroin, and a fourth involved powder cocaine. Among arrests for outdoor drug dealing, 79 percent were for crack, 17 percent involved heroin, and 3 percent involved powder cocaine (Beckett, Nyrop, and Pfingst 2006, figure 1).

The researchers concluded that the disparity was the result of the police department's emphasis on the outdoor drug market in the racially diverse downtown, its lack of attention to other outdoor markets that were predominantly white, its relative disinterest in heroin sellers (who were predominantly white), and its emphasis on crack cocaine: "In over two-thirds of buy-bust operations (in which undercover enforcement officers solicit drugs from suspected drug dealers), officers requested crack cocaine. We even came across records of cases in which undercover officers were offered heroin and powder cocaine by street dealers (both black and white) and refused to purchase those substances, saying they only wanted crack" (Beckett et al. 2005, 429).

POLICE ARREST BLACKS FOR DRUG DEALING MUCH MORE OFTEN THAN THEY ARREST WHITES

Racial differences in arrest rates for drug offenses are enormous, as the findings of a 2009 Human Rights Watch analysis of state and federal arrest data show. The percentage of blacks among people arrested for drug offenses grew from 27 percent in 1980 to 35 percent in 2007 and ranged during the Bush I administration between 40 and 42 percent.[1] The white percentages were at their lowest of the past three decades during the Bush I administration (Human Rights Watch 2009, table 1).

Racial differences are as acute when expressed as rates. Figure 3.2 (see page 58) shows black and white arrest rates per 100,000 same race population. The differences are even more stark when rates are calculated only for adults. The drug arrest rate for black adults has ranged between 1,500 and 2,000 per 100,000 since 1990. Racial disparities in drug arrests exploded in the 1980s, as table 3.3 shows. In 1980 the black arrest rate of 658 per 100,000 was less than twice the white rate (367). By 2003 the black rate was 3.5 times higher and had grown by 225 percent. The white rate increased by 70 percent.

White arrest rates have recently slightly increased because of an emphasis on methamphetamine (Human Rights Watch 2009, figure 1). Higher drug arrest rates for blacks than for whites characterized every state in 2006, with differences ranging from a factor of 3 in several states to more than 11 in Minnesota and Iowa. More than 3 percent of black adults (i.e., more than 3,000 per 100,000) were arrested in California,

TABLE 3.3   Adult Drug Arrests per 100,000 by Race, 1980 and 2003

Race	1980	2003	Growth Rate
White	367	658	70 percent
Black	684	2,221	225 percent

Source: King (2008, table 3).

Illinois, Minnesota, Nebraska, and Oregon (Human Rights Watch 2009, table 4).

Undercover drug agents can relatively easily penetrate black urban drug markets in socially disorganized areas and make arrests almost at will. An undercover police officer can purchase drugs on the street from strangers. Even with street-level dealers who are more cautious, a minority officer working undercover can within hours or days become a familiar local figure. Most white drug dealing, by contrast, occurs within existing social networks in which people know one another and in private places—homes, locker rooms in factories, local bars—to which strangers cannot easily gain admission. Undercover agents have to invest much more time in establishing their bona fides. A stranger in a bar asking "Who here will sell me some coke?" is unlikely to find a willing seller. Getting into private homes or factories to buy drugs is even harder.

John Hagedorn, a sociologist, conducted ethnographic studies of black and white drug markets in Milwaukee. Black drug sales generally occurred openly in the inner city, on the streets, and often to strangers. In white suburban communities, where "nearly all drug transactions were at places of employment or at after-work leisure activities," the picture was different and more insular:

Drugs are sold mainly by "word-of-mouth" means in the suburbs and to white youth. There are no stable, neighborhood, drug-selling locales like [in the African American neighborhoods studied].... White youth and suburban drug dealers hire very few employees, and drug dealing is more part of a "partying" lifestyle than a job. Drugs are sold to whites through contacts at work, at taverns and athletic leagues, and at alternative cultural events....

These methods are more hidden from law enforcement than neighborhood-based sales. (Hagedorn 1998, 1–2)

The arrest yield from a fixed amount of time or effort is much lower when pursuing white than when pursuing black sellers. In a city in which drug arrests are emphasized, an individual officer's productivity in a given amount of time is much greater when black dealers are targeted. If the department wants to maximize arrests, the individual officer will also.

Equally important, police stop blacks more often on the sidewalks and on the streets, for less valid reasons, than they do whites. Blacks are more likely to be stopped on the sidewalk, regardless of whether rates are calculated according to the number of people living in the neighborhood or to the number of people passing through, and on the roads regardless of whether rates are calculated according to the resident population or to the numbers and characteristics of drivers who use the road.

Once stopped, blacks (and Hispanics) are more likely than whites to be searched, have force used against them, and be arrested. These three post-stop phenomena interact. Blacks are more likely than whites to be on bail, probation, or parole or to be subject to pending criminal charges. They are also more likely to feel unfairly treated and that they are victims of police disrespect, bias, or harassment, and to behave in a way that police can characterize as being disrespectful or resisting arrest. Once a suspect is stopped police can check to see whether there are outstanding warrants or parole or probation revocations. Even assuming police stops of blacks were as often made for valid reasons as for whites, the factors would result in more black arrests. Given that police stops of blacks are less often made for valid reasons, that amplification process is even more pronounced.

Critically important, percentages of stops resulting in seizures of "contraband" (a euphemism usually for drugs or guns), however, tend to be lower for blacks than for whites. This indicates that police stop blacks for less valid, often pretextual reasons (e.g., Engel and Calnon 2004, 77–81).

Stop and think about that: police stop blacks much more often than whites, and more often than is objectively justifiable, but are less likely on average to find contraband. Overall, however, because police stop so many more blacks than whites in relative terms, they find many more black people, relative to the population, who possess guns or drugs. Police arrest them.

Black arrest rates for drug crimes are high for two reasons. First, police invest more energy and effort in arresting people in inner cities and on the streets, circumstances that disproportionately target drug transactions involving blacks. Second, racial profiling in police stops of citizens identifies disproportionate numbers of black people possessing drugs who can be arrested. There is therefore no mystery as to why blacks are so much more often arrested for drug crimes than whites, even though they use drugs less often and sell drugs no more. It results from the ways the police choose to enforce drug laws.

BLACK DRUG ARRESTEES ARE MORE LIKELY THAN WHITES TO BE CONVICTED AND IMPRISONED

Once the arrests are made the machinery of the criminal justice system is set in motion. Racial disparities in imprisonment for drug crimes are vastly greater than can be explained by reference even to racially disparate patterns of arrest. Of all major crime categories for which people are sent to prison, as the Blumstein (1982) and Tonry and Melewski (2008) analyses show, drug arrests "explain" the lowest amount of racial disparity in imprisonment.

Blacks' much higher drug arrest rates lead to even greater disparities in imprisonment, as a series of Bureau of Justice Statistics reports on state court operations shows for 2006. Two-thirds of drug felony charges resulted in convictions, and two-thirds of drug felony convictions resulted in imprisonment. Although blacks constituted about a third of drug arrestees, they constituted 49 percent of drug felony defendants in 2006. Among people convicted of drug felonies, 71 percent of blacks were sentenced to confinement, compared with 63 percent of whites (Cohen and Kyckelhahn 2010). When all those higher black percentages are taken into account, a 2008 Human Rights Watch analysis of prison admissions for 2003 showed that relative to population, blacks were 10.1 times more likely than whites to be imprisoned for drug crimes.

A compounding is going on: blacks are arrested for drug crimes much more often than their participation in drug use or trafficking would justify, but then, in addition, they are sent to prison in numbers much greater than their arrests for drug offenses would justify. Why? There are two primary possibilities: prosecutors and judges are biased against blacks and as a result black drug offenders receive harsher sentences, or sentencing laws and guidelines treat the offenses blacks are arrested for more harshly than the offenses whites are arrested for.

National data sources provide no meaningful data on prosecutors, who possess enormous discretion. They can decide not to file charges or dismiss those police have filed. They can divert offenders to treatment programs, including, in many jurisdictions, to drug courts. They may decide that prosecution in a particular case should not be pursued for evidentiary reasons, or because as a matter of resource allocation office policies give higher priority to other kinds of cases. We do know, of course, that police arrest disproportionate numbers of blacks for drug crimes, but we don't know what prosecutors do with those cases.

Comparatively little empirical research has been done on the inner workings of prosecutors' offices. The tiny bit that has been done is not encouraging. The Vera Institute of Justice in New York City, a well-known law reform organization, for example, has worked with urban prosecutors in three cities to assess racial differences in case flows and in decisions to decline prosecution in cases in which police made arrests. In Milwaukee they found that prosecutors more often declined to prosecute white drug suspects than blacks. Forty-one percent of drug paraphernalia cases against whites were declined, compared with 27 percent against nonwhites. Among first-time marijuana possession cases, 16 percent involving whites were declined, compared with 12 percent involving nonwhites. For first-time cocaine possession, 12 percent of white cases were declined, and 7 percent of black cases (MacKenzie, Stemen, and Coursen 2009, 6). Another report showed that Milwaukee prosecutors "declined drug charges…against whites more often" (Miller and Wright 2008, 164). These reports put the findings in a positive light, since documentation of the racial differences led the prosecutor to change policies. Less optimistically, if such differences exist even in progressive and innovative offices that cooperate with Vera's Prosecution and Racial Justice Project, they are likely to exist and be worse in less enlightened places. Overall, the most plausible inference to draw is that prosecutors are tougher on black drug offenders than on whites.

Judges, however, appear to sentence black and white drug defendants relatively even-handedly, although there are not many sources of national data on court processes and operations, and those tend to be dated. The Bureau of Justice Statistics publishes two relevant data series. One, *Felony Defendants in Large Urban Counties*, collects court data from the seventy-five most populous U.S. counties (Kyckelhahn and Cohen 2008; Cohen and Kyckelhahn 2010). The other, *State Court Sentencing of Convicted Felons*, also available most recently for 2006, is based on a nationally representative sample of state courts from three hundred counties (Durose and Langan 2007). Tables 3.4 to 3.7 provide general descriptive information on processing of drug felony cases in state courts in 2006. For that year the FBI reported that 63.6 percent of people arrested for state drug offenses were white and 35.1 percent were black (Hispanics are included within racial categories). Because whites are underrepresented among drug arrestees and blacks are overrepresented, the racial difference is greater than the numbers suggest. Calculated as arrest rates per 100,000 same-race population, the black rate (1,500 per 100,000) in 2004, for example, was 3.6 times higher than the white rate (418 per 100,000; Human Rights Watch 2009, table 2).

Those arrest figures do not easily translate into felony court statistics. Some arrests are not followed by prosecutions. Some involve minors

TABLE 3.4   Race and Hispanic Origin of Defendants, Drug Felonies, Percentages, State Courts, 2006

Offense	Black, non-Hispanic	White, non-Hispanic	Hispanic	Other
Total	49	26	24	1
Trafficking	59	16	23	2
Other drugs	43	33	24	1

Source: Cohen and Kyckelhahn (2010, table A2).

who are handled in juvenile courts. Some are dismissed by prosecutors or judges. Some result in misdemeanor convictions.

Table 3.4 shows that blacks were much more heavily overrepresented among felony drug defendants in 2006 than their 35 percent share among arrestees appears to justify: 49 percent of felony drug defendants were non-Hispanic blacks, 26 percent were non-Hispanic whites, and 24 percent were Hispanic. Fifty-nine percent of those prosecuted for trafficking were non-Hispanic blacks. That racial breakdown is used in the original source. If Hispanics were allocated between the racial groups, the black percentage would be even higher.

Table 3.5 points up the disproportionate black presence among people convicted of drug offenses in 2006. Forty-four percent of people convicted of any drug offense were non-Hispanic blacks, as were 49 percent of those convicted for drug trafficking. Here as always, if Hispanics were included within racial categories, the black percentages would be higher.

Blacks convicted of drug offenses receive harsher sentences than whites. This is primarily because many more black than white offenders are arrested and convicted for crack cocaine offenses and because more blacks are affected by mandatory minimum sentence laws. The research on sentencing discussed in chapter two generally concludes that there are relatively few racial differences in sentences judges impose once the offense of conviction and past criminal records are taken into account. However, if blacks are disproportionately often convicted of offenses subject to mandatory sentence laws or that receive especially long sentences, substantial racial disparities in imprisonment are inevitable. That is what happens.

TABLE 3.5   Racial Characteristics of Persons Convicted of Drug Felonies, State Courts, 2006

Drug Offense	Black*	White*	Other
All drugs	44	55	1
Possession	36	62	2
Trafficking	49	50	1

Source: Rosenmerkel, Farole, and Durose (2009, table 3.2).

TABLE 3.6   Type of Sentence, Drug Felonies in Urban Counties, By Race, 2006, Percentages

Offense	Total Incarceration		Prison		Jail		Non-incarceration	
	Black	White	Black	White	Black	White	Black	White
All drug	70	61	43	31	27	30	30	39
Trafficking	70	59	46	33	25	26	30	41
Possession	71	63	38	28	33	35	29	37

Source: Rosenmerkel, Durose, and Farole (2009, table 3.4).

Table 3.6 shows the types of sentences received following drug felony convictions by black and white drug offenders in state courts in 2006. The general pattern is that blacks more often receive prison sentences and that whites more often receive jail and non-incarcerative sentences. The first two columns show that 70 percent of black drug felons receive incarcerative sentences compared with 61 percent of white drug felons. The last two columns show that 39 percent of whites receive nonincarcerative sentences compared with 30 percent of blacks. The intermediate columns show that slightly more whites receive (by definition, short) jail sentences. Blacks are much more likely to be sentenced to state prisons.

There are no good national data on racial differences in length of sentence for drug crimes. The available data do not show major differences in the lengths of sentences imposed. This is consistent with findings of research on sentencing but is misleading. The statistical systems sometimes combine data for jail and prison sentences, and generally combine data for men and women. Women receive shorter sentences than men. Black women make up a larger percentage of drug felons than do white women, which reduces the overall averages for blacks.

The best national data I have been able to find, shown in table 3.7, are for people released from prison in 2006. The mean average times served by released black drug felons are a third longer than for whites. The numbers are lower than someone new to the subject might expect (24 months time served overall for blacks and 18 months for whites), but they are misleadingly low. One reason is that the numbers refer to both men and women; the women's averages are lower and the men's are higher. A second is that the numbers are for people released during a one-year period.

TABLE 3.7   Time Served at First Release from State Prison in Months, 2006, By Race

Offense	White Median	Black Median	White Mean	Black Mean
All	12	15	18	24
Possession	10	13	14	19
Trafficking	14	18	20	27
Other drugs	12	14	18	22

Source: Bonczar (2010, table 11).

By definition they include relatively large numbers of people serving short sentences and relatively small numbers serving long ones: One hundred percent of the people serving one-year sentences will be released within a year but only ten percent of those serving ten-year sentences. A third is that the laws mandating sentences of 10 or 20 years or longer were passed from the mid-1980s to the mid-1990s and most of the people who received them were still in prison in 2006.

Even with all those qualifications, the numbers shown in table 3.7 are disturbing. They show that the average black drug felon spends a third longer in prison. When the effects of lengthy mandatory minimums, which heavily disproportionately affect blacks, are taken into account the real difference is much greater. Black drug offenders will accumulate in prison in disproportionate numbers if comparatively more of them receive especially long sentences. Under 100-to-1, truth-in-sentencing, and mandatory minimum sentence laws that's what happens.

So there it is. When all the relevant data are pulled together, it is clear that black people bear most of the brunt of the War on Drugs. It is also clear that racial disparities among people imprisoned for drug offenses arise primarily from racial profiling by the police, deliberate police policies to focus drug law enforcement on inner-city drug markets, and deliberate legislative decisions to attach the longest prison sentences to drug offenses for which blacks are disproportionately arrested. I have purposely not used the word *racism* to this point, but it is difficult not to wonder. Racial profiling is, after all, *racial* profiling and happens throughout the United States. Legislators enacting 100-to-1 and other mandatory minimum sentence laws for drug offenses are advised by smart, informed people and cannot have failed to foresee that mostly black people would bear the brunt of the "expressive" and "symbolic" laws they enacted.

The system responded when in the 1960s and 1970s it became clear that large numbers of young white people were being arrested and imprisoned for marijuana offenses and accumulating criminal records that could affect them for the rest of their lives. Arrests of young white people for marijuana offenses plummeted. Some states and more counties effectively decriminalized low-level marijuana dealing. The National Commission on Marihuana and Drug Abuse (1973) proposed decriminalization of marijuana, as did President Jimmy Carter and his primary drug advisor, Dr. Peter Bourne (Musto and Korsmeyer 2002).

The damage done to young black people by the federal 100-to-1 law and the disproportionate burdens placed by the War on Drugs on black people have been clear for two decades. And nothing has happened to change the police practices and sentencing policies that produce those results.

4

Race, Bias, and Politics

Racial disparities in the U.S. criminal justice system raise two important causal questions. The first is how they happened. Those answers are clear. Police practices and legislative and executive policy decisions systematically treated black offenders differently, and more severely, than whites. Policy makers emphasized law enforcement approaches to drug abuse over preventive approaches. Police concentrated on inner-city, primarily minority neighborhoods, where many black Americans live, and on crack cocaine, of which blacks are a large majority of arrested sellers. Police officers engaged in widespread racial profiling and stopped blacks on streets and sidewalks much more often than is justifiable in terms of objective, race-neutral criteria. Legislatures and administrative agencies established policies in the 1980s and 1990s that mandated sentences of historically unmatched severity for violent and drug crimes, for both of which blacks are disproportionately often arrested and prosecuted.

The second question is, Why? Possible answers range from deliberate antiblack racism to inadvertence. Racism in its most blatant forms is not the answer. Conscious racial discrimination is not so pervasive in the early twenty-first century, nor was it in the last two decades of the twentieth, that it is likely that policy makers and police officials were primarily motivated by invidious aims or beliefs.

Nor is inadvertence believable—that policies were chosen and practices were followed in good faith, and it simply never occurred to anyone that black Americans would disproportionately suffer. No credible case can be made that gross racial disparities were unforeseeable. Everyone, we know, sees the world through filters shaped by personal values and ideologies, and reasonable people accordingly differ in their assessments of the scientific evidence about the effectiveness of drug and crime control policies. Reasonable people, however, cannot have failed to recognize that policies adopted since the mid-1980s would produce foreseeable undesirable side effects.

No informed person could have failed, for example, to foresee that unprecedentedly harsh penalties for crack offenses would hit black drug dealers especially hard. Nor, since black arrest rates for serious violent crimes have long been higher than white rates, could any informed person have failed to understand that three-strikes laws, lengthy mandatory minimum sentences, truth-in-sentencing laws, and sentences of life without the possibility of parole would disproportionately send black offenders to prison and keep them there.

One possible explanation is uncomfortably close to racism: officials knew blacks would disproportionately suffer but did not care. For reasons of political self-interest, ideology, or partisanship they enacted disparity-causing policies anyway. At least for some policy makers this is what happened. They acted as if it were more important to score political and ideological points than to worry about the effects on individual human beings of the policies they promoted. Similar choices were made in many policy realms in recent decades, and there is little reason to doubt that this was the choice in relation to drugs and crime.

Americans have lived through three decades in which many conservative politicians at the federal level—and in some states, most notably California and Texas—adopted scorched earth political strategies in which ideological purity, frustrating Democratic policy initiatives, or obeisance to key constituencies have been more important to them than formulating sensible public policies. Examples outside the criminal justice system include the decision to shut down the federal government in the early 1990s rather than negotiate budget reforms, uncompromising opposition to health care reform during the early years of the Obama administration, and refusal over many years to support meaningful gun control legislation despite heavy public support for it. Examples inside the justice system are countless.

One stark example was the persistent refusal of federal policy makers for 24 years to amend or repeal the 100-to-1 law for sentencing of cocaine offenders.[1] No one questioned that the law produced unwarranted racial disparities, and almost everyone agreed that it was unjust. Three Republican administrations and Bill Clinton's, however, refused to change it. In 2008 former President Clinton called the law a "cancer" and said, "I regret more than I can say that we didn't do more on it" (Wickham 2008). However, his administration was unwilling to act, fearing to open itself to Republican accusations of softness. The Clinton White House rejected proposals by the U.S. Sentencing Commission, endorsed by Attorney General Janet Reno and "drug czar" Barry McCaffrey, to eliminate the 100-to-1 difference. Congress passed legislation to reject the commission proposal; Clinton signed it. That was more than fifteen years ago. The Obama administration reduced the differential to 18-to-1. The new law remains fundamentally unjust but will do slightly less damage.[2]

The challenge is to understand why for a quarter century most urban police leaders and many state and federal policy makers adopted and supported disparity-causing policies and practices. The answer is not uncomplicated, but it is becoming clearer. Three powerful forces interacted. The first is a psychology of American race relations characterized by stereotypes of black criminals, unconscious preferences for whiteness over blackness, and lack of empathy among whites for black offenders and their families. The second, which shaped the first, is a three-centuries-old pattern of economic, political, and social dominance of blacks by whites. The third, enabled by the first two, is the Republican Southern Strategy of appealing to racial enmities and anxieties by use of seemingly neutral code words.

Research on social stratification shows how contemporary drug and crime control policies helped sustain a historic pattern of white political and economic dominance. Few police officials and other policy makers have been consciously motivated by that goal. Instead they have viewed the world through what might be called white eyes. The minds behind the eyes, we know better than we once did, were influenced by stereotypes of black street criminals and drug dealers and saw disparities as chips falling where they may. Some, in a more melancholy mood, may have thought, "Life is unjust, but there is nothing we can do about it." The minds behind the eyes, we also now know better than before, often lacked empathy for black offenders, largely because of social distance and lack of personal contact, and partly because of widely held white resentments of black people in the aftermath of the civil rights movement.

A half dozen intertwined literatures on the psychology of race relations show that insensitivity to the interests of black people became a theme of crime and drug control policy. One demonstrates that the mass media—news and entertainment both—regularly portray criminals as black and victims as white and that those stereotypes seep into people's thinking. A second literature shows that, when asked to envision a drug addict or a violent criminal, most white people assume the typical offender to be black. Because these findings have long been known, and no doubt contribute to conscious and unconscious biases, I do not discuss them in detail. A third literature on "implicit bias" shows that most people, when asked to associate black and white with such qualities as pleasant and unpleasant, or dangerous and safe, associate black with unpleasant and dangerous, and white with pleasant and safe. These reactions are nearly instantaneous and unconscious but influence what people think and do. A fourth literature, on "colorism," shows that the darker the skin tone of a black suspect, the likelier victims and others are to believe him to be a criminal, and the more severely he is likely to be punished. A fifth, on "Afro-American feature bias," provides parallel findings concerning people whose facial features match prevailing African American stereotypes. Observers associate stereotypically black faces with crime and criminals. People with such faces get punished more severely, even unto death. Finally, a sixth literature on public attitudes and opinions shows that whites have much harsher attitudes toward offenders and that racial animus and resentment are the strongest predictors of those attitudes.

More important, however, than unconscious processes, though made easier by them, was the deliberate decision of Republican political strategists beginning in the 1960s to use stereotypes of black criminals and proposals for tough crime policies as devices to appeal to white voters. Kevin Phillips, the author of *The Emerging Republican Majority* and an architect of the Republican Southern Strategy, observed that liberalism and Democrats in the South "lost the support of poor whites" as the civil rights movement progressed: "The Negro socioeconomic revolution gave conservatism a degree of access to poor southern white support which it had not enjoyed since the somewhat comparable Reconstruction era" (1969, 206). In the social turbulence associated with the 1960s in general, and the civil rights movement in particular, conservative Republican politicians saw an opportunity to appeal to southern and working-class white voters who traditionally voted Democratic, a group referred to later on as "Reagan Democrats." They did so by focusing on issues—states' rights, crime, welfare fraud, "forced" busing, affirmative action—that served as proxies for race, "wedge issues" as they have since become known (Edsall and Edsall 1991).

Elaborating on the logic of the Southern Strategy in an interview published in the *New York Times* in 1970, Phillips observed:

> From now on, the Republicans are never going to get more than 10 to 20 percent of the Negro vote and they don't need any more than that...but Republicans would be shortsighted if they weakened enforcement of the Voting Rights Act. The more Negroes who register as Democrats in the South, the sooner the Negrophobe whites will quit the Democrats and become Republicans. That's where the votes are. (Boyd 1970, 106)

In a 1981 interview Lee Atwater, the first President Bush's Karl Rove and the developer of the Willie Horton ads used in the 1988 presidential campaign against Michael Dukakis, told a blunter story:

> You start out in 1954 by saying, "Nigger, nigger, nigger." By 1968 you can't say "nigger"—that hurts you. Backfires. So you say stuff like forced busing, states' rights and all that stuff. You're getting so abstract now [that] you're talking about cutting taxes, and all these things you're talking about are totally economic things and a byproduct of them is [that] blacks get hurt worse than whites.
>
> And subconsciously maybe that is part of it. I'm not saying that. But I'm saying that if it is getting that abstract, and that coded, that we are doing away with the racial problem one way or

the other. You follow me—because obviously sitting around saying, "We want to cut this," is much more abstract than even the busing thing, and a hell of a lot more abstract than "Nigger, nigger." (quoted in Herbert 2005; Lamis 1999, 8)

The Southern Strategy is no longer official Republican Party policy, but it need not be. It achieved its short-term aim—winning elections. In the long term, however, it helped shape and reinforced prevailing negative white attitudes toward black people. As time passed, most white people abandoned ideas about black racial inferiority but replaced them with racial resentments: that disadvantaged black people have received too much support from the state and are responsible for the adverse social and economic conditions of their lives.

The rest of this chapter tells those stories. The first part examines recent writing on the social psychology of American race relations in connection with crime and punishment. It documents mental processes that lead officials and others to engage in "statistical discrimination," and to treat black people more severely on the basis of skin tone and distinctive African American facial characteristics. A literature on public opinion and attitudes examines the causes and correlates of racial differences in attitudes toward punishment. The key findings are that much larger percentages of whites than blacks support harsh punishments, including the death penalty, for reasons that include widely held resentments toward and stereotypes about black criminals.

The second part examines the history of American race relations. Scholars who study social stratification and racial hierarchy have shown that American social, economic, and legal institutions have evolved in ways that maintained white dominance and protected the interests of whites as a class. When one mechanism for maintaining white domination broke up, another replaced it. Slavery did the job for centuries, until the Civil War. Within decades after the war Jim Crow laws restored overwhelming white predominance. Millions of blacks moved north to escape Jim Crow; the big-city ghettos, housing and employment discrimination, and racial bias kept them in their subordinate place. Contemporary wars on drugs and crime took over more recently.

The third part says a bit more about the Republican Southern Strategy. Some of its most influential designers and practitioners in retrospect repudiated it and expressed regret for the roles they played. It has, alas, done lasting damage. The appeals to overt racism made by the George Wallaces and Lester Maddoxes in the 1960s were followed by the appeals to racial animus made by Richard Nixon, Ronald Reagan, and George H. W. Bush. Beliefs in the inferiority of black people were succeeded by beliefs that unfair efforts were made to help blacks overcome the legacies of slavery and racial discrimination, and that blacks failed to take advantage of them. Ideological battles over affirmative action, busing, quotas, and reverse racism shaped many white people's beliefs that the time for remediation is past and that further efforts to help disadvantaged black people unfairly deny jobs, school admissions, opportunities, and resources to whites. Those racial resentments are a principal reason why so many whites support drug and crime control policies that do so much damage to black people.

THE SOCIAL PSYCHOLOGY OF AMERICAN RACE RELATIONS

Some Americans, including no doubt some public officials and practitioners, are racists and are biased against blacks. Larger numbers are affected by conscious stereotypes ("Many young black men are dangerous, and this young black man probably is also"). Almost everyone, black Americans included, is influenced by subconscious negative associations of black people with crime and criminality. Different terms are used to describe those influences—*colorism, Afro-American feature bias, implicit bias*—and different groups of researchers study them. In the end they come to the same conclusion: Americans, especially white Americans, are predisposed to associate blackness with crime and dangerousness and are prepared to treat black offenders especially harshly as a result.

Sociologists use the term *statistical discrimination* to describe one outcome of those predispositions. Statistical discrimination is the attribution to individuals of traits that characterize groups of which they are members. In *The Truly Disadvantaged: The Inner City, the Underclass, and Public Policy* (1987), the Harvard sociologist William Julius Wilson showed how this operates in employment. Many young black inner-city men have not been socialized into habits that employers want: coming to work on time, sticking with monotonous jobs, dressing in mainstream ways, speaking in mainstream English, observing conventional forms of politeness. As a consequence employers are skeptical about hiring young black men. They may be correct that young minority men who dress in trousers with drooping crotches and affect stereotypical ghetto behaviors are on average more likely than other people to be unreliable workers. However, those preconceptions in many cases lead them to reject job applicants who would be reliable workers. Extensive subsequent research, most prominently by sociologist Devah Pager (2007), has confirmed Wilson's assertions. Pager conducted a series of projects in which black and white applicants sought the same jobs and presented identical résumés and submitted identical applications. The white applicants were much more likely to be hired.

The novelist Tom Wolfe in *Bonfire of the Vanities* describes the power of statistical discrimination in the criminal courts. Stereotypes matter. The lawyer for a young black defendant has tried, with some success, to persuade the judge that his client is a nice kid, young, impressionable, and salvageable; he played a minor role in a street robbery, and deserves a break. Then the defendant appears:

> He had the same pumping swagger that practically every young defendant in the Bronx affected, the Pimp Roll. Such stupid self-destructive macho egos, thought Kramer [a prosecutor]. They never failed to show up with the black jackets and the sneakers and the Pimp Roll. They never failed to look every inch the young felon before judges, juries, probation officers, psychiatrists, before every single soul who had any say in whether they went to prison.... The defendant's comrades always arrived in court in their shiny black thermal jackets and go-to-hell sneakers. That was very bright too. That immediately established the fact that the defendant was not a poor defenseless victim of life in the ghetto but part of a pack of remorseless young felons. (1987, 13–14)

The defendant doesn't get the break.

Statistical discrimination is a central problem in racial profiling by the police. If many young black men in particular neighborhoods, who adopt a particular style of dress are involved in gang activities or drug dealing, police seeing a young man in that neighborhood who fits that pattern may believe it likely that he is a gang member or drug dealer and stop him, even if the individualized basis for a stop that the law requires does not exist.

The situation with court officials is somewhat different. Judges worry about the possibility that cultural differences and stereotypos will influence their decisions. They discuss it often among themselves and with others. Judges, however, are no doubt affected by unconscious stereotyping.

NEGATIVE STEREOTYPES

It is not surprising that the racial profiling literature documents excessive and poorly justified stops of black people. Two decades of research document that the media commonly portray a world of black offenders and white victims and that, when asked to describe typical violent criminals and drug dealers, white Americans describe black offenders (e.g., Entman 1992; Reeves and Campbell 1994; Beckett and Sasson 2004). Psychological processes much subtler than the crude stereotypes Tom Wolfe describes, however, are also at work. Research on the influence of skin tone and African American features shows that negative stereotypes are deeply embedded in American culture, and operate to the detriment of blacks in the criminal justice system. They cause black offenders to be punished more severely than whites, and among blacks they cause dark-skinned people, and people with distinctively African American facial features, to be punished more severely than light-skinned people and people with more European features.

Colorism is the "tendency to perceive or behave toward members of a racial category based on the lightness or darkness of their skin tone" (Maddox and Gray 2002, 250). The research field is comparatively new, but the phenomenon is old. More than sixty years ago Gunnar Myrdal observed in *An American Dilemma: The Negro Problem and Modern Democracy*, "Without any doubt a Negro with light skin and other European features has in the North an advantage with white people" (1944, 697). A few years earlier an American Council on Education report observed, "What is really crucial behind the color point is class; the implication that light color goes with higher status, and Negroid appearance with lower status, is what makes these characteristics so important" (A. Davis, Dollard, and American Youth Commission 1946, 137).

Among American black people, dark-skinned people are at a comparative disadvantage. Jennifer Hochschild, a political scientist at Harvard and one of the leading scholars on the subject, offered this summary: "Relative to their lighter-skinned contemporaries, dark-skinned blacks have lower levels of education, income, and job status. They are less likely to own homes, or to marry; and dark-skinned blacks' prison sentences are longer. Dark-skin discrimination occurs within as well as across races" (Hochschild and Weaver 2007, 644).

There has not been much research on the effects of colorism on people suspected or accused of crimes, but what there is suggests that dark-skinned people are more likely to be suspected and are punished more severely. Dark skin evokes fears of criminality (Dasgupta, Banaji, and Abelson 1999) and is a more easily remembered characteristic of a purportedly criminal face (Dixon and Maddox 2005).

An analysis of more than 67,000 male felons incarcerated in Georgia for their first offense from 1995 through 2002 showed that dark skinned blacks received longer sentences than light-skinned blacks. Overall white sentences averaged 2,689 days. The black average was 378 days longer. When the figures for blacks were broken down, however, light-skinned black people received sentences three and a half months longer than the white average, medium-skinned blacks received a year longer, and dark-skinned blacks a year and a half longer. Controlling for type of offense, socioeconomic characteristics, and demographic factors, light-skinned black defendants received sentences indistinguishable from those of whites. Medium- and dark-skinned black defendants received longer sentences (Hochschild and Weaver 2007, 649).

Scholars of Afrocentric feature bias take the analysis one step further (Blair, Judd, and Chapleau 2004). If skin tone affects stereotypes about crime and criminals, analysts hypothesized that stereotypically African American facial features (e.g., dark skin, wide nose, full lips) would also influence decision makers' judgments. The evidence confirms the hypothesis. One study found that the larger the number of Afrocentric features an individual possessed, the more criminal that individual appeared to be in the eyes of observers (Eberhardt et al. 2004).

Several important studies have tried to assess the significance of Afrocentric feature bias. Blair et al. (2002) found that individuals with more Afrocentric features were judged by college undergraduates to have stereotypical African American traits. Blair, Chapleau, and Judd (2005) found that observers believed individuals with more Afrocentric features were more likely than others to behave aggressively.

Jennifer Eberhardt and three colleagues asked 182 police officers to examine photographs of male students and employees at Stanford University. Half were shown white faces and half were shown black faces. One third of the officers were asked to rate the stereotypicality of each face on a scale, that is, how stereotypical each face was of members of that person's race. Another third, told that some of the faces might be of criminals, were asked to indicate whether the person "looked criminal." The last third were asked to rate attractiveness on a scale. Each officer completed only one of the three measures.

More black than white faces were thought to look criminal. Black faces rated above the median for stereotypical black features were judged as criminal significantly more often than were black faces rated below the median. The authors concluded that the police officers thought black faces looked more criminal and that "the more black, the more criminal" (Eberhardt et al. 2004, 889).

Blair, Judd, and Chapleau (2004) analyzed the faces of inmates in the Florida Department of Corrections to learn whether facial features were associated with longer sentences. They asked undergraduates to rate the faces of a randomly selected sample of 100 black and 116 white inmates in terms of the "degree to which each face had features that are typical of African Americans" (676). After controlling for race and criminal history, stereotypical facial features were a significant predictor of sentence length. Within each race more stereotypical black features were associated with longer sentences. Even those whites who had facial features that "looked black" had received longer sentences than other white prisoners.

Pizzi, Blair, and Judd (2005) also investigated the effect of facial features on sentencing, starting from the presupposition that conscious bias is not likely to be a significant cause of disparities. They reasoned that judges and prosecutors have learned to be sensitive to the possibility that they treat blacks differently and have become sensitive to some stereotypical differences. They concluded, however, that practitioners treat offenders differently on the basis of Afrocentric features: "Racial stereotyping in sentencing decisions still persists. But it is not a function of the racial category of the individual; instead, there seems to be an equally pernicious and less controllable process at work. Racial stereotyping in sentencing still occurs based on the facial appearance of the offender. Be they white or African American, those offenders who possess stronger Afrocentric features receive harsher sentences for the same crimes" (351).

Even the chance that offenders will be sentenced to death is influenced by facial features. Looking at cases in Philadelphia in which death had been a possible sentence, Eberhardt et al. "examined the extent to which perceived stereotypicality of black defendants influenced jurors' death-sentencing decisions in cases with both white and black victims" (2006, 383). Stanford undergraduates were shown photographs of forty-four defendants who were eligible for the death penalty. The photos were presented randomly and edited for uniformity, and the students were asked to rate the stereotypicality of each black defendant's appearance. With stereotypicality as the only independent variable, 24.4 percent of black defendants rated below the median had been sentenced to death, compared with 57.5 percent of black defendants rated above the median.

Yet another source of evidence comes from the Implicit Association Test (IAT), which was developed by psychologists to assess people's implicit attitudes toward different groups. The IAT, which by 2008 had been taken by 4.5 million people on the Internet and elsewhere, asks individuals to categorize a series of words or pictures into groups.[3] Two of the groups are racial, "black" and "white," and two of the groups are characterizations of words as "good" or "pleasant" (e.g., *joy, laugh, happy*) or "bad" or "unpleasant" (e.g., *terrible, agony, nasty*). To test for implicit bias one version of the IAT asks respondents to press one key on the computer for either "black" or "unpleasant" words or pictures and a different key for "white" or "pleasant" words or pictures. In another version respondents are asked to press one key for "black" or "pleasant" and another key for "white" or "unpleasant." Implicit bias is defined as faster responses when "black" and "unpleasant" are paired than when "black" and "pleasant" are.

The results have consistently shown that implicit bias against blacks is "extremely widespread" (Jolls and Sunstein 2006, 971). The consensus view is that the IAT results demonstrate the existence of unconscious bias by whites against blacks (Rachlinski et al. 2009). Almost all demographic groups show a significant implicit preference for whites over blacks. The major exception is blacks: equal proportions show implicit preferences for blacks and for whites, but, unlike whites, do not show a preference for their own group.

The consensus view of the existence of implicit racial bias is based on the results of millions of tests of every imaginable group in the population. It would be remarkable if criminal justice practitioners were not affected by it. As a consequence much recent research investigates the effectiveness of possible ways to alert officials to their implicit biases so that they can attempt to reduce the biases' influence in the same ways that practitioners have learned to be sensitive to cruder stereotypes based on dress or hair styles (e.g., Levinson 2007).

Some research has explicitly examined practitioners' possible biases. Jeffrey Rachlinski and his colleagues (2009) recruited 133 judges from three jurisdictions to take implicit bias tests and to sentence hypothetical cases in which the defendant's race varied. The bias test, as expected, revealed implicit biases against blacks among white judges and no clear pattern among black judges. The sentencing exercise also showed a statistically significant (though not large) relationship between individual judges' biases and the sentences they said they would impose.

Other research has focused on police. In one study participants were shown pictures of black and white criminal suspects who were and were not carrying guns. Participants were told to imagine they were police officers and that they should shoot suspects holding guns. The findings strongly confirmed hypotheses about implicit bias. Among suspects carrying guns, whites were less likely than blacks to be "shot;" among suspects not carrying firearms, blacks were more likely to be shot (Plant, Peruch, and Butz 2005).

When George H. W. Bush used images of Willie Horton to symbolize Michael Dukakis's softness on crime in the 1988 presidential election he was pushing a button that was waiting to be pushed, one that manipulated deeply engrained predispositions among whites to associate blackness with criminality.

RACIAL RESENTMENTS AND PUBLIC OPINION

White Americans, especially political conservatives and fundamentalist Protestants, tend to support harsh punishments, including the death penalty. Black people tend to support harsh punishments at much lower rates. Whites have substantially greater confidence in the justice system and its practitioners than do blacks. Researchers repeatedly find that racial animus and resentment are strong influences on whites' punitive attitudes. Reciprocally, low levels of confidence in the fairness of the justice system are a major influence on blacks' attitudes. Most black Americans believe the criminal justice system is racially biased and that black suspects and defendants are treated unfairly. Most whites disagree.

A substantial literature on racial differences in attitudes toward and opinions about crime control policy shows that whites have rationalized a criminal justice system that is disparately severe toward blacks. Early research on the influence of race on attitudes toward the criminal justice system found that racial prejudice (measured by support for racial segregation and belief in black inferiority) was associated with whites' support for harsh sentencing (Cohn, Barkan, and Halteman 1991), as were negative racial stereotypes (Hurwitz and Peffley 1997), and racial antipathy (a preference for maintaining social distance from blacks; Gilliam and Iyengar 2000).

More recent work has tried to disentangle the influence of racial beliefs and attitudes, distinguishing among racial bigotry, racial resentments, and negative racial stereotyping. Findings consistently show that whites' belief in inherent black inferiority has almost disappeared. Encouraging as that is, however, findings also demonstrate widely shared white resentments of post–civil rights era efforts to integrate blacks into mainstream American society, and a powerful association between those resentments and support for the crime control and drug policies that have ensnared so many black Americans.

The relevant literature has grown rapidly. The initial focus was on racial differences in support for harsh sentencing policies and for the death penalty. The death penalty literature began to develop after the U.S. Supreme Court decided *Furman v. Georgia*, 408 U.S. 228 (1972), which suspended use of capital punishment in the United States, and *Gregg v. Georgia*, 428 U.S. 153 (1976), which reinstituted it. Researchers examined a wide range of issues, including characteristics of death penalty supporters and opponents, whether people's views changed if they learned more about the subject (sometimes), whether the availability of sentences of life without possibility of parole changed opinions (sometimes), and whether blacks and whites had different views (yes, very).

The most comprehensive survey of that literature shows that there was a racial gap of 30 points in support for capital punishment in 2004 (whites, 72.5 percent; blacks, 41.7 percent). That gap had not changed since 1974 (whites, 69.8 percent; blacks, 39.9 percent), and held steady in between. The obvious question is, What explains the gap? The strongest predictor of whites' support for capital punishment in our time is racial resentment: "Taken together, the extant studies reach remarkably consistent results: negative views toward African Americans—what scholars in this area have called 'racism' or 'racial animus'—predict a range of political attitudes, including greater support for capital punishment" (Unnever, Cullen, and Lero Jonson 2008, 53).

Efforts have been made to see whether people's attitudes change when they learn that blacks disproportionately occupy death row cells and that the race of the victim is a primary determinant of whether a murderer is sentenced to death. The most sophisticated study of racial attitudes about the criminal justice system, the National Race and Crime Survey, interviewed a representative sample of 600 white and 600 black Americans (Peffley and Hurwitz 2010). Randomly selected subgroups of the respondents were asked in three different ways whether they favor or oppose capital punishment for persons convicted for murder and whether they held their views strongly. In the first version of the question, they were simply asked their views. Sixty-five percent of whites said they strongly or somewhat favored capital punishment compared with 50 percent of blacks.

In the second version of the question, respondents were first told "Some people say that the death penalty is unfair because most of the people who are executed are African Americans" and were then asked whether and how strongly they favor capital punishment. The percentage of black respondents favoring capital punishment fell to 38 percent, but the white percentage in favor *increased* to 77 percent. In the third version, before being asked their views respondents were told that some people "say the death penalty is unfair because too many innocent people are being executed." The white percentage was strongly or somewhat in favor (64 percent) and was unchanged from whites' answer to the first version. Black support fell further, to 34 percent (see table 5.1).

Summarizing those patterns of response, the white percentage was unchanged when reminded that some innocent people are believed to be executed, and it increased substantially when reminded that blacks make up a disproportionate share of those executed. Blacks' overall support of the death penalty was lower to begin with and fell when respondents were reminded of racial disparities and risks of executing innocent people.

The explanations for those discordant patterns were teased out from analyses of a large number of other variables relating to respondents' characteristics. Blacks' lower levels of support are related to the widespread belief that the criminal justice system treats black defendants unfairly; being reminded of problems of racial disparities and possible executions of innocents heightened those anxieties and led to lower levels of support. Few whites, however, believe that the system treats blacks unfairly. Instead, when whites are confronted with an argument about racial bias, "they reject it with such force that they end up expressing more support for the death penalty than when no argument is presented at all" (Peffley and Hurwitz 2010, 175).

In an earlier study, Lawrence Bobo and Devon Johnson (2004) examined blacks' and whites' support for capital punishment and the crack cocaine 100-to-1 law and the extent to which opinions changed in light of information about the racial dimensions of those problems (e.g., the disproportionate presence of blacks on death rows; that killers of whites are much more likely to be sentenced to death than killers of blacks; that most crack dealers are black). In general, except concerning the 100-to-1 law, information did not significantly affect whites' opinions. Racial resentment was strongly related to whites' support for the death penalty:

> The most consistent predictor of criminal justice policy attitudes is, in fact, a form of racial prejudice. While racial resentment does not ever explain a large share of the variation in any of the attitudes we have measured, it is the most consistently influential of the variables outside of race classification itself. This pattern has at least two implications. It further buttresses the concern that some of the major elements of public support for punitive criminal justice policies are heavily tinged with racial animus and thus quite likely to be resistant to change based on suasion and information-based appeals. (171–72)

James Unnever and colleagues have tried to isolate the influence of racial resentments on other issues. One analysis examined data from the 2006 African American Survey undertaken for the *Washington Post*, the Henry J. Kaiser Foundation, and Harvard University to explore people's explanations for racial disparities in imprisonment. This is a huge survey of 1,328 African American men, 507 African American women, and 1,029 members of other racial and ethnic groups. Blacks were substantially likelier than whites to cite denial of jobs and bad schools as "big reasons" for the disparity, but the largest differences concerned bias in the legal system. Seventy-one percent of blacks, but only 37 percent of whites, believed police bias was a primary cause of disparities. Similarly, 67 percent of blacks blamed "unfair courts," but only 28 percent of whites (Unnever 2008, table 1). The degree to which black respondents had personally experienced what they perceived as racial discrimination "predicts whether African Americans believe that criminal injustices, such as whether the police target black men and whether the courts are more willing to convict African-American men, are reasons for the high incarceration among black men" (527).

The racial difference in perceptions of bias in the justice system that Unnever found is echoed in findings from many other projects. The leading scholar of the subject, Lawrence Bobo, a Harvard sociologist, organized two representative national surveys on race, crime, and public opinion. The 2001 Race, Crime, and Public Opinion Study is a survey of 978 non-Hispanic whites and 1,010 non-Hispanic blacks living in American households. Only 38 percent of whites said they believed the criminal justice system is biased against blacks; 89 percent of blacks said it was. Only 8 percent of blacks said that the justice system "gives blacks fair treatment"; 56 percent of whites said it did. Seventy-nine percent of whites expressed confidence that judges treat blacks and whites equally, compared with only 28 percent of blacks. Concerning police the gap was even bigger: 68 percent of whites expressed confidence in the police, and only 18 percent of blacks did (Bobo and Thompson 2006, 456). The findings of the Peffley and Hurwitz (2010) survey discussed above are similar. Seventy percent of blacks but only 18 percent of whites believed that police and courts treat blacks unfairly (189).

Approaching the same kinds of issues from another angle, Unnever, Cullen, and Jones (2008) analyzed data from the 2000 National Election Study to investigate racial differences in support for social policies to address economic and social causes of crime. Respondents were asked whether they thought "the best way to reduce crime is to address social problems or to make sure criminals are caught, convicted, and punished, or something in between." A series of follow-up questions asked whether the preferred approach was a "much" or "somewhat" better way to reduce crime. Their main aim was to investigate whether and how people's attachment to egalitarian beliefs influenced their attitudes toward adoption of nonpunitive anticrime policies (yes, a lot). Their premise was that people with strong commitments to equality are more likely than others to support social policies aimed at preventing crime by reducing the social and economic inequalities associated with it. A variety of demographic (age, sex, race, education, place of residence) and attitudinal (egalitarian beliefs, racial stereotypes, racial resentment) variables were analyzed. Blacks were much more likely than whites to support social policy approaches to crime reduction. Whites with racial resentments toward blacks were much more likely to oppose social policy approaches and to support criminal justice approaches. Here, too, the findings reported by Peffley and Hurwitz (2010) are similar: twice as large a percentage of whites as blacks preferred harsh punishments over social welfare programs as a crime control strategy (162).

Devon Johnson (2008) carried out a particularly comprehensive analysis of the reasons for racial differences in attitudes toward punishment. I describe it in considerable detail to show the basis of the conclusions she drew. The data came from the 2001 Race, Crime, and Public Opinion Study (Bobo and Thompson 2006). A "punitiveness index" was calculated on answers to four questions on a 1–4 scale (1 = "strongly disagree"; 4 = "strongly agree"): Do you favor life sentences for third-time felons? Should parole boards be more strict, less strict, or continue current practices? Should fourteen- to seventeen-year-olds accused of violent crimes be tried and sentenced in adult courts? Are current punishments for violent crimes too harsh, too light, or just about right? Whites were much more likely than blacks to favor three-strikes laws and trying young people as adults, to believe parole boards should be more strict, and to believe that punishments for violent crimes are too light.

To find out whether and how racial attitudes and beliefs influence punitive attitudes, Johnson developed a measure of perceived racial bias in the justice system and various measures of racial prejudice. Perceived racial bias was calculated from responses to three questions about confidence that the police, prosecutors, and judges treat blacks and whites equally.

Racial prejudice was measured in three ways. To calculate "racial resentment," respondents were asked to agree or disagree with six propositions (shortened and paraphrased here):

1. Members of other ethnic groups have overcome prejudice and succeeded; blacks should do the same without special favors.
2. Blacks in recent years have gotten less than they deserve.
3. Government officials pay less attention to requests and complaints from black than from white people.

4. Blacks who receive welfare could get along without it if they tried.
5. If blacks would only try harder, they'd do as well as whites.
6. Generations of slavery and discrimination created conditions that make it hard for blacks to work their way out of the lower class.

To calculate "negative affect" in general attitudes to black people, respondents were asked two questions: How often have you felt sympathy for blacks? How often have you admired blacks?

Finally, to calculate "racial stereotypes," respondents were asked to characterize on a 1–10 scale as accurate or inaccurate four negative descriptions of black people: as lazy, aggressive or violent, preferring to live on welfare, and complaining.

The analysis took account of demographic characteristics of the survey respondents, including age, sex, income, education, and place of residence, and of other characteristics such as political beliefs, fear of crime, and having a relative or friend imprisoned. When all these characteristics were taken into account, two factors stood out. For blacks, perceptions of racial bias in the system were the major distinguishing characteristic. For whites, it was racial resentment. The other two measures of prejudice—negative affect and racial stereotypes—had discernible effects that were dwarfed by the power of racial resentment.

It might in some sense seem encouraging that whites are less likely than in earlier times to harbor beliefs about racial inferiority or about race-based negative characterizations of laziness, violence, and querulousness. Their displacement by racial resentment is no cause for celebration. The consequence in some ways is more pernicious, especially in light of what we now know about statistical discrimination, colorism, Afro American feature bias, and implicit bias. Widespread beliefs that blacks are racially inferior have been replaced by beliefs that the conditions of life that lead some black people to crime are their own fault and they deserve whatever punishment they get. Put differently racial resentments provide a powerful basis for lack of sympathy for people caught up in the legal system. If disproportionate numbers of blacks are arrested for drug dealing and for violent crimes, they've no cause to complain.

Devon Johnson summed up where things stand:

Given the association between race and crime in political discourse, in media accounts, and in the minds of many whites, it is probable that racial prejudice will continue to play a significant role in whites' support for punitive policies for some time. Moreover, in light of the...inability of those in privileged positions to perceive racial discrimination in the administration of justice (or their unwillingness to acknowledge it), it is unlikely that blacks' cynicism toward the criminal justice system will markedly improve in the short term. (2008, 205)

That seems right. The explanation for whites' attitudes can be found in the history of American race relations.

THE HISTORY OF RACE RELATIONS

Ideas about statistical discrimination and social stereotyping, and about the unconscious effects of colorism and Afrocentric facial features, may be unfamiliar to some readers, but they are not difficult to grasp. Similarly pernicious effects of social stereotypes and unrecognized biases about women and gay and lesbian people were in due course recognized, and social attitudes, actions, and policies changed as a result. Few people any longer believe that menstruation makes women emotionally unstable and unsuited for leadership positions or that women lack the physical stamina and self-discipline to participate in physically demanding work or sports. Likewise few people any longer believe that gays' and lesbians' lives are governed by their sexual appetites (or no more, anyway, than is true of heterosexuals) or are incapable of being successful parents. No similar changes have occurred concerning the experiences of black people in the criminal justice system. Stereotypes about racial inferiority may have been replaced by racial resentments, but to disproportionate numbers of blacks on death row or in prisons, or to black defendants in crack cocaine cases, that is a distinction without a difference.

So the question is, Why do the effects of racial resentments persist and make many whites unsympathetic to the experiences of blacks in the criminal justice system? The most likely explanation for adoption of disparity-causing policies, and their continuation long after their effects became known, and why racial resentments have such blinding power, is the hardest and most uncomfortable to grasp. It is that we white Americans as a class are so accustomed to seeing the world from the perspective of our own self-interest that we unconsciously support policies that ensure our social, political, and economic dominance. Anti-immigrant policies are a vulgar recent example. People hostile to immigrants may talk about the rule of law and illegal immigration, but their real, underlying concerns relate to competition for jobs, fear of social change, and worry that their own well-being will suffer. Much can be said in favor of increased immigration. A country with an aging population needs more young people to support a growing economy and to pay taxes to support government spending, including Social Security and Medicare for the elderly. A sizable body of research shows that the popular belief that immigrants are an economic burden is wrong: after only a few years in the country immigrants add to national wealth. Rational analyses of economic and social effects of immigration, however, are for many people beside the point. Drug and criminal justice policies that destabilize poor black communities and maintain white dominance are a subtler instance of a similar phenomenon.

The stereotyping, resentments, and attributions discussed in the preceding section are unlikely by themselves to have produced and perpetuated racial profiling and 100-to-1, three-strikes, and similar laws. Police officials and other policy makers are sometimes influenced by base political considerations, but comparatively few are likely to be motivated by invidious racial bias. Conscious stereotypes and statistical discrimination no doubt play roles, especially in explaining police decisions to stop citizens on the street and judges' sentencing decisions to send to prison people they believe (often wrongly) to be dangerous. Unconscious stereotyping no doubt operates at the level of the individual case, and people with typical black features suffer as a result. All of these factors, however, are likely to be most important in individual cases. They are unlikely to explain the passage of laws and policies that treat black people especially severely.

A literature that has developed over the past twenty years explains what happened. Contemporary drug and crime control policies are in large part products of unconscious efforts by the white majority to maintain political, social, and economic dominance over blacks. American cultural practices and legal institutions have operated to keep whites on top for three centuries. Until the Civil War slavery did the job. Within thirty years after the war, the practices and legal forms of discrimination known as Jim Crow laws restored white dominance. In the Great Migration in the early twentieth century millions of southern blacks moved north to escape Jim Crow; the big-city ghettos, housing discrimination, and other forms of discrimination kept blacks in their subordinate place (Lieberson 1980). Federal civil rights laws and Supreme Court decisions in time outlawed Jim Crow and forbade most forms of racial discrimination. For poor and disadvantaged black people, the victories were short-lived. Deindustrialization and the flight of jobs and the middle class to the suburbs left disadvantaged blacks marooned in the urban ghettos; the modern wars on drugs and crime took over and kept them there (Wacquant 2002a, 2002b).

Wacquant has explained how that happened:

> Unlike Jim Crow, then, the ghetto was not dismantled by forceful government action. It was left to crumble onto itself, trapping lower-class African-Americans in a vortex of unemployment, poverty, and crime, abetted by the joint withdrawal of the wage-labor market and the welfare state.... As the ghetto lost its economic function and proved unable to ensure ethno-racial closure, the prison was called upon to help contain a population widely viewed as deviant, destitute, and dangerous. (2008, 65)

Wacquant is not alone in suggesting that contemporary American criminal justice practices are the latest in a series of social policies that operate to keep poor blacks in their places. Douglas Massey, the author (with Nancy Denton) of *American Apartheid* (1993), a widely praised and decidedly nonpolemical account of housing discrimination, argued in *Categorically Unequal*, his book on social stratification, that crime policy supports white interests:

Whether whites care to admit it or not, they have a selfish interest in maintaining the categorical mechanisms that perpetuate racial stratification. As a result, when pushed by the federal government to end overt discriminatory practices, they are likely to innovate new and more subtle ways to maintain their privileged position in society. If one discriminatory mechanism proves impossible to sustain, whites have an incentive to develop alternatives that may be associated only indirectly with race and are therefore not in obvious violation of civil rights law. The specific mechanisms by which racial stratification occurs can thus be expected to evolve over time....

[The] new emphasis on retribution and punishment...was achieved through the deliberate racialization of crime and violence in public consciousness by political entrepreneurs. (2007, 54, 94)

Glenn C. Loury, a Brown University economist who was in the 1980s and early 1990s generally regarded as one of America's preeminent conservative black intellectuals, observed in *The Anatomy of Racial Inequality* that "the deeper truth is that, for some three centuries now, political, social, and economic institutions that by any measure must be seen as racially oppressive have distorted the communal experience of the slaves and their descendants" (2002, 104). Later, in introducing his 2007 Tanner Lectures at Stanford, he elaborated:

We have embraced what criminologist Michael Tonry (1995) calls a policy of "malign neglect," and in doing so we, as a society, have stumbled more or less wittingly into a God-awful cul de sac....The connection of this apparatus to the history of racial degradation and subordination in our country (lynching, minstrelsy, segregation, ghettoization) is virtually self-evident....The racial subtext of our law and order political discourse over the last three decades has been palpable. (2007; references omitted)

More recently Loury has written, "Mass incarceration has now become a principal vehicle for the reproduction of racial hierarchy in our society" (2008, 36–37). The finding, discussed earlier, that racial resentment is the strongest predictor of whites' support for severe punishment policies, led Bobo and Johnson to conclude, "This pattern reinforces the claim . . . that one major function of the criminal justice system is the regulation and control of marginalized social groups such as African Americans" (2004, 171–72).

These are functionalist arguments about what criminal justice policies and practices do, rather than political ones about what they are intended to do. The argument is not that a self-perpetuating cabal of racist whites consciously acts to favor white interests, but that deeper social forces collude, almost as if directed by an invisible hand, to formulate laws, policies, and social practices that serve the interests of white Americans. Thought of that way, it is hard not to see that the machinery of the criminal justice system produces devastatingly reduced life chances for poor black Americans. If its aims were to reduce black men's chances of earning a decent living, or being successfully married and a good father, or being socialized into prosocial values, it has been successful (Western 2006). There has to be a reason why the criminal justice system treats American blacks so badly, why its foreseeable disparate impacts on blacks and whites are disregarded. Wacquant's and the others' analyses provide a better explanation than any other that has been offered.

Once the analysis of racial hierarchy and status anxiety that Wacquant, Massey, Loury, and Bobo and Johnson offer is recognized, much else falls into place. David Garland, in his writing on lynchings in America during their 1890–1930 heyday, observes, "The penal excess of the lynching spectacle said things that a modernized legal process could not. . . . It reestablished the correlative status of the troublesome black man, which was as nothing, with no rights, no protectors, no personal dignity, and no human worth" (2005, 817).

There are plenty of other policy realms in which similar things happened. Housing policy offers an example. Federal policies of the 1950s and 1960s, though proposed and explained in neutral terms of credit risk and sound stewardship of federal dollars, blocked blacks from moving into newly developing white suburbs and, through red-lining "risky neighborhoods," denied federally insured mortgages to residents of urban minority neighborhoods. The effect was to lock black people into deteriorated inner-city areas. In retrospect those federal policies have been discredited and are widely recognized to have been a significant contributor to perpetuation of racially segregated housing (Massey and Denton 1993).

Nineteenth-century temperance and prohibition movements provide another example of a conflict over crime and drug policy that appeared to be about one thing (the dangers of alcohol) but was really about status conflicts between ethnic groups. Proponents claimed that they were motivated to address the problems precipitated by and associated with alcohol use. In retrospect nineteenth century prohibition was in large part a proxy for social and status conflicts between Protestant descendants of earlier waves of British and German settlers, anxious to protect their newly acquired social status and political power, and newly arrived Irish Catholics. Many of the earlier settlers were teetotalers; many of the bibulous Irish were enthusiastic drinkers. Moralistic crusades against alcohol served as devices for expressing disapproval and social distance from newcomers that was sometimes unacknowledged or unrecognized by the prohibitionists themselves. Attacking drinking as immoral was a way to assert the moral superiority of the attackers, and the moral inferiority of the attacked (Gusfield 1963).

Criminalization of particular substances reflected similar ethnic group dynamics each time it happened in the twentieth century. When heroin and cocaine were criminalized by the federal Harrison Act in 1914, the prevailing images of the immorality of drug use were provided by groups other than the white majority: Chinese users of opiates and black users of cocaine (Courtwright 1982; Musto 1999). The Marijuana Tax Act, the first federal criminalization of marijuana, was aimed at pot-smoking Mexican laborers whose migration into western states in search of work precipitated hostile reactions from whites not unlike those occurring early in the twenty-first century (Whitebread and Bonnie 1974). In the 1980s the targets of unprecedentedly tough laws aimed at crack cocaine were inner-city blacks (Massing 1998, chap. 14)

A similar dynamic, though between generations rather than between ethnic groups, characterized recent drug wars. The first was announced by President Nixon on July 14, 1969, in his "Special Message to the Congress on Control of Narcotics and Dangerous Drugs." The primary status conflict of the time concerning drugs was not between whites and blacks or between members of other ethnic minorities, but between generations. The alcohol-using and -abusing generations that moved in the corridors of power in the 1960s were befuddled by a troubling and disrupted world and threatened by challenges to their political and moral authority. Marijuana and hard drug use by young people encapsulated those challenges. Marijuana was widely available and widely used. LSD and cocaine had visible, influential, and outspoken proponents. Officials said, and probably believed, that they wanted to protect young people from the ravages of drug use, and in any case that drug use is irresponsible and immoral. Young people believed the dangers were slight and that the choice should be theirs, not the state's, to make. As was true of nineteenth-century prohibition, recent disagreements about legal enforcement of important moral standards can as readily be understood as conflicts over whose moral standards are to be preferred, and expressed in the criminal law. The words of the planners of successive modern drug wars may have been about safety and responsibility, but the music was about protection of their views of the world and of the places in it of people like them (Musto and Korsmeyer 2002, 60).

Harvard philosopher Tommie Shelby has observed, "It is a truism about human nature—one emphasized by Max Weber—that the privileged want to believe that they merit their advantages and that the disadvantaged deserve all their hardships" (2008, 80). Concerning the criminal justice system, whites can take comfort in racial stereotypes, such as that black Americans are especially criminal or that blacks more often than whites freely choose to behave in immoral ways that violate the criminal law. So of course huge numbers of black people are in prison.

At some level, however, most people understand that black human beings are not inherently morally weaker and worse than whites. At some level, everyone understands that discrimination and disadvantage play at least *some* role in explaining why human beings become involved in ordinary crimes and drug dealing. A simple test of this is to think of someone you know well—your child, or a friend's or neighbor's—who has gotten into trouble, and to think about how you explain it. The explanation almost always will include something other than only willfully immoral choices. Family circumstances, drug or alcohol problems, mental health issues, and depression are the kinds of things you would probably think about. If in playing this mental game, you imagine that you are black and poor, you would think about the social and economic disadvantages and discrimination your or another's child has experienced. In real life, black people do think about such things. That is why, as the research discussed earlier shows, blacks distrust the criminal justice system and especially police officers, and it is why they favor social welfare over punishment approaches for preventing crime.

Large majorities of whites, however, are unable to step back from problems of racial disparity in the justice system and try to think about it as they would were they black parents. The reasons for that are well understood. The problems seem intractable and they make people uncomfortable. When thought of empathetically, they are hard to reconcile with many white people's political ideology.

A number of psychological devices enable human beings to rationalize awkward realities. The best known is the psychological concept of cognitive dissonance. The psychologist Leon Festinger, who invented the term, observed that people are uncomfortable in situations in which part of the mind wants something and another part knows it is a bad idea. Smokers know lighting up is bad for their health and the health of those around them. What to do? The options are to give up smoking or find a way to explain why you are not quitting. Typical rationalizations are that it is not really dangerous or is only a little dangerous if only a few cigarettes are smoked each day, or the damage will reverse if smokers stop when they reach fifty, or the damage is already done and there's no point stopping now. When we find ourselves in situations of dissonance, Festinger said, our choices are to change the situation, or to rationalize it. By coincidence, here is the first example he gives in the opening sentences of what became a landmark book:

> It has frequently been implied, and sometimes even pointed out, that the individual strives toward consistency within himself. His opinions and attitudes, for example, tend to exist in clusters that

are internally consistent. Certainly one may find exceptions. A person may think Negroes are just as good as whites but would not want any living in his neighborhood. (Festinger 1957, 1)

Two more recent psychological theories offer fuller explanations. Proponents of "just world theory" assert that "people need to believe that the world is a just place in which individuals get what they deserve" (Hafer and Bègue 2005, 128). A socially concerned mother is run over by a motorist while picketing to support a local cause. One observer demands harsh punishment for the driver. Another blames the victim because she was blocking traffic and interfering with the driver's "freedom of movement." Both are fitting the events into personal—but irreconcilable—scripts in which the driver and the dead picketer get what they deserved.

System justification theory "posits a general human tendency to support and defend the social status quo, broadly defined" (Blasi and Jost 2006, 1123). Regardless of their situation, people try to rationalize the injustices and inequities they see. Stereotypes (such as that the rich are smart, the poor are lazy, and blacks are criminal) are often employed to demonstrate that all members of society deserve their status. People who can reconcile discordant features of their lives and come to believe in a world that is just by and large experience more positive emotions than people who believe it unjust. For example, poor people who blame themselves for their own poverty are happier and more satisfied with life in general.

These several theories help explain why and how white Americans rationalize stark racial inequities in the American criminal justice system. Many white Americans unthinkingly assume, or persuade themselves, that the problem is not in the policies they and people like them set and enforce, but in social forces over which they have no control or in the irresponsibility of individual offenders.

That is not good enough. Current crime and drug control policies were not written by an invisible hand. They were enacted and implemented by human beings influenced by mixed motives, some idealistic, some cynical, some self-serving. Insofar as they were enacted as fruits of the Republican Southern Strategy they represented deliberate manipulations of racist biases and fears, and racial stereotypes and attributions, to achieve partisan political aims.

THE SOUTHERN STRATEGY

The Republican Southern Strategy is commonly said to date from the 1960s and Kevin Phillips's *The Emerging Republican Majority* (1969) is generally described as its basic text. Both things are true. The term of art was used to characterize Republican Barry Goldwater's 1964 presidential campaign, and Phillips was a strategist in Nixon's 1968 campaign who later published a book making a case for it. Both statements, however, are oversimplications. The foundations were laid two decades earlier.

Proposals that southern segregationist Democrats combine with Republican conservatives were first seriously promoted in the 1940s, when civil rights advocates began to win legal and political victories and white supremacists began to worry. On June 25, 1941, Democratic President Franklin Delano Roosevelt signed Executive Order 8802, which established the Federal Employment Practices Commission. The order forbade racial discrimination by federal contractors and empowered the FEPC to investigate complaints. After Roosevelt's death segregationists hoped Harry S. Truman would be more sympathetic. Truman had been a U.S. senator from Missouri, a border state with an almost Southern history of troubled race relations. Many southerners hoped he would be more sensitive to segregationist concerns than Rossevelt had been. Instead, within two months of taking office, he proposed legislation to make the FEPC permanent. Truman later appointed a biracial Committee on Civil Rights which, in *To Secure These Rights* (1947), recommended enactment of antilynching, anti–poll tax, and fair employment legislation. The Committee also proposed prohibition of discrimination in interstate transportation and desegregation of the armed forces. In his January 7, 1948, State of the Union address Truman announced his intention to carry out the Committee's proposals (Lowndes 2008, chap. 2).

Segregationist southern Democrats were stunned. Senator James Eastland of Mississippi declared, "The South we know is being swept to its destruction." Southern governors convened to denounce Truman's desegregation effort and approved a resolution mostly written by Governor Strom Thurmond of South Carolina warning that the South would not "stand idle and let all of this happen" (Lowndes 2008, 27). Among the results were opposition to Truman's bid for reelection and the nomination of Thurmond as the "Dixiecrat" candidate for president in 1948. He received 20 percent of the southern vote and carried Alabama, Mississippi, Louisiana, and South Carolina.

I stop retelling the story at that point and skip to the 1960s. A number of fine books tell it in detail and carry it forward from the 1940s (Carter 1996; Black and Black 2002; Murakawa 2005; Lowndes 2008). My aim in going back to the 1940s is to show that what became widely known as the Southern Strategy had its roots in earlier efforts by segregationists to maintain white supremacy in the South.

Barry Goldwater's 1964 campaigns first for the Republican nomination and then for the presidency were the first national campaigns in which Republicans openly played the race card. The Republican National Committee since 1961 had been pouring money into "Operation Dixie," an effort to reach out to conservative and segregationist southern Democrats, and recruiting segregationist candidates. Goldwater trod a fine line. He condemned President John F. Kennedy for sending troops to the University of Mississippi in 1962 to assure admission of the first black students. He supported voting rights for black people, but also insisted on southerners' right to control their own destiny. The historian Joseph Lowndes observes, "As long as Goldwater held high the banner of states' rights, he could appear to split real questions of racial domination from an abstract commitment to the Tenth Amendment, and allow conservatives to show clean hands while building a segregationist party in the South" (2008, 67).

Other Republicans knew what was going on, and objected loudly. New York's Republican senator Jacob Javits accused Operation Dixie "and what was now being called the 'southern strategy' of wrecking the party by appealing to the worst in southern racial sentiment" (Lowndes 2008, 63). At the Republican Convention the young Republicans' Ripon Society declared that the party had to choose "whether or not to adopt a strategy that must inevitably exploit the 'white backlash' to the Civil

Rights Movement in the South and the suburbs of the North" (*New York Times* 1964, 31).

The historical accounts make it clear that Goldwater meant to appeal to white supremacist voters. Conservative scholars Stephan and Abigail Thernstrom, for example, refer to use of race-coded issues as "rhetorical winks" that allowed "a variety of candidates—for instance, Barry Goldwater, with his talk of states rights—to play on white racial resentment" (1997, 309).

Goldwater lost dismally, winning only 38.5 percent of the vote and six states (Arizona, Louisiana, Mississippi, Alabama, Georgia, and South Carolina), but the pattern was set. In 1968 George Wallace ran as a third party candidate appealing openly to antiblack sentiments. Nixon ceded the segregationist Deep South to Wallace. Goldwater showed that conservative Republicans could win elections in the Deep South by use of veiled appeals to race. However, he also showed that the ugliness of open racism could alienate voters elsewhere. Former President Richard Nixon, in a 1988 interview, observed of Goldwater that he "ran as a racist candidate . . . and he won the wrong [southern] states" (Lowndes 2008, p. 115). By this Nixon meant that openly or barely disguised racist appeals that were successful in the Deep South would not win elsewhere unless made more subtly.

Goldwater, however, had cast the die, and conservative Republicans continued to cast them for another twenty-five years. Nixon's code words were *law and order* and *busing*. The historical accounts make it clear that in 1968 he tried to walk a fine line between repudiating the vulgar, overtly racist appeals of Wallace while appealing to whites' racial resentments and animus. One of the gentler critiques observes that supporters of the Southern Strategy, "including southern politicians and Richard Nixon and his aides, seem to have been quite conscious of the fact that the voters they targeted for mobilization were white and had racial concerns" (Mendelberg 2001, 11).

Racial appeals did not play a big role in the 1972 (Nixon and McGovern) or 1976 presidential campaigns, but reappeared prominently in the 1980 campaign between Ronald Reagan and Jimmy Carter. Reagan's campaign was launched in Philadelphia, Mississippi, a town notorious in the history of the civil rights movement for the 1964 murders of civil rights workers James Cheney, Michael Schwerber, and Andrew Goodman. Reagan assured those present of his adamant support for states' rights, a term then widely understood to refer to white segregationists' resistance to civil rights pressures coming from the federal government. Lowndes observes, "Reagan could now seamlessly combine conservatism, racism, and antigovernment populism in a majoritarian discourse—and with it founded the modern Republican regime" (2008, 160).

Reagan staked out a similar position on welfare. In his unsuccessful 1976 campaign against Gerald Ford for the Republican presidential nomination, and again in his successful 1980 campaign, Reagan regularly referred to the "welfare queen" who was said to exemplify all the problems of welfare. The person caricatured was Linda Taylor, a black Chicago woman who reportedly received benefits under several aliases and, as mythology has it, traveled to the welfare office in a rented limousine to collect her checks (Tonry 1995, 10).

The low point in race-coded political symbolism occurred in the Bush I–Dukakis presidential campaign in 1988 and centered on Willie Horton.[4] Horton had been convicted of a particularly gruesome murder in Massachusetts in 1974. He was released under a Massachusetts prison furlough program that had been signed into law in 1972 by Republican Governor Francis W. Sargent. He did not return to the prison. Months later he broke into a Maryland couple's suburban home where he raped the woman and assaulted and tied up the man before stealing their car. A photograph of the bleary-eyed, unshaven, and disheveled Horton, taken shortly after his arrest, was repeatedly used in the campaign to symbolize Dukakis's softness on crime (Anderson 1995).

Lee Atwater, the creator of the Willie Horton strategy and others later denied they were playing a race card, but subsequent reconstructions make it clear that they were. A focus group of thirty people who had voted for Reagan in 1984 but planned to vote for Dukakis was convened in Paramus, New Jersey in late May 1988, a time when Bush was running far behind Dukakis in the polls. Small numbers of participants reacted negatively to Dukakis when they learned that he opposed capital punishment and as governor of Massachusetts had vetoed legislation permitting prayers in schools. And then, "pay dirt," as historian Dan

Carter describes it. On learning the Willie Horton story "fifteen of the thirty voters said they had changed their minds. They would never vote for Dukakis. Lee Atwater had found his silver bullet" (1996, 72–73).

A few days later, on Memorial Day 1988, Atwater showed films of the focus group's discussions at a campaign strategy meeting at Bush's summer home in Kennebunkport, Maine, and proposed a campaign strategy. Within ten days, first in Texas, then elsewhere, Bush began mentioning Horton in his campaign speeches.[5] The campaign arranged for *Reader's Digest* to run a July story on Horton, and Atwater under the aegis of the Bush Re-election Committee developed and released a hard-hitting television commercial. Another Republican group, Americans for Bush, blanketed CNN with Bush campaign advertisements showing a picture of Horton staring dully into the camera. Dukakis never recovered.

The Republican Southern Strategy, and its more subtly coded successors, cynically manipulated the anxieties of southern and working-class whites by focusing on issues like crime and welfare fraud that served as code words for race. The times were ripe in the decades after enactment of the Civil Rights Act of 1964. Life in the United States was turbulent. The civil rights movement continued; busing to integrate schools, aggressive legal efforts to assure employment and housing opportunities for black people, and political developments like the emergence of the Black Panthers and Elijah Muhammad's Nation of Islam followed in its wake. Riots broke out in black areas of cities across the country in the late 1960s. The Vietnam War ripened, provoked years of demonstrations and resistance, and ended ignominiously. Robert Kennedy and Martin Luther King were assassinated in 1968, and George Wallace was permanently crippled in an assassination attempt in 1972. The women's and gay liberation movements became newly assertive and challenged long-standing social practices and norms. OPEC declared its first embargo in the 1970s, and the first major modern economic restructuring, disproportionately affecting unionized and low-level white-collar workers, took place.

People were on edge and ready to look for scapegoats. It was a time when virtuous political leaders should have tried to reassure people, to develop practical solutions to troubling problems, and to foster improved race relations. Conservative politicians instead fostered racial conflict. It worked. David R. Roediger, a leading historian of American race relations, recently observed that "Reagan's sure command of divisive code words such as 'state's rights,' 'welfare moms,' 'quotas,' and 'reverse racism' came to be seen as key to his success at winning over 'Reagan Democrats' via racial appeals" (2008, 207).

In our time politicians must tread a fine line. Appeals to race can mobilize white voters but, as Nixon understood, they will fail if they are seen as overtly racist. Most Americans no longer believe in the racial inferiority of black people, and most believe racial discrimination is wrong. Reflecting the conclusions of most scholars who study race relations, Thernstrom and Thernstrom (1997, 498–501) report that from the 1970s onward large majorities of whites favor integrated schools, do not object to having blacks of their own social class as neighbors, and believe that blacks are of equal intelligence.

The most thoughtful and detailed analysis of the role of racial issues in American politics surveys the research on racial attitudes and concludes that Americans' endorsement of norms of racial equality are nearly universal:

> In the age of equality, neither citizens nor politicians want to be perceived or to perceive themselves as racist. The norm of racial equality has become descriptive and injunctive, endorsed by nearly every American. For most white Americans, it is a personal norm as well. Whites do not simply pay lip service to equality and continue to derogate blacks in private. Almost all whites genuinely disavow the sentiments that have come to be most closely associated with the ideology of white supremacy— the immutable inferiority of blacks, the desirability of segregation, and the just nature of discrimination in favor of whites. In this sense, nearly every white person today has a genuine commitment to basic racial equality in the public sphere. (Mendelberg 2001, 18–19)

If it is true, as I believe it is, and as Mendelberg and the Thernstroms conclude, that most Americans believe in racial equality and that base forms of invidious racism are no longer commonplace in American life, how is it possible that coded allusions to race and racial resentment so long remained so common and so effective? Part of the answer can be found in the psychology of race relations that I discussed earlier. White Americans are influenced by stereotypes of black criminals, as the research on colorism, Afro American feature bias, and implicit bias shows. And, as the research on public opinions and attitudes shows, overtly racist attitudes have been replaced by racial resentments, which are the most powerful explanation for why many more whites than blacks support harsh criminal justice policies.

Coded racial appeals have long been effective in American politics precisely because they are coded, as Mendelberg (2001) shows in an exhaustive analysis of the media's handling of the Willie Horton advertisement in the 1988 presidential campaign and afterward. The key distinction is between explicit and implicit appeals to race. Because of Americans' commitment to norms of racial equality, explicit appeals no longer work. They backfire, and their practitioners are widely disparaged. The successive campaigns for Louisiana governor and U.S. senator by a former Ku Klux Klansman, David Duke, provide a vivid illustration.

Implicit appeals, however, can work:

> White voters respond to implicitly racial messages [such as Willie Horton and Reagan's "welfare queen"] because they do not recognize these messages as racial and do not believe that their favorable response is motivated by racism. In fact, the racial reference in an implicit message, while subtle, is recognizable and works most powerfully through white voters' racial stereotypes, fears, and resentments. (Mendelberg 2001, 7)

Appeals to racial issues in modern American politics, once explicit, became implicit. White segregationists in the 1960s and 1970s, who were not reconciled to the success of the civil rights movement, were motivated by invidious considerations and made explicit racial appeals when they could. Opponents of the civil rights movement, rather than continue openly to fight battles they had lost, and whose loss made open appeals to bigotry no longer politically acceptable, "shifted attention to a seemingly race-neutral concern over crime" (Loury 2008, 13). A historian of law-and-order politics in the 1960s similarly observed, "For conservatives, black crime would become the means by which to mount a flank attack on the civil rights movement when it was too popular to assault directly" (Flamm 2005, 22). Vesla Weaver explains: "Much of the legislative activity on crime came out of the same hand that fed the early opposition to civil rights.... Through a frontlash, rivals of civil rights progress defined racial discord as criminal and argued that crime legislation would be a panacea to racial unrest" (2007, 265).

Other activists, influenced by the history and social psychology of American race relations, and blinded by political opportunism, were unable fully to appreciate the implications of what they were doing. Some, especially in hindsight, recognized those implications and expressed regret for their earlier actions and blindness. The most striking refutation came from Lee Atwater, creator of the Willie Horton campaign. On his death bed Atwater apologized for the "naked cruelty" of the attacks on democratic candidate Michael Dukakis: "In 1988, fighting Dukakis, I said I would 'strip the bark off the little bastard' and 'make Willie Horton his running mate.' I am sorry for both statements" (Associated Press 1991, 16).

At the end of an article on racial attitudes toward the justice system, Unnever, Cullen, and Jones offered an assessment of the consequences of the Southern Strategy:

> The disturbing part of our research is that we found not only that Americans with racial resentments were more likely to endorse the punitive approach to resolving the problem of crime, but also that racial animus was the most robust predictor.... We did not find any evidence that having negative stereotypes of African Americans was predictive of how individuals perceive solutions to reducing crime.... Together, these findings are suggestive that the Republican political elites' southern strategy "worked." (2008, 25–26)

There are no easy paths out of the racial dead end in which American criminal justice policy finds itself. The damage has been done to living black Americans: lives have been blighted, life chances diminished, families fractured, communities undermined. Even radical changes in

American crime policies cannot undo the damage. Chapter 6, however, shows how that unnecessary damage can in the short term be reduced and in the long term prevented.

First, though, chapter 5 goes one level deeper into American history and culture to explore the still bewildering questions of how and why the racial politics of the past half-century unfolded as they did.

Ideology, Moralism, and Government

IN TRYING TO UNDERSTAND THE AMERICAN CRIMINAL JUSTICE system, race matters. It helps explain why imprisonment rates are so high, why profiling by the police continues, and why the federal 100-to-1 law so long endured. Race relations, however, do not explain why American drug and crime control policies are so severe. The damage done to black Americans would be much less if the criminal justice system were not so harsh. If the American imprisonment rate were the same as the average of other developed countries, around 100 per 100,000 people, rather than approaching 800, the absolute numbers of black Americans entangled in the arms of the law would be vastly lower. There would be many fewer devastated lives, fatherless children, and fractured families. Many more young black offenders would have had the chance to do what most other young offenders do: put their mistakes behind them and get on with living normal lives.

Crime has always been preponderantly a young man's game, everywhere and at every time, and most young men age out of it. They find love, or God, or a decent job, and realize that's what they really want. Many hundreds of thousands of young black American men have been unable to do that. When—if—they leave prison, many face obstacles that make living a conventional, satisfying life an impossible dream.

The history of American race relations, the social psychology of race and crime, and the politics of racial resentment explain much that is wrong with the American criminal justice system and why it does such disproportionate damage to black people. They do not, however, explain why it is so harsh. Nor can they explain why the American justice system is so much harsher than those of other countries with which the United States might ordinarily be compared.

Deeper forces are at work. One is a historical tendency in American life to political extremism. It has appeared time and again in popular political movements aimed at immigrants, ethnic minorities, commu-nists, and foreign enemies. It appeared in the Red Scares of the 1920s, isolationism and xenophobia in the 1930s, Japanese internment in the 1940s, McCarthyism in the 1950s, and backlash to the civil rights movement in the 1960s, 1970s, and 1980s. It reappeared in the Tea Party movement in 2009.

A second is a tendency toward moralistic excess predicated on reli-gious certainties, particularly of the fundamentalist Protestant kind. A wide range of recurring hotly contested political issues—abortion, school prayer, capital punishment, governmental support of religion—are distinctively, almost uniquely American. Those issues prompt dis-agreements everywhere, but only in the United States have they produced powerful, enduring single-issue interest groups, nonnego-tiable politics, and long-term gridlock. Only in the United States have they resulted in adamant refusal to accept unfavorable court decisions and, in the cases of abortion and school prayer, decades-long campaigns to change constitutional doctrines. They are intelligible to outsiders only when the force of religious beliefs in American life is understood.

A third is a structure of government that makes U.S. jurisdictions uniquely vulnerable to influence by extreme emotions and political pas-sions. Only in America and Switzerland are judges and prosecutors elected. Only in America are they chosen in partisan elections or selected according to openly political criteria. And only in America have drug and crime control policies been enduring and central political issues in national politics for nearly fifty years. If political extremism, religion-based beliefs, or short-term emotion make Americans excited, the structure of American government gives elected officials powerful incentives to respond. If drug use and crime are seen as raising primarily moral issues, and drug users and criminals are conceived of primarily as moral reprobates, it should not be surprising that governmental policies lack moderation and balance. Only the United States, as a result, has "wars" on drugs and crime, capital punishment, three-strikes-and-you're-out laws, life sentences without the possibility of parole, truth in sentencing laws, and Megan's laws that are at least as important for the moral messages they express and the political concerns they symbolize as for any effects they might have.

The self-righteousness, emotionalism, and lack of empathy and proportionality that characterize America's metaphorical wars on drugs and crime also characterize the "War on Terror." Many Americans are ashamed of things their national government has done, or has permitted to be done, in the name of protecting national security. If we understood better the underlying causes of inhumane excesses in the War on Terror, we would better understand why American drug and crime control policies are so severe. Seeing ourselves through others' eyes might help.

For most of my adult life I've had the good fortune to spend part or all of each year in small towns on the coast of Maine. European friends often come to visit. In recent years each in one way or another has asked the same question. They are bewildered by the contrast between the friendliness, openness, and decency of the people they meet on the street, in stores, and on front porches, and the inhumane values, dishonesties, and brutalities of the national governments those people repeatedly elected. In recent years what they've had in mind are Guantánamo, Abu Ghraib, rendition, and torture.[1] "How does that happen?" they wonder.

What they don't at first understand is that many American drug and crime control policies, of which typically they know little, are as oblivious of basic decencies and human rights as are many elements of the American War on Terror. At its most populated, for example, Guantánamo housed 680 inmates. In 2009 more than 30,000 souls lived in American super maximum-security prisons under conditions in many instances bordering on sensory deprivation. Every country has high-security prisons, but they hold tens or hundreds of inmates and under far less harsh conditions.

In the Bush II administration's plans Guantánamo inmates were to be held for indefinite periods, potentially until the end of the War on Terror, without charges, access to courts, or opportunity even for independent judicial review of whether there were adequate grounds to hold them. In 2008 nearly 42,000 American prisoners were serving sentences of life without the possibility of parole; that number will soon reach 50,000. Few other Western countries authorize sentences that require an offender to spend the rest of his life behind bars. In those that do, the numbers of affected prisoners are in single or double digits.

One of many human rights objections to Abu Ghraib Prison in its worst years was that it was grossly overcrowded. More than 7,000 prisoners were held in a facility designed for less than half that number (Schlesinger et al. 2004, p. 60). California prisons in recent years have continuously operated at 200 percent of capacity. On June 30, 2007, California housed 166,277 inmates in prisons designed to accommodate 84,653 (California Department of Corrections 2008, tables 4, 5). Many prisoners are held in open dormitories filled with bunk beds, often in spaces previously used as cafeterias, gymnasiums, and corridors. Few other developed countries house more inmates than their prisons are built to hold, and many for human rights reasons forbid holding more than one prisoner in a cell.

Add to those examples the American practices of prosecuting children as adults (in many countries, the minimum age of criminal responsibility is fifteen or higher), sentencing children to lifetime sentences without parole (impossible in any European country), and executing criminals (impossible in any other developed Western country). The differences are stark, and they are not to America's credit.

Nor are racial disparities to America's credit. International organizations have repeatedly decried disparities in American prisons. Examples can be found in several reports prepared by the Committee on the Elimination of Racial Discrimination (CERD) of the United Nations, created to review compliance with the International Convention on the Elimination of All Forms of Racism. The United States has ratified the convention and is obliged to file periodic reports on American compliance with it. Twice, in 2001 and 2008, CERD reminded the United States that the convention forbids discrimination in any form, including as a result of practices not motivated by discriminatory intent. In 2008,

taking particular note of racial profiling and disparities in adult imprisonment, youth confinement, and capital punishment, CERD reminded
the United States that ratifying states are required to "prohibit and eliminate racial discrimination in all its forms, including practices and legislation that may not be discriminatory in purpose, but in effect" (2008, 2).[2]

Governments in the end can operate only within the "boundaries of
political permission" that citizens set (Yankelovich 1991). Governmental
actions and policies outside those boundaries lack legitimacy and are in
the long term unsustainable. America's policies toward its foreign
enemies are thus possible only because American citizens support or at
least accept or tolerate them. Abu Ghraib, Guantánamo, rendition, and
water-boarding fell within the boundaries permitted by American
political culture in the first decade of the twenty-first century. No one
has ever suggested that the Bush administration was in danger of losing
the 2004 election because of them, or that government officials who
supported them were in political jeopardy. That is also true concerning
capital punishment, sentences of life without the possibility of parole,
three-strikes laws, decades-long mandatory minimums, and prosecution of children as if they were adults. Support for such policies has not
imperiled their supporters' reelection. Opposition to them has.

All of these policies, foreign and domestic, operate as if on the
premise that the individual human beings they affect need not be
regarded with sympathy and respect. The German idealist philosopher
George Wilhelm Friedrich Hegel, writing about punishment, distin-
guished between treating criminals as human beings or as animals (1991,
126, 160). He meant by this that human beings are moral agents whose
capacity for moral choice should be respected and whose wrongs should
be addressed in moral terms. Animals, by contrast, lack moral agency
and may be dealt with instrumentally. If they are dangerous they may be
isolated or killed. If they do things people don't want them to do they
may be retrained or restrained. Ethicists argue over whether particular
harms to animals can be justified—killing them for food or fur, factory
farming, removing their claws and voice boxes for human conve-
nience—but the objections do not relate to animals' capacities for moral
choice. That is a uniquely human capacity.

In Hegel's terms American policies directed at foreign and domestic
"enemies" treat people as if they are animals. Treating them as human

beings requires that we respect human rights and deal with them fairly. It also requires that we deal with them in ways that are proportionate to the moral character of their wrongdoing. To treat offenders or external enemies as human beings requires that they be treated as individuals, and that what is done to them be capable of justification by reference to the moral character of their actions.

More recently, the American philosopher Ronald Dworkin (1986) observed that the fundamental and irreducible requirement of the notion of equality before the law is that legal institutions and practices accord equal respect and concern to all people. This means that their individual stories should be heard and given fair consideration, and that they should be treated as others like them are. This test is no better satisfied by confinement of citizens in prison for the rest of their natural lives than by confinement of foreigners in Guantánamo for so long as the U.S. government chooses.

Modern Americans give their leaders political permission to operate within much wider human rights boundaries than citizens of other countries allow their leaders. How come? The answers are becoming clear. Two recurring features of American history—what the historian Richard Hofstadter (1965) called the "paranoid style" in American politics and the influence of Protestant fundamentalism—have in our time combined with outmoded features of U.S. constitutional arrangements to produce policies incomparably harsher than those in other Western countries. And the peculiar history of American race relations has meant that the burdens of those policies are disproportionately borne by disadvantaged black Americans, which, to the white and middle-class majority, makes them relatively easy to bear. As Stan C. Proband has often observed, Americans have a remarkable capacity to endure the suffering of others.[3]

It may simply have been colossally bad luck for black Americans that the success of the civil rights movement coincided with a period of acute social anxiety. There were similar periods earlier in the twentieth century. In the period 1920–40 the aftermath of World War I coincided with the Roaring Twenties, Prohibition, the Great Depression, the Russian Revolution, and the rise of Nazism and fascism. The Red Scares of the 1920s and the xenophobia of the 1930s were among the results, but blacks were not especially targeted (immigrants and foreigners were), and the criminal justice system did not become vastly more repressive. The period 1945–60 coincided with the end of World War II, the descent of the Iron Curtain, nuclear war anxieties, and the breakup of colonial empires. The McCarthy era and hysterical anticommunism were among the results, but this time also blacks were not targeted (foreign enemies and their purported sixth columns were), and the criminal justice system was little affected.

The most recent period of heightened social anxiety is typified by globalization and economic restructuring, political terrorism, increased population diversity, and the social movements emblemized by civil rights, women's rights, and gay rights. Some refer to our time as "late modernity," a time characterized by rapid social change, economic disruption and uncertainty, and moral skepticism (Garland 2001).

In each of these periods the paranoid style has been manifest, exacerbated in the last two by the rigid moralism of Protestant fundamentalism. In each period the organization of American government has meant that few devices existed to insulate government policies and practices from the influence of political extremism, ideological excess, and emotionalism. Legislative elections are frequent. Most judges and prosecutors, almost uniquely among developed countries, are elected. Many worry about how the media or interest groups will respond to their decisions and, being human, sometimes make different—and harsher—decisions than they otherwise would.

In recent decades some judges and many prosecutors have responded to public passions and emotions with demagogic election campaigns. Incumbents were often attacked for "leniency." In the 1980s it was not uncommon for judicial candidates to emphasize how punitive they would be if elected, and for campaign advertisements to show candidates standing before slamming jailhouse doors.

What has been different in recent decades, however, has been the targeting of behaviors for which black Americans are disproportionately arrested. Those criminal justice system policies and practices provided enemies within—enemies with whom most white Americans do not identify. Because of the history and social psychology of American race relations white Americans do not extend the same solicitude and sympathy to disadvantaged black people that they extend to people like themselves.

This chapter develops the arguments and evidence on which the preceding observations are based. The first two sections briefly demonstrate that American crime and drug control policies, like American practices in the War on Terror, are incomparably harsher than those of other Western countries, and that the explanations for why that is so must be sought in American history and culture. The third section finds those explanations in the paranoid streak of American political culture, the moralism of evangelical Protestantism, and the structure of American government.

INCOMPARABLE AMERICAN CRIME CONTROL POLICIES

Most people with even superficial knowledge of American crime control policies know that only the United States among Western countries retains capital punishment and that American imprisonment rates are four to ten times higher than those of comparable countries. Table 5.1, offering those comparisons and others, shows that American criminal justice policies are incomparably more severe than those elsewhere.

IMPRISONMENT RATES

When American imprisonment rates began their unprecedented climb in 1973 they were around 160 per 100,000 population, jail inmates included, not much different from those in other Western countries and lower than some, as they had been for most of the twentieth century.[4]

In 2010 American rates were around 780 per 100,000, four to five times higher than those in Spain, England, and New Zealand (150 to 200 per 100,000) and seven to ten times higher than those in most other Western countries (70 to 110 per 100,000; International Centre for Prison Studies 2010).

CAPITAL PUNISHMENT

America has capital punishment; no other Western country does (Hood and Hoyle 2008, 2009). The 3,270 residents of American death

TABLE 5.1   American Crime Control Policies Compared with Those of Other Countries

Subject	United States	Western Countries*
Imprisonment rate (2009)	780 per 100,000	70 to 150 per 100,000
Capital punishment	Yes	No
On death row (July 1, 2009)	3,297	None
Average, 2000–2010	70 killed per year	None
Life without parole	Yes	No
How many (2008)	41,000	100 est.
Three-strikes, etc.	Yes, 26 states	No (minor qualifications)
Age of responsibility	Varies, 10–12	Varies, 10–18
Juvenile waiver	Yes	Varies
Breadth	Wide	Mostly none or narrow
How many per year	30,000 per year	Tiny numbers
War on drugs	Yes, since 1970	No; policies vary
Procedural protections	Weakening since 1970	Strengthening since 1960s

* *Western Europe: fifteen original European Union countries plus Australia, Canada, and New Zealand.*

rows at the beginning of 2010 had no equivalents in other developed Western countries. The differences are starker, however. Only in the past decade, in hotly contested decisions with spirited dissents, has the Supreme Court declared unconstitutional the execution of people who are mentally handicapped or who were younger than 18 when their offenses were committed (respectively, *Atkins v. Virginia*, 536 U.S. 304 [2002]; *Roper v. Simmons*, 543 U.S. 551 [2005]).

LIFE WITHOUT THE POSSIBILITY OF PAROLE

Here too America has it and few other countries do. Few prisoners in other developed countries correspond to the 42,000 poor souls in prison in 2008 who were doomed to spend the rest of their lives there (Nellis and King 2009). Children as young as twelve have been sentenced to lifetime without parole (Canedy 2001; Liptak 2007a); until recently there were no limits. In *Graham v. Florida*, 130 S. Ct. 2011 (2010). the U.S. Supreme Court held that life without the possibility of parole for offenses other than homicide committed by juveniles violates the Eighth Amendment's prohibition of cruel and unusual punishments. This does not mean that people sentenced for crimes committed as a juvenile will not be held until they die. All that is required is that there be a possibility of release. LWOP sentences for juveniles convicted of homicide remain constitutional.

In many European countries the longest sentence that may be imposed for a single offense, including murder, is fourteen years (and that's usually before automatic time off for good behavior). When the German Parliament enacted a law authorizing real life sentences, the Federal Constitutional Court struck it down (van Zyl Smit 2002). The court reasoned that hope for the future, belief in the possibility of a better life, is a basic human right. It ruled that a meaningful review of the need for continued confinement, affording a realistic possibility of release, must be afforded every inmate within fourteen years following confinement. German law was changed accordingly. The other Anglo-Saxon countries tend to be tougher than that but are in no way comparable to the United States. Statutes in a few other countries call for real-life sentences under narrowly specified conditions, and a few people are serving them, but no other country's practices are even vaguely comparable to American life sentences without parole (Appleton and Grøver 2007).

Three-Strikes and Mandatory Minimum Sentence Laws

More than half the states have three-strikes laws, including, most notoriously, the California law that applies to tens of thousands of cases and requires twenty-five-year sentences, or longer, following conviction for any third felony, no matter how minor, and for some misdemeanors. Classic cases, which were unsuccessfully appealed to the U.S. Supreme Court, involved robbery of several slices of pizza (Associated Press 1995), theft of a couple of DVDs from K-Mart (*Lockyer v. Andrade*, 538 U.S. 63 [2002]), and theft of three golf clubs (*Ewing v. California*, 538 U.S. 11 [2003]). Every American state has mandatory minimum sentence laws, many calling for sentences measured in decades. With a few minor exceptions in other English-speaking countries, other Western countries do not have such laws (Tonry 2009).

The Age of Responsibility

In the United States, the age of criminal responsibility, the age at which a person is deemed developmentally capable of committing a crime, is generally ten to twelve. In most of continental Europe that age is higher. In the Netherlands it is twelve; in Germany fourteen; in the Scandinavian countries fifteen; in Belgium eighteen. No matter what they do, twelve- and thirteen-year-olds in most countries, and fourteen-year-olds in many, cannot be criminally prosecuted. The state must find other, more constructive ways to respond to its most troubled young people (Tonry and Doob 2004).

Juvenile Waivers

It is very rare in most countries that have juvenile courts for juveniles to be prosecuted and punished in adult courts. Most Western countries forbid it. That happens to tens of thousands of young Americans each year. Some states, such as New York, do it by dropping the top age of juvenile court jurisdiction to fifteen, well below the developmental ages of emotional and cognitive maturity. Others do it by making all serious violent crimes triable in adult courts. Still others do it by giving prosecutors and judges wide discretion to transfer young people to adult courts (Tonry and Doob 2004).

There are thus stark differences between American criminal justice systems and those of other Western countries in their absolute severity and in the importance they attach to the human rights of individual citizens. Cross-national criminal justice comparisons usually focus on imprisonment rates. As these differences demonstrate, the gap is far wider.

WHY ARE AMERICAN PENAL POLICIES SO HARSH?

The question usually asked is narrower than that: How can we explain national differences in imprisonment rates? None of the commonly offered answers provides much illumination.

Crime rates and trends are not the explanation. Crime trends have been much the same throughout the Western world since 1970: rises through the early or mid-1990s and declines since. There is no relationship, however, between crime rates and imprisonment rates. Since 1973, in the face of similar crime rate trends in most Western countries, imprisonment rates increased five-fold in the United States and doubled in England and Spain, but declined by more than half in Finland, held steady in the rest of Scandinavia, Germany, Switzerland, Austria, and Belgium, and zigzagged in France and Italy (Tonry 2007). In Canada, where since 1980 crime trends have closely paralleled those in the United States, the imprisonment rate has fluctuated around 100 per 100,000 for fifty years (Webster and Doob 2007).

Nor is public opinion the answer. In the English-speaking countries at least, penal policies and imprisonment rates vary enormously, but public opinion has stayed much the same. Majorities of the public believe crime rates are rising when they are falling. Large majorities believe judges are too lenient, on the basis of mistaken underestimates of the severity of punishments. The sentences citizens say they believe are appropriate are typically less severe than those judges actually impose. When citizens are asked whether they prefer more punitive policies or increased investment in rehabilitative programs, majorities usually prefer rehabilitation (Roberts et al. 2003).

David Garland in his 2001 book, *The Culture of Control*, attributes toughened penal policies in England and America to a number of conditions of "late modernity." These include the limited capacities of governments to affect crime rates, the destabilizing effects of economic globalization, increasing population diversity, increased sensitivity to risks of all kinds, and increased vulnerability to crime of privileged segments of the population. The result, he suggests, is a proliferation of "expressive" policies meant more to reassure the public and show that government is doing something, anything, than to reduce crime.

The insuperable difficulty for the analysis is that, if Garland is correct, all Western countries should have experienced steeply rising imprisonment rates and steadily harshening penal policies. The developments he describes happened everywhere; imprisonment rates and policy trends, however, diverged dramatically.

Recent research looks deeper and tries to explain imprisonment trends and penal policy differences in terms of such factors as income inequality, citizens' perceptions of the legitimacy of governmental institutions, citizens' trust in each other and in government, the strength of the welfare state, and the structure of government. All these things matter. Moderate policies and low imprisonment rates are associated with low levels of income inequality, high levels of trust and legitimacy, strong welfare states, professionalized as opposed to politicized criminal justice systems, and consensual rather than conflictual political cultures (Lappi-Seppälä 2008). For each of those factors the United States falls at the wrong end, the end associated with more punitive policies and practices, but that's the beginning, not the end, of the search for explanations. The question is, Why is the United States at the wrong end of every distribution?

WHY ARE HUMAN RIGHTS CONCERNS SO WEAK IN THE UNITED STATES?

That is the $64,000 question. American politicians, and therefore ultimately American citizens en masse, do not much care about the human rights of opponents in the War on Terror. And, as I demonstrated earlier, Americans do not much care about the human rights of their domestic enemies in the wars on drugs and crime.

If we Americans did care much about human rights we would want to know that every human being accused of crime and threatened with punishment is treated, in Dworkin's terms, with equal respect and concern. We would want to know that every human being accused of crime and threatened with punishment is treated, in Hegel's terms, as a human being, not as an animal, in accord with his or her personal merits and demerits. We would oppose ham-fisted, one-size-fits-all policies that ignore offenders' humanity and the circumstances of their offenses and their lives. We would demonstrate the characteristics that Winston Churchill, home secretary of England and Wales in 1910, said "are the symbols which in the treatment of crime and criminals mark and measure the stored up strength of a nation, and are the sign and proof of the living virtue in it." These include "constant heart-searching by all charged with the duty of punishment, a desire and eagerness to rehabilitate in the world of industry all those who have paid their dues in the hard coinage of punishment, tireless efforts towards the discovery of curative and regenerating processes, and an unfaltering faith that there is a treasure, if only you can find it, in the heart of every person" (quoted in Gilbert 1992, 214).

There are four major reasons why American cultural attitudes and political practices accord so little value in our time to basic human rights even of our own citizens. Two—what has been called "the paranoid style" in American politics and a Manichaean moralism associated with fundamentalist religious views—are recurring characteristics of American society. The third is the obsolescence of the U.S. Constitution and a political culture that allows raw public emotion to drive governmental action and policy. The fourth, aggravating and aggravated by the first three, is the distinctive history of race relations in America.

POLITICAL PARANOIA

Richard Hofstadter, the great mid-twentieth-century American historian, described "the paranoid style" as a recurring characteristic of American politics. What is deeply disapproved is seen as evil or immoral, and few means are off-limits in pursuit of its eradication. Distinguishing clinical definitions of paranoia from the paranoid style in politics, Hofstadter wrote:

> The clinical paranoid sees the hostile and conspiratorial world in which he feels himself to be living as directed specifically *against him*; whereas the spokesman of the paranoid style finds it directed against a nation, a culture, a way of life whose fate affects not him alone but millions of others.... His sense that his political passions are unselfish and patriotic, in fact, goes far to intensify his feelings of righteousness and his moral indignation. (1965, 4, emphasis in the original)

American political paranoia waxes and wanes and finds different targets at different times. It manifests itself on the left and the right, though in recent decades mostly on the right. In the twentieth century it waxed three times. The first was in the 1920s and 1930s and is exemplified by Prohibition, the Red Scares of the 1920s, and the xenophobia of the entire period. It wound down only when the onset of World War II gave people more important things to worry about. The second was in the late 1940s and 1950s and is exemplified by Senator Joseph McCarthy, the House Un-American Activities Committee, and the John Birch Society. It waned only when the optimism and idealism of the 1960s pushed it aside. The third, still ongoing, dates from the late 1960s and is exemplified by the recent decades' wars on drugs, crime, welfare recipients, and illegal immigrants, and most recently by the Tea Party movement.

Hofstadter, and many other writers, most famously Daniel Bell (1963), were trying in the 1950s and 1960s to explain the excesses of the McCarthy era and what Hofstadter called the "pseudo-conservative politics" of the emerging radical right wing of the Republican Party associated with Barry Goldwater. Here is how he described the political paranoid:

> The paranoid is a militant leader. He does not see social conflict as something to be mediated and compromised, in the manner of the working politician. Since what is at stake is always a conflict between absolute good and absolute evil, the quality needed is not a willingness to compromise but the will to fight things out to a finish. Nothing but complete victory will do. (1965, 31)

The National Rifle Association and major elements of both sides of the abortion debate are contemporary single-issue examples, unwilling ever to give an inch or to acknowledge even a trace of merit in their opponents' arguments and fearful that the slightest political loss will lead to a slippery slope on which all will be lost. As seen from the right, if banning or tighter regulation of semi-automatic weapons is countenanced every heirloom hunting rifle will soon be confiscated. As seen from the left, any tighter controls or additional conditions on second- or third-term abortions will lead inexorably to the disappearance of women's "right to choose."

Every political battle is crucial, Hofstadter observed. The proponents of morality will fight to the end: "The central image [held by practitioners of the paranoid style] is that of a vast and sinister conspiracy, a gigantic and yet subtle machinery of influence set in motion to undermine and destroy a way of life" (1965, 29).

The right wing of the Republican Party deserves most of the blame for the impoverishment of American criminal justice policy since the 1970s and the diminution of human rights values in it, just as it deserves the blame for Abu Ghraib, Guantánamo, rendition, and the "torture memo." I can remember as a boy in the 1950s wondering what the "Impeach Earl Warren" billboards were about. They were placed beside American highways throughout the country by the John Birch Society. Warren's impeachable offenses, I much later came to understand, related to *Brown v. Board of Education*, 347 U.S. 483 (1954), the Supreme Court's landmark decision declaring segregated schools unconstitutional, and the Court's early, halting efforts to strengthen the procedural protections afforded criminal defendants.

In the 1950s the John Birch Society was widely seen as a radical fringe group. By the 1960s many of its views had been adopted by Goldwater and the (then) far right wing of the Republican Party. Hofstadter observed that Goldwater "arrived at the position, far from conservative in its implications, that the decisions of the Supreme Court are 'not necessarily' the law of the land.... It is only in our time, and only in the pseudo-conservative movement, that men have begun to hint that disobedience to the court is not merely legitimate but the essence of conservatism" (1965, 99–100).

By the 1970s such views became mainstream Republican doctrine. The John Birch Society's effort to impugn the integrity of the courts and to reduce their legitimacy in the eyes of the American people has remained a prevailing theme of the American right, with pernicious effects.

One consequence has been the declining legitimacy of the courts and the legal system in the eyes of the American public, as the John Birch Society and its successors wanted. "Impeach Earl Warren" was followed by forty years of attacks on "activist" and "lenient" and "liberal" judges who were said to be frustrating the will of the people. This is a bit odd inasmuch as conservative Republican presidents have appointed most sitting federal judges since 1968, and Democratic President Bill

Clinton never fought very hard to appoint liberal judges. Nor so far has President Barack Obama. Republican presidential aspirants' speeches even in 2008 regularly decried "activist" "liberal" judges.

Research on public opinion about punishment tells a subtle story about the effects of conservatives' efforts to undermine the legitimacy of the judicial system. Tom Tyler (2006) and others have demonstrated the importance of the perceived legitimacy of legal institutions in the eyes of people they affect. People who believe that police and judges treat them impartially and fairly, consider their interests, and listen to their stories are more likely to respect legal institutions and to accept adverse decisions as appropriate than are people who believe they are treated unfairly. Neither Hegel nor Dworkin would be surprised by this. A different conception of legitimacy instructs that citizens who believe institutions operate fairly and honestly are more likely to respect them in general than are people who do not believe these things. Duhh!

The unhappy consequences of a half-century's effort to undermine the legitimacy of the courts can be seen when Americans' attitudes are compared with those of people in other countries. In both the United States (Roberts et al. 2003) and the Netherlands (Elffers and de Keijser 2006), for example, public opinion research has examined whether citizens believe judges sentence too severely, too leniently, or just right, and what sentences citizens say they themselves would impose in particular cases. The findings from English-speaking countries show that large majorities of citizens believe judges sentence too leniently. However, when the sentences citizens say they would impose are compared with those judges do impose, the comparison almost always shows that judges impose longer sentences than citizens say they would. Citizens' beliefs about sentences are not based on the ordinary run-of-the-mill cases that make up the bulk of court dockets, but on aberrant or special cases that are distinctive or sensational enough to attract media attention. As a result most people systematically underestimate the sentences typical offenders receive.

A parallel but more nuanced body of research in the Netherlands produces similar and also strikingly different findings. Do Dutch citizens believe judges sentence too leniently? Yes. Do judges know that citizens believe this? Yes.

So far the story is the same, but then it diverges. Do Dutch judges impose sentences less severe than Dutch citizens would? Yes. Dutch citizens, unlike American citizens, are right: judges are less severe than citizens say they would be.

But now the corker: Do Dutch citizens believe judges should impose harsher sentences in order to reflect citizens' preferences? No. That last finding is unimaginable in the United States. For decades voters have been electing politicians who run against "lenient" judges.

How do Dutch citizens explain this finding, which to Americans is bizarre? It's easy. They trust their judges. They say that it is the judge's job to consider the facts of cases, consult the relevant laws, and then in good faith make decisions he or she believes to be right. For a judge to do anything else would be to make a decision he or she believed to be wrong, and that's incompatible with what an honest, conscientious judge is supposed to do.

Why would Americans have such a different outlook? To a large extent it is because conservative politicians' efforts for fifty years to delegitimize judges have sunken in. And partly it is because many American judges and prosecutors are blatantly political. Dutch judges, like those of most developed countries, are apolitical career civil servants who are selected meritocratically. Most American judges are chosen in partisan political elections, and for limited terms. Many run for office spending campaign funds donated by lawyers who practice before them, and most of the rest are appointed in partisan political ways. It doesn't take a great deal of cynicism for Americans to believe that what prosecutors and judges do is influenced by their political self-interest and the possible effects of their decisions on future electoral or other political prospects.

If judges cannot be trusted to handle cases brought against alleged terrorists and criminals, then other agencies of government must do it. If alleged terrorists and offenders and drug dealers and illegal immigrants and welfare recipients are evil, the embodiment of immoral behavior, then of course their interests need not be taken into account in deciding how to address the threats they represent.

All of us in our personal lives want to be treated with equal respect and concern in proceedings that affect us and our interests and our loved ones and their interests. The paranoid style, however, has too often led policy makers to forget that their enemies are human beings and to abandon the sympathy and mutual respect that distinguish human beings from animals. From that forgetting come Guantánamo and Abu Ghraib and three-strikes laws and life sentences without the possibility of parole for children.

RELIGION AND MORAL INTOLERANCE

Several of the British colonies in America were established by people fleeing religious intolerance—the Puritans in Massachusetts Bay, the Quakers in Pennsylvania, and Roger Williams's nonconformists in Rhode Island are the classic examples. Even so, within a half century people were being killed for religious reasons. Kai Erikson's *Wayward Puritans* (1966) is most famous for its account of the Salem witch trials. It also describes, however, a gradual descent into intolerance in Massachusetts that led to the maiming and execution of Quaker missionaries who dared express divergent religious views. And, lest we forget, the "witches" in Salem were executed because they were adjudged to be heretics.

A sizable historical literature on nineteenth-century America recounts recurring episodes of religion-based intolerance (e.g., Myers 1943; D. B. Davis 1960). Usually these were related to the status anxieties and xenophobia of established groups triggered by the in-migration of new ethnic groups, often bringing their own religions and worldviews. The temperance movements in the middle and again in the late nineteenth century, for example, usually involved status conflicts between abstemious descendants of earlier Protestant settlers and newly arrived, more bibulous Catholics (Gusfield 1963). In much the same way moralistic crusades against drugs and crime in our time have provided devices for fundamentalist Protestants to express disapproval of and social distance from people different from them, including black Americans.

Similar patterns existed in other times. David Garland (2005) has demonstrated that lynchings in America during their peak period, 1890–1930, were in significant part the product of status anxieties among southern white Protestants. In the 1920s the Ku Klux Klan defined itself primarily as a campaign to preserve Christian values: "The Klan drew heavily on white evangelical Protestants for its mass membership, and evangelical clergy were disproportionately prominent among the leadership" (Wald and Calhoun-Brown 2007, 208).

When Hofstadter wrote in the 1960s it was apparent that the fundamentalist Protestant groups, which were rapidly expanding and becoming prosperous, made up one important strand of the paranoid style of his era. He observed, "Most prophetic of the future of the right wing was [McCarthy's] strong appeal for fundamentalist-oriented Protestants" (1965, 70).

In our time it is clear that some (though definitely not all) fundamentalist Protestant groups are among the strongest proponents of the paranoid style of contemporary politics concerning issues ranging from the war in Iraq, support for Israel against the Palestinians, and opposition to abortion and gay rights to support for capital punishment and severe criminal justice policies. The notion that these are issues of good versus evil, of absolute right and absolute wrong, helps explain the religious right's fervor and its intolerance. When added to the resurgence in recent decades of the paranoid style in American politics it is small wonder that the interests of people seen as enemies or threats typically receive short shrift.

Taken together these events and ideas make the success of the Republican Southern Strategy, and its effects on crime control policy and black Americans, more understandable. The civil rights movement produced status anxiety among white southerners, worried about maintaining their traditional higher status than that of blacks, and among working-class white voters, worried about economic and social threats newly empowered blacks might pose. Because politicians after 1970 no longer could openly appeal to antiblack sentiments they used code words, one of which was *crime*. The wars on drugs and crime rapidly expanded as politicians kept their promises. Because it was disproportionately black people who went to prison white voters felt able comfortably to pay that price, especially since it perpetuated the economic and social tradition of white dominance over a socially disorganized black underclass.

The sizable political science and religion literatures on religion and politics in the United States are silent, except in passing, on the influence of Protestant fundamentalism on American crime policy generally. They focus on abortion, women's and gay rights, and separation of church and state. None of the major recent works includes the terms *crime* or *capital punishment* in its index (e.g., Layman 2001; Green 2007). One leading work, however, *Religion and Politics in the United States* (Wald and Calhoun-Brown 2007), explains how and why Protestant fundamentalism shaped American crime control and punishment policies for three decades. Whereas Catholics and mainstream Protestants espouse a commitment to social welfare consonant with their belief in "a warm, caring god," the fundamentalist "image of a cold and authoritative deity lends support to government's role in securing order and property" (121). Richard Snyder, a former dean at New York Theological Seminary, explains the fundamentalist vision this way: "If we believe that all persons are essentially corrupt save for the extraordinary intervention of God's grace in their lives, it is a simple step to think that those who are poor, or sick, or in trouble with the law, or different from us in any way are somehow evil. The redeemed are God's children; the unrepentant are children of Satan" (2001, 14).

Fundamentalists are "characterized by a quest for certainty, exclusiveness, and unambiguous boundaries" and attempt "to chart a morally black and white path out of the gray zones of intimidating cultural and religious complexity" (Nagata 2001, 481). In its 1995 Contract with the American Family Pat Robertson's Christian Coalition accordingly called for increased penalties for convicted criminals (Wald and Calhoun-Brown 2007, 351). A year later Bennett, DiIulio, and Walters (1996) produced the fullest elaboration of fundamentalist crime control policy analysis ever published.

The near absence of crime control and punishment from the politics and religion literature is odd. The nexus seems self-evident. The Republican resurgence of the past forty years is attributable in large part to the Southern Strategy. The political influence of the religious right on Republican politics is well known (e.g., Green 2007). As one major review of the literature on fundamentalism and conservative politics observed, "The [religious right] enjoys something like a veto power in the Republican Party" (Woodberry and Smith 1998, 48).

By contrast the criminology literature, though small, has ferreted out the connection. Unnever, Cullen, and Applegate's examination of attitudes toward capital punishment concludes that those fundamentalists "who have a rigid and moralistic approach to religion and who imagine God as a dispassionate, powerful figure who dispenses justice are more likely to harbor punitive sentiments toward offenders" (2005, 304). A slight but fascinating article based on a representative survey of Oklahoma City residents showed that Protestant conservatives viewed nearly all crimes as "very wrong" and thus did not differentiate among them in terms of seriousness (Curry 1996, 462). This finding goes a long way toward explaining why traditional ideas about proportionality in punishment are irreconcilable with many modern three-strikes, mandatory minimum, and life without the possibility of parole laws.

Constitutional Structure

"It can be argued, of course," Hofstadter observed, "that certain features of our history have given the paranoid style more scope and force among us than it has had in many other countries of the western world" (1965, 7). Outmoded constitutional arrangements are among the most important of those explanatory features. Those arrangements provide little insulation from the influence of paranoid politics, fundamentalist moralism, and short-term emotionalism when they arise.

Major elements of the U.S. constitutional system are designed to address eighteenth-century problems. They make the United States almost uniquely vulnerable to the policy excesses associated with the paranoid style and religious fundamentalism.

Extreme politicization of criminal justice policy is directly related to whether prosecutors and judges are selected politically or meritocratically, whether they are career professionals or political opportunists, and whether political and constitutional conventions allow elected politicians to participate in decision making about individual cases. These three considerations fundamentally differentiate the United States from most other Western countries. Almost nowhere else are judges or prosecutors politically selected; usually they are career civil servants who begin specialized training in law school. And almost nowhere do prevailing conventions justify a direct political voice in punishment decisions (Tonry 2007).

The U.S. Constitution was written to address eighteenth-century problems and reflects eighteenth-century ideas. The colonists were angered by governance by a distant British Parliament in which they were not represented (remember from elementary school the revolutionary-era slogan "No Taxation without Representation"?); capricious actions by imperious local representatives; and the inability of citizens to seek redress for grievances. The principal solutions centered on protection of individual liberty and insulation of citizens from the power of an overweening government. Protection of individual liberty was addressed by adoption of the Bill of Rights, creating fundamental personal rights (speech, religion, redress for grievances) and entitlements (jury trials, representation by counsel, no unreasonable searches and seizures, no cruel and unusual punishments).

Protection from an overweening government was sought in two ways. First, complicated systems of checks and balances were created to fragment governmental power, principally by creating a strong horizontal separation of powers among the three branches of the federal government, and by a vertical differentiation of the spheres of interest of the federal and state governments (which in turn have their own systems of horizontal and vertical separations of power). Second, provisions in the federal Constitution calling for frequent elections to the House of Representatives (two years) and presidency (four years), and in state constitutions for frequent elections at county levels for state legislators, judges, and prosecutors, were meant to push major elections to local levels, to require them at short intervals, and thereby to make officials accountable to local opinion.

The results more than two hundred years later include in many states partisan elections of judges and prosecutors who run for office on the basis of emotive appeals. If the public is anxious about crime or angry at criminals, or if particular cases become notorious, there is nothing to stop prosecutors from seeking personal political benefit by posturing before public opinion or handling cases in particular ways only because they have become notorious. Because local prosecutors are accountable through elections and are in the executive branch of government, the U.S. Supreme Court has held that their discretionary decisions are effectively immune from judicial review (allegations of corruption are the principal exception; *Bordenkircher v. Hayes*, 434 U.S. 357 [1982]). Judges also are elected in most states and know that decisions that are highly unpopular with much of the public can lead to their defeat.

Most chief prosecutors and many judges aspire to be elected or appointed to higher political or judicial office, which means that they worry about controversies that might diminish their future professional prospects, and no doubt sometimes deal with particular cases in particular ways to curry popular approbation or avoid popular condemnation. Criminal justice issues are openly politicized and polemicized in local elections of judges and prosecutors. It is not surprising that candidates for state and federal legislatures and governor and president do likewise, even though they have no direct roles to play in handling individual cases.

Constitutional arrangements place the United States at one end of a continuum distinguishing consensual from conflictual political systems (e.g., Lijphart 1999). Consensual political systems are usually characterized by more than two major political parties, coalition governments, proportional representation, and multiseat electoral districts. Major policy decisions are based on broad consultation within and outside the coalition government. Even after elections resulting in changes of government, major policy decisions are seldom altered abruptly. This is partly because a new coalition government is likely to contain parties from the old coalition, and partly because parties newly in power are likely to have been involved in the development of policies of the former government.

Conflictual political systems are typically characterized by two major parties, single-party governments, first-past-the-post electoral systems, and single-member districts. Elections are winner-take-all events. Parties that are out of power often define their positions in opposition to those of the government of the day and, not having played a major role in developing existing policies, have no particular reason to maintain them. Dramatic changes in direction are much more common in conflictual than in consensual systems, partly because the newly elected government campaigned against existing policies and feels obligated to change them.

Its eighteenth-century governmental institutions have made the United States the paradigm case of a conflictual system. Most European constitutions by contrast took shape in the twentieth century and aimed to assure broad-based political representation. They diffused rather than concentrated political power and provided for parliamentary representation of any party receiving votes above a designated minimum, often 5 percent.

No other Western country has a constitution primarily designed to address eighteenth century problems. All except that of England and Wales include entrenched bills of rights. Most were designed to address the challenges of pluralistic societies and call for electoral systems of proportional representation. Most are generally governed by multiparty coalitions. Policy making on important subjects is generally based on wide consultation within the coalition, with other political parties, criminal justice professionals, NGOs, and interest groups. This takes time. Several years often elapse between initial proposals for changes and their eventual enactment. Changes based primarily on political impulses, overwrought emotions, and short-term political considerations happen, but they are not common.

The constitutional features of American government, by contrast, make the United States uniquely susceptible to the wholesale politicization of criminal justice policy. The structure of American government was meant to tie officials closely to community needs and beliefs, and democratic ideology celebrated the importance and influence of public opinion, even if it was ill-informed, mercurial, or mean-spirited. Constitutional draftsmen worried about the dangers that passing passions would sometimes produce unjust laws. If public emotions become generally inflamed, as happened after the events of September 11, the inflammation is likely to be widespread. James Madison, in Federalist Paper No. 10, observed, "The form of public government...enables it to sacrifice to its ruling passion or interest both the public good and the rights of other citizens.... A common passion or interest will, in almost every case, be felt by a majority of the whole; a communication and concert result from the form of government itself; and there is nothing to check the inducements" to adopt rash, unwise, or unjust policies (Hamilton, Madison, and Jay 2006 [1818]).

Democracies ultimately have no protection against majorities' oppression of minorities, Madison admitted, but he took solace in the protections offered by the dispersion of political power: "The influence of factious leaders may kindle a flame within their particular States, but will be unable to spread a general conflagration through the other States." Unjust laws might be enacted in Illinois, but that does not mean they will be enacted anywhere else. When Madison wrote and for nearly two centuries later, he was right. Travel across the United States took time, there were no electronic media, newspapers dealt mostly in local news, and advocacy groups could not develop the infrastructure to be active throughout the country.

The problems Madison worried about did not fully take shape until late in the twentieth century, when ubiquitous electronic and broadcast media meant that detailed reports of horrible incidents anywhere, and ensuing emotionalism could sweep across an entire continent. Most Americans, probably most citizens of the world, saw pictures of airplanes hitting the World Trade Center. Most Americans quickly learned of the tragedies of Polly Klaas and Megan Kamka, and of the villainies of Willie Horton. A form of government that is designed to respond quickly to changes in public opinion is not well placed to resist emotional calls to enact harsh laws to punish bad people or to protect good ones.

Crime rates rose throughout the United States for twenty-five years beginning in the 1960s. The Republican Southern Strategy placed crime at the center of the political agenda. Conservative politicians campaigned repeatedly for tougher laws and longer sentences. Small wonder that nearly every American state enacted harsher laws and experienced sharp rises in the number of people in its prisons.

Race

The history, psychology, and sociology of American race relations, discussed in chapter 4, combine into the fourth explanation. Unlike the first three its logic applies more to domestic than to foreign enemies, unless lack of empathy for the minority enemies in the wars on drugs and crime, people who look and seem different from the majority white population, is extended by analogy to the enemies in Iraq and Afghanistan and elsewhere, who also seldom look much like the white American middle class.

American political culture has still not come to grips with the legacy of slavery and Jim Crow. I used to get a bit impatient with people who seemed to see the half-empty glass of American racial progress rather than the half-full one of enduring injustice, but I am now convinced that I was wrong.

Obliviousness to the interests of black Americans continues to characterize American drug and crime control policies. Racial disparities in imprisonment continue to be driven by policy choices that should have been foreseen when enacted, and are indubitably recognized now, to affect disadvantaged black Americans disproportionately.

These sad patterns of racial insensitivity, however, make sense in light of the other three explanations. If crime and drugs are matters of good and evil, and criminals and drug users are evil, then there is little reason to expect sympathy or solicitude toward them from the holders of those views. If many whites harbor racial resentments of black people and are affected by unconscious stereotypes of black criminals there is little reason to expect them to sympathize with black suspects, defendants, or prisoners. People on death row or serving lifetime without the possibility of parole or decades-long prison terms deserve what they get, and once they get it there is no reason to think further about them.

Analyses of social stratification and racial hierarchy discussed in chapter 4 make it clear how and why the race card was played, as Hofstadter predicted more than forty years ago. Although, he observed, Republicans historically had sympathy with the plight of blacks in the South,

By adopting "the Southern strategy," the Goldwater men abandoned this inheritance. They committed themselves not merely to a drive for a core of Southern states in the electoral college but to a strategic counterpart in the North which required the search for

> racist votes. They thought they saw a good mass issue in the white
> backlash which they could indirectly exploit by talking of violence
> in the streets, crime, juvenile delinquency, and the dangers faced
> by our mothers and daughters. (1965, 99)

What is distinctive about our time, compared with the 1950s and 1960s about which Hofstadter wrote, and compared with earlier periods of American history, is that the paranoid style of American politics moved from the fringes to the center and has for much of the past thirty years set the tone for policies concerning internal and external enemies. The only way the paranoid style will lose its power is if Americans stop electing its practitioners and thereby show that the boundaries of political permission within which government may operate have narrowed. Thus the answer to the question I asked at the outset—"How does it happen that American governments routinely violate the human rights of their enemies, domestic and foreign?"—is that majorities of American voters have allowed them to do so.

One of the things most people know about Socrates is the aphorism "The unexamined life is not worth living." Among the things the aphorism means is that we should know who we are and how and why we are and what we believe, and that knowing those things we will want to make ourselves better. The same should be true of countries, and for some countries it is. After World War II, Europeans learned the dangers of the too-powerful state and the importance of protecting individuals from it. That's one reason why European governments and institutions have been reluctant to deny procedural protections to people alleged to be terrorists and why most European governments loudly condemn Abu Ghraib, Guantánamo, rendition, and the use of torture. And it's a reason why other Western countries have abolished capital punishment and why they have not followed the American lead in adopting life without the possibility of parole, three-strikes laws, and prison sentences measured in decades, and why they refuse to treat children as if they were adults. Other Western countries have decided that human rights matter and, using a metaphor long ago proposed by Ronald Dworkin (1977), should be treated as trumps when they conflict with what governments want to do.

Winston Churchill also observed, "The mood and temper of the public in regard to the treatment of crime and criminals is one of the most unfailing tests of the civilisation of any country" (quoted in Gilbert 1992, 214). The United States fails by a huge margin to pass Churchill's test, and more than anyone else, black Americans bear the burdens of that failure.

Doing Less Harm

From a race relations perspective the election of Barack Obama as president of the United States was a wonderful thing. It occurred, however, in a country in which a third of black baby boys are bound for prison, and a third of black men in their twenties are in prison or jail or on probation or parole—more than a half century after the U.S. Supreme Court decided *Brown v. Board of Education*, declaring segregated public education unconstitutional, and more than four decades after passage of the Civil Rights Act of 1964.

Whether Obama's election portends changes in American social policy that will distribute the fruits of the civil rights movement more widely and changes in American criminal justice policy that will reduce the damage it does to poor black Americans remains to be seen. It would be Pollyannaish to assume that the election as president of a smart, articulate, and transparently decent black man, a graduate of Columbia College and Harvard Law School, means there will be wider empathy for poor black people who have been left behind.

Winston Churchill observed that the ways a society deals with crime and the criminal are symbols of the "stored-up strength of a nation" and proof of the "living virtue within it" (quoted in Gilbert 1992, 214). Turned around, that is a bleak view. It implies that little can be done to make the American criminal justice system, which offers few signs of "living virtue," less cruel and destructive in general or in relation to black Americans. It is on this account as it is precisely because it reflects and results from predominant social values. Swiss, Scandinavian, and German criminal justice systems by contrast are more respectful of offenders' human rights, punishments are less severe, and prisons are relatively decent places because they reflect those countries' strong social welfare and human rights values (e.g., Whitman 2003). The American justice system is incomparably severe among Western nations, and its prisons are pretty awful places because they reflect punitive, moralistic, and racially insensitive American social values.

In this chapter I discuss ways that the American justice system can be made less punitive, less destructive, and less harmful to the interests of black Americans. Those aims are inextricably connected. It is the severity of the American justice system that makes it so destructive. The severity affects everyone it touches. Because relatively so many more black people are touched it does special damage to them. Reducing severity is the single most effective way to diminish that damage.

Here is a thought experiment that shows why. If the United States locked up its citizens at the same rate Canada locks up its citizens, around 100 per 100,000 consistently for the past forty years, the number of black prisoners would decline by 70 to 90 percent, even if current racial disparities in imprisonment were unchanged. This is not so far-fetched as it may seem to some. In 1973, when American crime rates were higher than they were in 2010, the American imprisonment rate was only a little higher than Canada's. Black Americans would remain six to seven times likelier than whites to be in prison, but the absolute number of blacks in prison would be a tiny fraction of what it is now.

That is a chastening realization. The causes of extreme levels of racial disparity in American prisons—racial profiling by police, police drug arrest priorities, unprecedentedly long prison sentences for offenses for which blacks are disproportionately arrested, the force of stereotypes of black criminals—are unjust and objectionable in themselves, but it is severity, not disparity, that does most of the damage.

American imprisonment rates are unlikely to match Canada's in my lifetime. The thought experiment, however, demonstrates that the unjust burdens the criminal justice system places on black people, and the damage it does to the national aspiration of racial equality, cannot be eliminated or substantially ameliorated unless the severity of

American sentencing is reduced and the causes of racial disparities are addressed.

This chapter shows how those goals can be pursued. Because the greatest benefits will come from reducing the justice system's overall severity, I begin there. The things that need to be done include reduction in the use of prison sentences and in the lengths of sentences; repeal of most three-strikes, mandatory minimum sentence, truth-in-sentencing, and life-without-the-possibility-of-parole laws; creation of emergency mechanisms for shortening sentences of many currently imprisoned offenders; and reconstitution of permanent institutions to oversee release of offenders whose continued confinement serves no valid public purpose. These proposals inexorably raise the question of whether, if adopted, they would significantly diminish public safety. The answer is no. To show why that is so, I survey current knowledge about the effectiveness of contemporary drug law enforcement strategies and about the crime prevention effectiveness of severe penalties in deterring crime and incapacitating offenders.

Only after that has been done do I turn to changes that need to be made to reduce racial disparities per se. These include elimination of racial profiling by the police, abandonment of police departments' emphasis on street-level drug arrests, repeal and amendment of laws that punish offenses for which black people are disproportionately often arrested especially severely, reduction of the influence of previous convictions on the lengths of prison sentences, expansion of current efforts to educate and sensitize practitioners about the power of racial stereotypes, and development of racial disparity impact analyses and audits as an indispensable part of policy-making processes.

I should say something about public opinion before I discuss those proposals. Substantial evidence exists that public anxiety about crime and support for severe policies in the late twentieth century was shaped by politicians' and media preoccupation with crime, rather than vice versa (e.g., Beckett 1997). Politicians and the media in the 1970s through the 1990s often did not respond to public anxiety, but provoked it in order to win elections, sell papers, and attract viewers and listeners. Table 6.1 summarizes survey results of Americans' views about the most important problems facing the country over a quarter century beginning

TABLE 6.1 Most Important Problems Facing the Country, Percentages of Respondents Based on Gallup Polls, 1984–2008 (even years)

	1984	1986	1988	1990	1992	1994	1996	1998	2000	2002	2004	2006	2008
High living cost	10	4	2	2	8	4	11	7	15	2	10	8	22
Unemployment	29	23	9	3	25	18	13	5	2	8	13	8	5
Crime, violence	4	3	2	1	5	37	25	20	13	1	2	2	under 0.5
Terrorism	N/A	N/A	N/A	N/A	N/A	N/A	N/A	N/A	N/A	12	27	20	15
Government spending	12	13	12	21	8	5	15	5	4	1	3	4	2
Poverty	N/A	6	7	7	15	11	7	12	5	4	3	4	2
Drugs	N/A	6	7	7	15	11	7	10	5	3	1	1	N/A
Quality of education	N/A	N/A	2	2	8	7	13	13	16	7	4	6	3
Health care	N/A	N/A	N/A	N/A	12	20	10	6	8	6	6	8	7

Source: Bureau of Justice Statistics (various years-d, table 2.1).

in 1984. Crime ranked high only during the mid-1990s, when candidates competed to endorse the toughest anticrime policies and legislatures rushed to enact three-strikes, truth-in-sentencing, mandatory minimum, and Megan's laws. After the anticrime politicking stopped, crime dropped to the bottom of citizens' concerns. A similar pattern appears for drugs. The bigger picture, however, is that for a time the public did become concerned, whatever its reasons for doing so. As a result it is commonly said that current policies are as they are because the public demanded them. If that were true in the early and mid-1990s, it is true no longer.

Contemporary public opinion cannot be invoked as justification for the injustices of the American justice system. Crime and drugs no longer rank high as matters of public concern. Between 2002 and 2008 only 1 to 3 percent of Americans named crime or drugs the most important problem facing the nation. In the twenty-first century concerns about crime or drugs rank far below the economy, unemployment, terrorism, health care, and education.

Crime has not featured prominently in an American presidential election since 1988, and in recent years has only occasionally been a major element in state and local elections. The flurry of adoptions of unprecedentedly severe sentencing laws ended in the mid-1990s. Many states have since enacted amendments mitigating some effects of these laws.

If policy making were animated primarily by rational and humane values the second decade of the twenty-first century would be an auspicious time to remake American criminal justice and drug policies. Racial justice in the American criminal justice system can be improved, though it will not be easy. Americans continue to be influenced by unconscious associations of blackness with crime. The cynicism that underlay the Republican Southern Strategy, and the related willingness to deal unjustly with black offenders in order to appeal to white voters, have not disappeared. Nor has the risk averseness of many Democratic politicians to any action that might be characterized by Republicans as soft on crime. The Clinton administration notoriously supported a federal three-strikes law, new mandatory sentencing laws, and fifty-eight new death penalty provisions in the mid-1990s, and did only by stealth such few good things as it did in relation to crime policy. At the time of this writing the Obama administration and Congress have done nothing significant to roll back the policy excesses of the 1980s and 1990s, so it is not clear whether the Democratic Party even now has set aside its unwillingness to stand up for what is right.

Nonetheless if counsels of despair are allowed to dominate our thinking nothing will change, and there are many historical examples of successful against-all-odds social and political changes concerning other subjects. Franklin Roosevelt's New Deal, which created the Social Security System, the Tennessee Valley Authority, and many other still surviving governmental programs and institutions, and revived the American economy after the Great Depression, is one. The civil rights movement is another. Lyndon Johnson's Great Society, which in the aftermath of John F. Kennedy's assassination produced Medicare and Medicaid and much of the major civil rights legislation, is yet another. Barack Obama's successful effort to create a national system of medical insurance and medical care is a historical accomplishment. Compared with changes of those magnitudes the criminal justice system is small potatoes. Here is what needs to be done.

RADICALLY REDUCE THE USE OF IMPRISONMENT

Efforts to reduce the influence of bias and stereotyping in official decision making are being made throughout the United States and should continue. Unfortunately, even if they were completely successful they could have only modest effects. Table 6.2 shows why. Prison disparities do not result primarily from biased or unconsciously stereotyped decisions. The top row of Part A shows black and white non-Hispanic imprisonment rates per 100,000 population for jail and prison combined in 2006. The second row shows what would happen if black rates were decreased by 10 percent—a high estimate of the degree to which bias and stereotyping enhance disparities—while white rates were left unchanged. The black imprisonment rate would fall from approximately 2,661 per 100,000 to 2,395, and the ratio of black-to-white imprisonment rates would fall from 5.5:1 to 5.0:1. The number of black people locked up would fall by about 100,000.

If instead, as Part B shows, the prison population were cut by half across the board, disparities would not be reduced, but the black

TABLE 6.2   Hypothetical Reduction in Incarceration Rates

	Black	White	Ratio
A. Disparity Reduced 10%			
Imprisonment rate, 2006	2,661	483	5.5:1
10% less disparity	2,395	483	5.0:1
Reduction in prison per 100,000	266	0	
Reduction in black prisoners	101,000		
B. Use of Imprisonment Halved			
Imprisonment rate, 2006	2,661	483	5.5:1
Imprisonment halved	1,330	241	5.5:1
Reduction in prison per 100,000	1,330	241	
Reduction in black prisoners	505,400		
C. Return to 1980 Imprisonment Rates			
Imprisonment rate, 1980	827	134	6.2:1
Reduction in prison per 100,000	1,834	349	
Reduction in black prisoners	697,000		

Source: Tonry and Melewski (2008, table 5).

imprisonment rate would fall from 2,661 to 1,330. Or if, as Part C shows, imprisonment rates were cut to 1980 levels, disparities would not be reduced and the black imprisonment rate would be 827 per 100,000.

The differences in the projected effects of these alternative approaches are enormous. The U.S. Census Bureau estimated that 38.34 million U.S. residents in 2006 were black. If the number of people in prison were halved, but nothing else changed, the black imprisonment rate would fall from 26,613 per million to 13,306. More than 500,000 fewer black Americans would be in prison or jail. Returning to the 1980 level would mean 700,000 fewer black Americans behind bars.

Of course every effort should be made to eliminate bias and stereo-typing. Their diminution will reduce injustices, disparities, and the absolute size of the bite prisons take out of the black population. In absolute terms, though, that will only nibble at the problem. Only radical reduction in the scale of imprisonment can make a big difference. To attempt to limit damage done to people now entangled in the arms of the criminal justice system, devices need to be created for reducing the lengths of prison sentences and releasing hundreds of thousands of people serving unnecessarily long terms. Sentencing laws and guidelines need to be changed to reduce the emphasis on imprisonment, and new programs need to be created to divert many people from prison or jail into community correctional programs. New systems of parole, pardon, and commutation need to be developed, as do programs of social welfare and support to ease people's transitions back into the free community.

None of these changes need be focused on black offenders or on black prisoners. Although disparities are largely the result of contemporary drug and sentencing policies, black imprisonment rates are so absolutely high because American imprisonment rates are so absolutely high.

The prison population cannot be substantially reduced overnight or in a year, but it can be reduced relatively quickly and in ways that do not significantly impair public safety. The imprisonment rate in 1980, after all, was 221 per 100,000, and the violent crime rate was a third higher than it was in 2008. The imprisonment rate in 1970, when violent crime rates were not much lower than in 2010, was 161 per 100,000. All of these rates are significantly higher than those of any other country with which American citizens would ordinarily want their country to be compared. To return to 1980 rates would mean that U.S. rates would continue to be three times those of the Scandinavian countries, twice those in Canada, Germany, and France, and significantly higher than those in England and Wales, Spain, and New Zealand.

There is no good reason to believe that ambitious reduction in the scale of imprisonment would worsen American drug and crime problems. Much of what is done now is counterproductive. The mistaken belief that current drug and crime policies can achieve their aims has impoverished searches for other, more effective approaches.

Repeal Ineffective Crime and Drug Control Policies

Repeal or fundamental alteration of ineffective crime control and drug policies will benefit Americans of every race. The 100-to-1 federal law for sentencing crack cocaine offenses and its 18-to-1 successor are classic—

and extreme—examples. No one has ever made a credible case for that law's effectiveness at reducing drug use or trafficking. However, there are other laws and policies that do as great damage and that also cannot be shown to produce more than offsetting benefits. Three-strikes, mandatory minimum sentence, and truth-in-sentencing laws and the drug war's emphasis on inner-city drug dealing are examples.

DRUG WARS

Police emphasis on inner-city drug markets, the 100-to-1 law, and mandatory minimum sentence laws for drug crimes were all premised on the idea that aggressive law enforcement will reduce drug use or trafficking. A quarter-century's work by drug policy specialists makes it clear that this premise is wrong. Three recent articles by Peter Reuter, Mark Kleiman, Jonathan Caulkins, and Robert MacCoun, America's four most preeminent drug policy scholars, explain why (MacCoun and Martin 2009; Caulkins and Reuter 2010; Caulkins and Kleiman forthcoming).

Drug law enforcement is unusual among anticrime policies in that a single metric of its effectiveness is available: changes in the street prices of drugs. The Drug Enforcement Agency for decades has systematically purchased drugs in street markets in order to assess changes in their purity and price. In calculating prices adjustments are made for purity: one gram of pure heroin packs the same punch as two grams that include an equal amount of another substance and as four grams that contain three grams of another substance. As figure 6.1 shows, cocaine prices have fallen for nearly three decades. They have never risen for an extended period. The lesson to be drawn comes straight from Economics 101: if drug law enforcement were making drugs harder to find or purchase the resulting scarcity would cause prices to rise. Because prices have been falling continuously only the opposite conclusion can be drawn: the drug wars have had no effect on prices and therefore on availability and potential use.

The reasons are straightforward. Some illicit substances are so widely used, and therefore distributed, that a dealer's or user's chances of punishment are small. Caulkins and Reuter (2010) estimate that a

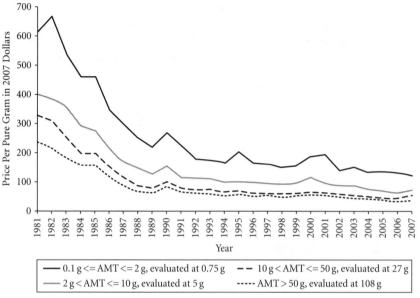

FIGURE 6.1 *The price of cocaine, 1981–2007.*
Source: Caulkins and Reuter (2010, figure 3, based on data from Office of National Drug Control Policy 2008).

marijuana user faces a risk of one hour of imprisonment for each year of use. This should not be surprising. According to the National Survey on Drug Use and Health, by 2008 46 percent of Americans aged twelve and over had used illicit drugs in their lifetimes and 14 percent in the preceding year. Nearly 41 percent had used marijuana at some time and 14 percent had used each of cocaine and hallucinogens (Office of Applied Studies 2010, table 1.1B). Police are not inclined to invest substantial resources in attacking middle-class drug use or cocaine and marijuana dealing behind closed doors, so people engaged in those trades face little risk.

By contrast crack cocaine dealers face significant chances of apprehension, conviction, and punishment, but that has little effect on the availability or prices of drugs. The potential profits of drug dealing, modest though they are in reality for most dealers, look awfully good to disadvantaged young people in the inner city who have few realistic legitimate opportunities for improving their lives. With only modest time lags, arrested dealers are quickly replaced by willing successors. On one notorious street corner in Milwaukee, for example, police in one three-month period arrested ninety-four drug dealers. That had enormous implications for criminal court dockets and correctional budgets, but none at all for the availability of drugs at the corner of Ninth and Concordia. A police officer observed, "These arrests were easy to prosecute to conviction. But despite the 2-year prison terms routinely handed down by the sentencing judges, the drug market continued to thrive at the intersection" (Smith and Dickey 1999, 8). Caulkins and Kleiman observe, "The incarceration of a drug dealer generally creates a niche for another dealer to enter the trade. . . . The key observation is that dealers have to compete for customers, thus making the demand side of the market the determining factor in drug volume" (forthcoming).

The realities just summarized have been widely recognized and have not changed for at least twenty years. In 1990 James Q. Wilson, then and now America's most influential conservative crime scholar, admitted, "Significant reductions in drug abuse will come only from reducing the demand for those drugs. The marginal product of further investment in supply reduction is likely to be small. . . . I know of no serious law enforcement executive who disagrees with this conclusion. Typically police officials tell interviewers that they are fighting either a losing war or, at best, a holding action" (534). Senator Daniel Patrick Moynihan, another of the leading neoconservatives of the late twentieth century, similarly wrote, "Interdiction and 'drug busts' are probably necessary symbolic acts, but nothing more" (1993, 362).

Jack Lawn was head of the Drug Enforcement Agency during the Reagan and Bush I administrations. Asked by then Senator Joseph Biden whether he was happy with that year's budget, Lawn replied, "Well I have enough for this year, but we will have to build more jails because we're going to arrest more people, we're going to convict more people, we're going to seize more drugs, we're going to seize more assets. But until someone gets serious about education, prevention, and treatment, we're the last line of resistance." When Biden responded, "Jack, that's heresy coming from a law enforcement officer," Lawn replied, "No, ask law enforcement people. The other components are indeed missing" (Whitford and Yates 2009, 97–98).

Robert Stutman (2008), special agent for the DEA during the Reagan and Bush I administrations, more recently observed, "Dollars we spend on treatment and prevention give us a far greater return than dollars we spend on enforcement. The general point is that we have never adopted the strategy that a lot of people think is truly a winning strategy. No one has yet demonstrated that enforcement will ever win the war on drugs."

The observations made here are not ones about which reasonable, informed people disagree. Conservative and liberal academics, technocratic specialists like the drug policy scholars quoted, and experienced practitioners agree: current antidrug policies focusing on street arrests of inner-city drug dealers and lengthy prison sentences for drug offenders do not reduce drug trafficking, use, or prices. That being so, police practices that have resulted in millions of arrests of street-level drug dealers make no drug policy sense and in the past twenty years have resulted in millions of young black people being sent to prison.

Likewise lengthy mandatory minimum sentences for street-level drug dealers make no sense. A case for significant punishments can be made concerning large-scale importers and the Mr. Bigs who head major distribution networks. For the small fry who deal in small quantities, often to support their own drug dependence, the deterrent logic underlying such laws is wrong. The threat of long prison sentences does not dissuade disadvantaged or desperate people from trying to make money selling small quantities of drugs.

DETERRENCE

The situation with three-strikes, truth-in-sentencing, and mandatory minimum sentence laws for other crimes is the same. The logic behind them is that they make the United States a safer place by deterring people from selling drugs and committing crimes, and in some cases by holding them behind bars so they cannot commit crimes outside. However, the clear weight of the evidence for more than thirty years is that harsh punishments, compared with lesser punishments, have few if any deterrent effects, and that lengthy prison terms are at best an inefficient and inhumane way to prevent crimes through incapacitation. Accumulating evidence shows that, all else being equal, sending people to prison makes them more likely to commit new crimes than if they were punished in some other way. Some people find God in prison, a few are rehabilitated, and some would have ceased offending whether or not they were sent to prison. For many others the experience of prison makes them more likely to reoffend. Young prisoners are exposed to antisocial role models and are immersed in a culture in which many of the people they see every day are chronic offenders. The time in prison effectively stops their lives in terms of education and developing a work record. Most on exiting find they are legally barred from many jobs and experience discrimination because they are ex-convicts. Minority ex-convicts experience even greater discrimination as they look for work (Pager 2007).

The most recent assessment of research on the crime-preventive effects of imprisonment, and much the most exhaustive and authoritative, concludes, "Most studies of the impact of imprisonment on subsequent criminality find no effect or a criminogenic effect....Existing research is not nearly sufficient for making firm evidence-based conclusions about the effectiveness of prison at reducing ex-prisoners' subsequent offending" (Nagin, Cullen, and Jonson 2009, 121). Sending people to prison makes them more likely to commit crimes after they are released, not less.

No one doubts that society is safer having some criminal penalties rather than none, but that choice is not at issue. The practical question is whether increases in penalties, or having more rather than less severe penalties, significantly reduces the incidence of serious crimes. The answer is no.

There are three main sources of authoritative evidence on those subjects. First, countries have asked advisory committees or national commissions to survey knowledge of the deterrent effects of criminal penalties in general. Second, a sizable number of surveys of the findings from the research literature on deterrence have been published. Third, evaluations have been conducted of the deterrent effects of newly enacted mandatory penalty laws.

Governmental advisory bodies are unanimous in expressing doubts. The U.S. National Academy of Sciences Panel on Research on Deterrent and Incapacitative Effects, after carrying out the most exhaustive examination of the evidence ever undertaken, concluded, "We cannot assert yet that the evidence warrants an affirmative conclusion regarding deterrence" (Blumstein, Cohen, and Nagin 1978, 7). Daniel Nagin, a principal draftsman, was less qualified: "The evidence is woefully inadequate for providing a good estimate of the magnitude of whatever effect may exist....Policymakers in the criminal justice system are done a disservice if they are left with the impression that the empirical evidence...strongly supports the deterrence hypothesis" (Nagin 1978, 135–36).

Fifteen years later another National Academy of Sciences panel, this one on violence, reached the same conclusion. After showing that the average prison sentence per violent crime tripled between 1975 and 1989 the panel asked, "What effect has increasing the prison population had on levels of violent crime?" Its answer: "Apparently very little" (Reiss and Roth 1993, 6). Average lengths of prison sentences for violent crimes have doubled again since then.

Similar bodies in other countries reached similar conclusions. A British Home Office white paper is a statement explaining why the government proposes to enact new laws. One issued by Prime Minister Margaret Thatcher's government expressed extreme skepticism:

Deterrence is a principle with much immediate appeal....But much crime is committed on impulse, given the opportunity presented by an open window or unlocked door, and it is committed by offenders who live from moment to moment; their crimes are as impulsive as the rest of their feckless, sad, or pathetic lives. It is unrealistic to construct sentencing arrangements on the assumption that most offenders will weigh up the possibilities in advance and base their conduct on rational calculation. (Home Office 1990, 6)

Likewise elsewhere. The Canadian Sentencing Commission: "Evidence does not support the notion that variations in sanctions (within a range that reasonably could be contemplated) affect the deterrent value of sentences. In other words, deterrence cannot be used with empirical justification to guide the imposition of sentences" (1987, xxvii). The director of the Finnish Ministry of Justice's National Research Institute of Legal Policy arrived at the same conclusion: "Can our long prison sentences be defended on the basis of a cost/benefit assessment of their general preventative effect? The answer of the criminological expertise was no" (Törnudd 1993).

Alfred Blumstein, chairman of National Academy of Sciences panels on deterrence and incapacitation (Blumstein, Cohen, and Nagin 1978), sentencing research (Blumstein et al. 1983), and criminal careers (Blumstein et al. 1986), and long America's leading authority on crime control research, explained why three-strikes and similar laws (and by implication all mandatory penalties) are misconceived even for serious crimes:

> However hard it is for rational folks to conceive of it, there are some people who simply do not respond to whatever threat is presented to them.... For people who see no attractive options in the legitimate economy, and who are doubtful that they will live another ten years in any event, the threat of an extended prison stay is likely to be far less threatening than it would be to a well-employed person with a family. (Blumstein 1995, 415)

The literature surveys reach similar conclusions. Philip J. Cook, one of a handful of American economists who has specialized on crime topics, surveyed the literature in 1980. He concluded that existing studies "do *not* demonstrate that all types of crimes are potentially deterrable, and certainly they provide little help in predicting the effects of any specific governmental action" (215, emphasis in original). Daniel Nagin, revisiting the subject twenty years after his work for the National Academy of Sciences panel on deterrence and incapacitation, observed that "a number of studies have credibly identified marginal deterrent effects," but that it is "difficult to generalize from the findings of a specific study because knowledge about the factors that affect the efficacy of policy is so limited" (1998, 4). In a report commissioned by the British Home Office of Tony Blair's government, Andrew von Hirsch and his colleagues concluded, "There is as yet no firm evidence regarding the extent to which raising the severity of punishment would enhance deterrence of crime" (1999, 52).

And so on. The Canadian scholars Anthony Doob and Cheryl Webster concluded, "There is no plausible body of evidence that supports policies based on this premise [that increased penalties reduce crime]" (2003, 146). A meta-analysis by Travis Pratt and his colleagues concluded in more technical language, "The effects of severity estimates and deterrence/sanction composites, even when statistically significant, are too weak to be of substantive significance (consistently below –.1)" (2006, 379). The latest survey of the deterrence literature, at the time of this writing not yet published, concludes, "There is little evidence that increases in the severity of punishment yield general deterrent effects that are sufficiently large to justify their social and economic costs" (Apel and Nagin forthcoming).

Evaluations of the effects of mandatory minimum sentencing laws also conclude that deterrent effects cannot be shown. Most evaluations were done between the mid-1970s and the mid-1990s. The findings are strong and consistent. Because the question has been answered decisively, there has been little research on it since. The evaluators of New York's Rockefeller Drug Laws, the first major modern mandatory minimum penalty law in the United States—and one of the toughest—tried to establish effects on drug use or drug-related crime. They found none (Joint Committee on New York Drug Law Evaluation 1978).

A number of studies were made of the crime-preventive effects of a Massachusetts law requiring a one-year minimum sentence for people convicted of possession of an unregistered firearm. They concluded that it had either no deterrent effect on the use of firearms in violent crimes (Beha 1977; Rossman et al. 1979; Carlson 1982) or a small short-term effect that quickly disappeared (Pierce and Bowers 1981). An evaluation of a mandatory sentencing law for firearms offenses in Detroit concluded that the mandatory sentencing law "did not have a discernible effect on the level or the pattern of violent crime" (Loftin, Heumann, and McDowall 1983, 309–10). Assessments of the deterrent effects of mandatory penalty laws in Tampa, Jacksonville, and Miami, Florida, "concluded that the results did not support a preventive effect model" (Loftin and McDowall 1984, 256–57). The results of evaluations of the crime-preventive effects of mandatory penalty laws in operation in

Pittsburgh and Philadelphia "do not strongly challenge the conclusion that the statutes have no preventive effect" (McDowall, Loftin, and Wiersema 1992, 382).

The most notorious modern sentencing law is California's three-strikes law, which requires mandatory minimum sentences of twenty-five years to life for third felony convictions. Table 6.3 summarizes the findings of fifteen empirical assessments of California's and other states' three-strikes laws. Only two concluded that crime rate were reduced. Three concluded that enactment of three-strikes laws led to *increases* in homicide rates. Of the two studies concluding that the three-strikes law had reduced crime rates, Chen's findings were weak and her conclusions were hedged.[1] Shepherd produced the only assessment purporting to find significant effects.

The fundamental problem with Shepherd's (2002) work, however, and that of some other but by no means all economists who study deterrence, is that it assumes what other social scientists investigate: that increased penalties reduce crime rates. Shepherd, for example, observes that her "model *predicts* that the offenses covered by two- and three-strikes legislation *will be deterred*" (174, emphasis added). Ronald Coase, a Nobel Prize winner and one of the founders of the law and economics movement, long ago wrote, "Punishment…can be regarded as the price of crime. *An economist will not debate whether increased punishment will reduce crime*; he will merely try to answer the question, by how much?" (1978, 210, emphasis added). Isaac Ehrlich, one of the few economists to work on deterrence issues throughout his career, observed that the "'market model'…builds on the assumption that offenders, as members of the human race, respond to incentives….*At least in the economic literature*, there has been little controversy concerning this approach" (1996, 43–44, emphasis added).

In the case of California's three-strikes law, however, even among economists, Shepherd is the exception. Other economists concur with the conclusions of noneconomists that such laws have no deterrent effects (Marvell and Moody 2001; Kovandzic, Sloan, and Vieraitis 2002; Moody, Marvell, and Kaminski 2003). Many economists' minds are just not open. One economist, for example, commenting on a conclusion by three other economists that econometric studies provide no credible

TABLE 6.3 California's Three-Strikes Law: Effects on Reduced Crime Rates

Authors	Method	Deterrent Effect
Schiraldi and Ambrosio (1997)	Yes/no three-strike state comparisons	None
Stolzenberg and D'Alessio (1997)	Time series: 10 largest California cities	None
Males and Macallair (1999)	California age-group comparisons	None
—	California county comparisons	None
E. Y. Chen (2000, 2008)	Time series: 50 states	None
—	Time series: California	Not significant
Austin et al. (2000)	California county comparisons	None
—	Yes/no three-strike state comparisons	None
Caulkins (2001)	National econometric model	None
Marvell and Moody (2001)	Time series: 50 states	None: increased murder rates
Moody, Marvell, and Kaminski (2003)	Time series: 50 states	None: increased murder rates
Zimring, Hawkins, and Kamin (2001)	California county comparisons	None
—	California age-group comparisons	None
Shepherd (2002)	California econometric model	Yes
Ehlers, Schiraldi, and Ziedenberg (2004)	California county comparisons	None
—	Yes/no three-strike state comparisons	None
Kovandzic, Sloan, and Vieraitis (2004)	Model U.S. cities	None: increased murder rates
Justice Policy Institute (2004)	Yes/no three-strike state comparisons	None
Tonry (2004)	Time series: 10 populous states	None
Legislative Analyst's Office, California (2005)	California county comparisons	None

Source: Tonry (2009).

evidence of the deterrent effect of capital punishment, plaintively observed, "It would be incredible and a violation of the law of demand if the chance of execution did not deter" (Rubin 2009, 858).

INCAPACITATION

The evidence concerning incapacitation is little stronger. No one questions that some crimes in the community are avoided because would-be offenders are locked up, but that is not the issue. There would be no crime in the community if everyone were in prison, and relatively little if all males aged fifteen to thirty-five were. Those are not options. The question is whether enough crimes are averted by current practices to justify having so many people in prison. The answer is no.

There are five good reasons to conclude that there are too many people in prison from an incapacitative perspective. First, crime is a young man's game. Most who commit crimes in their teenage years or early twenties will soon stop because they get tired of it or realize they have too much to lose: a wife or girlfriend, a family, a job. Imprisoning people at times in their lives when they are unlikely to offend prevents few crimes. If recent research findings are correct, and imprisonment increases later offending, then holding people past their criminally active age increases, not reduces, crime.

Second, crime is seldom an old man's game. This is not simply a restatement of the first point. Research on criminal careers shows that most offenders stop committing crimes at an early age (Blumstein et al. 1986). Most stop in their teens or early twenties. Very few remain criminally active after their mid-thirties. Almost by definition, with only a few exceptions, confinement of people older than thirty-five is irrelevant from a crime-prevention perspective. Yet at the end of 2008, American state and federal prisons held 150,000 men and 8,700 women aged 50 and over. Some states were operating geriatric prisons, and many prisons had geriatric wings. This is particularly a waste concerning the many people serving decades-long sentences for minor offenses.

Third, for many behaviors locking up a single offender is unlikely to prevent crimes. The "replacement problem" concerning drug dealers is the clearest reason: drug markets provide sufficient incentives to wannabes that filling an open street corner is seldom difficult. In recent years a quarter to a third of state prisoners and more than half of federal prisoners, have been convicted of drug offenses. The evidence of declining drug prices since 1980 means that the billions of dollars spent on their confinement have contributed little or nothing to the reduction of drug problems in the United States.

There are other circumstances in which removal of an offender from the community is unlikely to reduce crime rates. Where youth gangs are active new recruits are generally available to replace those who have been immobilized, unless the gang itself has disbanded. Kids generally do things in groups, including committing crimes, so locking up one or some will not change that reality and is unlikely to alter the group dynamic.

Fourth, among the quarter to a third of prisoners who were convicted of drug crimes, many were convicted of street-level dealing or possession. Most do not present significant risk of other forms of criminality. Especially in light of the high probability of their replacement in drug-trafficking roles, confining them serves little public purpose.

There is a fifth, not separate but supplemental reason why incapacitative considerations cannot justify current imprisonment levels. In every Western legal system, including generally in American systems, it is considered a requirement of justice that convicted offenders receive punishments that are proportionate to the seriousness of their crime. This means that offenders convicted of the same or comparable offenses should generally receive comparable punishments and that offenders convicted of serious offenses should receive severer punishments than people convicted of less serious crimes. Armed robbers should receive severer punishments than unarmed robbers; unarmed robbers should receive severer punishments than burglars; burglars should receive severer punishment than shoplifters, and so on. Every American sentencing guideline system respects that idea and apportions punishments to the seriousness of crimes. Most three-strikes and mandatory minimum sentence laws do not. As a result sellers of tiny amounts of drugs are sentenced more severely than many people convicted of burglaries, robberies, and sexual assaults. Similarly, as earlier examples demonstrate, three-strikes laws require prison terms for people convicted of minor crimes that are much longer than are served by most people convicted of rape, robbery, or murder. Simple justice requires that people not receive, or be expected to complete, disproportionately severe punishments.

Some people deserve to be sent to prison for serious crimes, but not for so long as many are now sent. Some people pose meaningful risks to public safety; from that perspective it is not unreasonable to confine them. There are, however, few such people, and very few of them remain dangerous past their mid-thirties. A large percentage of prisoners could safely be sent home.

From a crime prevention perspective, little would be lost if prisons held many fewer inmates. The savings in money and human suffering would be substantial, and the benefits for black Americans would be enormous.

TARGETING THE CAUSES OF RACIAL DISPARITIES

A wide range of contemporary criminal justice policies do unnecessary damage to black Americans. Some can be addressed by the police; others require administrative or legislative changes.

Years ago Alfred Blumstein (1993) showed that American practitioners and policy makers can respond quickly to racial disparity problems when they are motivated to do so. He observed that from 1965 to 1969 white and nonwhite arrest rates for young offenders were indistinguishable, that during the 1970s white rates exceeded nonwhite rates, and that thereafter until 1989 nonwhite rates nearly tripled and white rates halved, leaving nonwhite rates nearly four times higher. Figure 6.2 tells the story. Here is what Blumstein surmises happened:

> The decline [in white arrest rates] after the 1974 peak was undoubtedly a consequence of the general trend toward decriminalization of marijuana in the United States. A major factor contributing to that decriminalization was probably a realization that the arrestees were much too often the children of individuals, usually white, in positions of power and influence. These parents certainly did not want the consequences of a drug arrest

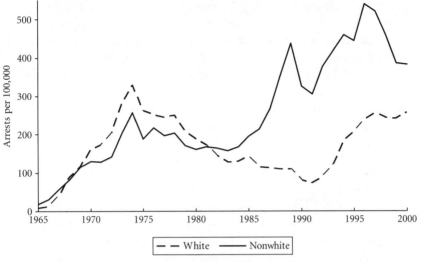

FIGURE 6.2 *Juvenile arrest rates for drug offenses, by race, 1965–2000.*
Source: Blumstein (1993); Blumstein and Wallman (2006).

to be visited on their children, and so they used their leverage to achieve a significant degree of decriminalization. Following the peak, arrest rates for both racial groups declined, and continued to decline for whites. On the other hand, for non-whites, the decline leveled out in the early 1980s and then began to accelerate at a rate of between twenty and twenty-five percent per year, until the peak in 1989. This clearly reflects the fact that drug enforcement is a result of policy choices. (758)

It is not completely cynical to wonder why soaring arrest rates for nonwhite kids in the 1980s and 1990s did not provoke the kinds of reactions that Blumstein attributes to soaring arrest rates of white kids in the 1970s and did not lead to a comparable policy adjustment. To the contrary, as economist Glenn Loury points out, so many black kids were sent to prison in order to dissuade white kids from drug use:

Significantly, throughout the period 1979–2000, white high school seniors reported using drugs at a significantly higher rate than black high school seniors. High drug-usage rates in white, middle-class American communities in the early 1980s account for the urgency many citizens felt to mount a national attack on the problem. But how successful has the effort been, and at what cost? Think of the cost this way: to save middle-class kids from the threat of a drug epidemic that might not have even existed by the time drug offense-fueled incarceration began its rapid increase in the 1980s, we criminalized underclass kids. (2008, 16–17)

Major policy improvements that do not require legislation could be made by police executives if they wished. These concern arrest policies for young people, police profiling, and drug arrest practices in the inner city. It has long been clear that police arrest young black people in circumstances when they do not arrest young whites, and that as a result young blacks accumulate criminal records from younger ages than whites do (Feld 1999). The earlier arrest records are stigmatizing, often unnecessarily interrupt young black people's educational careers, and reduce their chances of living conventional law-abiding lives later on. Convictions resulting from such arrests sometimes remove them from school altogether and always make it harder for them ever to get decent jobs.

RACIAL PROFILING

Racial profiling is per se unfair and puts black people at greater risk than whites of being arrested for reasons that would otherwise not come to the attention of the police. Some might say that the police should arrest people whenever there is evidence they have committed a crime, but sometimes not doing do so is a price free societies pay to protect liberty. Police could no doubt arrest many more white drug dealers if they were allowed to enter private houses without warrants, but few people believe that would be a good idea. Protection of privacy is why issuance of arrest and search warrants is tightly controlled and why they must, except in emergencies, be approved in advance by a judge. When an arrest results from an unlawful search or seizure the criminal charges must be tossed out.

Criminal charges resulting from arrests based on racial profiling should be dealt with in the same way. Because profiling arrests generally are made in public spaces and the police claim to have legitimate grounds for the stop, warrant requirements do not apply. Police incentives to engage in profiling would change substantially if after the fact every arrest arguably resulting from profiling were subject to the same degree of judicial scrutiny that warrants before the fact require.

Drug Arrests

Drug arrests are the second source of disparity that is within the power of police executives to alter. Police focus attention on inner-city drug markets for three reasons: arrests of dealers are relatively easy to make, street markets are visible so citizens complain about them, and police officials (and politicians who put pressure on them) like to be seen as "doing something" about drugs. However, we know that those policies have produced racial disparities between blacks and whites in drug arrest rates as high as 6 to 1 in some years, that arrested inner-city dealers are replaced by willing successors within days, and that whole-sale arrests have no effect on the price or availability of drugs. Police forces that retargeted their efforts to focus equally on white drug dealers would make an important symbolic statement about racial fairness, reduce racial disparities, and pursue the aims of drug law enforcement no less effectively. They would reduce racial disparities in arrests, convictions, and imprisonment in a stroke. They would free up large amounts of police resources to be redeployed in more socially constructive ways. They would also probably greatly reduce police emphasis on arrests of drug dealers. As happened with young whites arrested and convicted of marijuana offenses in the 1970s, white citizens would probably not tolerate substantial increases in the number of low-level white dealers who would be sent to prison. People sympathetic to young black drug dealers and worried about the damage done to them by recent arrest policies have had insufficient political influence to persuade police to deemphasize arrests in the inner city. People sympathetic to the interests of low-level white drug dealers do have that kind of influence.

CRIMINAL RECORDS

At the sentencing stage the damage-doing policies include heavy reliance on prior criminal records to aggravate punishments for new crimes and the effects of mandatory minimum sentences, life-without-possibility-of-parole sentences, and truth-in-sentencing laws. Heavy reliance on prior convictions in setting sentences means that convicted offenders receive much harsher punishments and longer prison terms than they otherwise would. Reducing the weight given previous convictions in sentencing would alleviate a major contributor to racial disparities in imprisonment.

Most of us share an intuition that people who have committed a previous crime should be punished more severely for a subsequent one, and most legal systems respect that intuition. In most other countries, legal doctrines tightly limit how much a punishment can be increased because of a previous conviction (sometimes they forbid any increase). The increases allowed are usually measured in months. In the United States, however, punitive increments to a punishment for a new crime imposed in respect of a criminal record are often measured in years or decades. Because black offenders are arrested more often and at younger ages than whites, they are more often affected by prior-record increments. And because they are more often sentenced for drug and violent crimes, they receive the longest increments.

Even in states with relatively low imprisonment rates, prior criminal records are a major cause of racial disparities in prison. Richard Frase has shown that Minnesota sentencing guidelines call for prison sentences for 39 percent of black convicted offenders but only 25 percent of whites: "The principal source of the increase in racial disproportionality from conviction to sentencing appears to be racial differences in average criminal history scores, combined with the heavy weight these scores have in determining which offenders are recommended to receive [prison terms]" (2009, 254). Differences in criminal records account for "about two-thirds of the black/white difference" (250).

An argument can be made, and often is made, that the book should be closed on an offense when an offender completes his sentence: Did the crime, did the time (Fletcher 1978; Singer 1979; Tonry 2010).

The basic argument parallels the logic of the double jeopardy rule that forbids retrying a defendant who was acquitted at the first trial. If you cannot be tried twice for the same crime, you should not be punished twice. Increasing the punishment for a new conviction because of an old conviction is, in effect, an additional punishment for the first crime.

A recent book of essays shows that no one has yet managed to provide a principled justification for why a person who has previously been convicted deserves a harsher punishment for a new crime (Roberts and von Hirsch 2010). Nonetheless the intuition that criminal records matter is strong, and I assume the practice will continue. But it should not result in vastly harsher punishments.

Other countries' legal systems limit the influence of criminal records. Sometimes they allow criminal records to be used to aggravate sentences only for designated crimes, as, for example, when the string of convictions shows a long-term pattern of specialization in a particular offense. In some countries criminal records are allowed to be used to justify longer sentences, but subject to a strict outer limit, often that the sentence may never be lengthened beyond what would be appropriate for the most serious version of the current offense.

American jurisdictions could also allow but limit the influence of prior convictions. One of the most important steps is to repeal three-strikes and other laws that predicate vastly longer sentences on prior convictions. A second is to establish caps, such as that a prior violent conviction can justify extension of a sentence up to but never beyond six months, and a prior nonviolent conviction can justify up to but not more than some shorter extension. Jurisdictions that operate sentencing guideline systems have an obvious and principled approach readily at hand: prior convictions could justify an aggregate sentence up to but not beyond the top of the applicable guideline range for the offense being sentenced.

The precise method used to limit the influence of prior convictions is not so important. What is important is recognition that current approaches greatly worsen racial disparities in imprisonment and that means must be found to lessen that effect.

Lengthy Prison Sentences

Mandatory minimum, LWOP, and truth-in-sentencing laws are a major contributor to racial disparities in prison. They mostly affect drug and violent crimes and so disproportionately affect black and other minority offenders. Most such laws were adopted primarily for symbolic or expressive purposes rather than, as my survey of the deterrent and incapacitative effects of severe punishments and punishment increases demonstrated, with any reasonable basis for believing they would significantly affect crime rates and patterns. They should be repealed, and no new ones should be enacted.

To address current overimprisonment, American jurisdictions need to establish principled new systems of sentencing guidelines that prescribe proportionate sentences for most crimes measured mostly in months, as in most other Western countries, and in years only for the very serious.

American jurisdictions also need to develop new mechanisms for shortening unduly, disparately, or disproportionately long prison sentences. Parole boards long performed that function. Many have been abolished. They should be reestablished. Most surviving parole boards became much more cautious. Often they do not release most eligible prisoners even though they have authority to do so, and they hold many prisoners far longer than is necessary. Half a century ago the Model Penal Code, the most influential criminal law document of the twentieth century, recommended a legal presumption that prisoners should ordinarily be released the first time they become eligible, and should be held longer only rarely and for very good reasons (American Law Institute 1962). Modern parole boards should adopt that policy.

Racial Bias and Stereotyping

Criminal justice executives have been working for decades to reduce racially biased and discriminatory patterns of decision making. Except at the police stage, where racial profiling remains rife and drug enforcement policy still targets inner-city drug markets, substantial progress has been made.

Many states in the 1990s and since have created racial equity task forces in their court systems. Innovative prosecutors' offices have established research programs to help them identify racial differences in case processing and to change them (Miller and Wright 2008). Continuing education programs attempt to sensitize judges and court and correctional personnel about the ubiquity and perniciousness of unconscious stereotyping and attribution. Programs such as these are as important for the normative messages they send—about the injustice of racial stereotyping, and the importance of treating people as equals—as for the improvements they produce in the quality of American justice. They need to continue and to be expanded to address subtler problems of unconscious bias against black offenders resulting from their skin tone or distinctively African American facial features. By itself, however, consciousness raising can make only a marginal contribution to the reduction of racial disparities in prison and to the damage American criminal justice does to its black citizens as a class. Larger changes are needed if major improvements are to be achieved.

PROPHYLACTIC MEASURES

U.S. governments have long used prophylactic measures to guard against unwanted effects of governmental decisions. To protect the public purse legislatures routinely require that legislative proposals be accompanied by or trigger fiscal impact statements. Some legislatures require that the assessment show that a proposed law's effects will be revenue-neutral before it can be considered. Others require that any proposal for a new law that would increase public expenditure contain within it provisions for raising the additional money required. Federal and state laws routinely require the preparation of environmental impact statements before building and other permits may be issued, and most states require archaeological impact assessments. Projects cannot go forward until the assessment has been completed and the proposed project's effects are shown to be benign. If that cannot be shown, the project must be reconsidered and either abandoned or made subject to amelioration or mitigation requirements.

Similar laws should be enacted concerning racial and other disparities in the criminal justice system (Tonry 1995, 2004; Mauer

2007). Proposals calling for the development of racial disparity audits and impact projections should be relatively uncontroversial. When differences are documented the next question is whether they can be justified, whether racial or ethnic disparities are a price appropriately to be paid to achieve, and are outweighed by, some greater public purpose.

If current or proposed policies create racially disparate effects, they should be considered inherently suspect. In most policy areas that proposition is self-evident. In employment law, for instance, the showing of a disparate effect of a hiring or promotion practice on minority groups or women creates a prima facie case of discrimination. The burden of showing that the practice is justifiable and that the disparity cannot be reduced is placed on the employer. Criminal justice policies should be subjected to similar scrutiny. Many would not survive.

The interests of people accused and convicted of crimes are no less important than those of people who apply for or are fired from jobs. Their interests are greater. What is at stake is not a livelihood but in the short term liberty and in the long term stigma and reduced chances of living a satisfying life. The standards for assessing racial and other disparities in the justice system should be no less demanding than those concerning disparities in employment.

Criminal justice system policy makers should be required to declare and justify disparate racial effects. Proposed new laws or policies should be accompanied by racial and ethnic impact projections that seek to identify foreseeable disparities and determine whether they can be justified. There should be strong presumptions against the law's or policy's adoption if it will disproportionately adversely affect members of minority groups. When disparities would be caused or worsened, the proposal should be abandoned or revised.

Current policies and practices should likewise be closely scrutinized by disparity audits to determine whether they operate in racially disparate ways. Clear and convincing evidence should be required that their other effects are substantially more important than the damage they do to the causes of racial neutrality in American law and racial justice in American society. When they cannot be justified, they should be revised or abandoned.

For many current policies the evidence has long been clear. Massive evidence documents the existence of racial profiling by the police, that they stop black people more often in cars and on the streets than they do whites, and for less cause. Police arrest policies in drug cases have long been known to target black and other minority drug dealers disproportionately and to place much less emphasis on white drug dealers. Sentencing laws for drug and some violent crimes have long been known to hit black offenders especially hard. Sentencing policies that make punishments much more severe for people with previous convictions are a significant contributor to racial disparities in prison. All of these policies should be reexamined.

The idea that proposed new laws affecting the criminal justice system should be accompanied by racial impact statements is no longer novel. Iowa has enacted such a law. Many criminal justice agencies now conduct disparity audits. The second edition of the *Model Penal Code* (American Law Institute 2007) requires them.

ARE MEANINGFUL CHANGES POSSIBLE?

Proposals for substantial reduction in America's prison population, abandonment of racially unfair practices, repeal of punitive but ineffective legislation, and the requirement of race and ethnicity impact statements may strike some readers as audacious. That is as it should be. Racial disparities and the damage they have done to millions of individual black Americans and their families, and to black Americans as a group, are pressing social problems. Audacity is called for.

There are pessimistic and optimistic ways to contemplate the future. The pessimistic way is to note the evolution of patterns of white dominance in American history and the succession of mechanisms by which it has been maintained. If slavery was succeeded by Jim Crow, which was succeeded by the racially segregated northern ghettoes, which was succeeded by mass imprisonment, it is hard not to wonder what will substitute for mass imprisonment or whether mass imprisonment will endure to keep patterns of racial hierarchy as they now are.

Likewise the psychology and history of American race relations pre-dispose white Americans to resent the progress black Americans have made, to believe that black Americans with dark skin tone and stereo-typically African American features are especially likely to be dangerous criminals, and to favor harsh crime control policies. It is hard not to wonder whether the goodwill and idealism exist to ameliorate the avoidable damage contemporary policies do.

The optimistic way forward is to focus on the good things the civil rights movement accomplished. Large numbers of black Americans have moved into the middle class and into positions of wealth and power. Some categories of black Americans—for example, young col-lege-educated women—earn higher incomes than comparable white Americans. Sixty years ago many white Americans, and most southern white Americans, believed that blacks were inherently inferior; that is no longer true. Today most white Americans, including most southern white Americans, reject ideas about white supremacy and believe in legal equality.

Fifty years ago, and for several decades thereafter, Republicans shamelessly pursued the Southern Strategy. In 2005 Kenneth Mehlman, chairman of the Republican National Committee, speaking before an annual meeting of the National Association of Colored People, apolo-gized for the Southern Strategy, saying, "Some Republicans gave up on winning the African-American vote, looking the other way or trying to benefit politically from racial polarization. I am here today as the Republican chairman to tell you we were wrong" (quoted in Benedetto 2005).

Few Americans thirty years ago, whether liberal or conservative, Democratic or Republican, would have chosen the criminal justice system we now have. The social psychology, sociology, and politics of American race relations have brought us to a place where no one should want to be. There is no good reason to stay here.

NOTES

CHAPTER I

1. The only significant partial exception is the replacement of the federal 100-to-1 crack cocaine law with an 18-to-1 successor. The amendment was not enacted because Congress accepted that the prior law was fundamentally unfair on its face or because of its effects but because a new administration with a black president and a black attorney general made a continuing issue of it. Republicans were unwilling under those circumstances flatly to oppose any amendment. They insisted, however, on a compromise that left the law's worst features intact. Most were also unwilling to go on record even in favor of that half-a-loaf change. The House of Representatives adopted the change unanimously and the Senate by a voice vote. No representative or senator had to signal support in a way for which he or she could be held politically accountable.

2. The psychology, sociology, and politics of American race relations are discussed in chapter 4; the paranoid streak, Evangelical Protestantism, and the structure of American government in chapter 5.

3. The black:white ratio is not higher than 5.5:1 because the table uses U.S. Bureau of Justice Statistics data that exclude Hispanics of either race and because it contains combined data on men and women. The disparity ratio for women in 2006 (3.8:1) was significantly lower that that for men (6.5:1; Sabol, Minton, and Harrison 2007, table 14).

4. Table 6.2 and the accompanying text present this analysis in greater detail.

5. Figure 6.1 presents these data and parallel data for other quantities of crack. The accompanying text discusses them in detail.

6. These literatures are discussed in detail in chapter 6.

Chapter 2

1. The method for redistributing Hispanics was determined by examining 1990 and 1995 data in which the Bureau of Justice Statistics reported black and white figures including Hispanics and also reported Hispanics separately. For 1995, for example, 17.6 percent of prisoners were classified as Hispanic. Excluding Hispanics, 45.7 percent of prisoners were black and 33.5 percent were white. Including Hispanics, 49.9 percent were black and 47.7 percent were white. Simple math shows that approximately 25 percent of Hispanics were counted as black and 75 percent as white (Tonry 2005, 1255 n. 99).

Chapter 3

1. Hispanics are not reported separately in these data; they are included among whites and blacks.

Chapter 4

1. This refusal is the more striking because the 100-to-1 law was the one contemporary crime control policy that whites opposed when they become aware of the racial disparities it causes. The level of whites' support for capital punishment does not significantly change when they learn that blacks are much more likely to be sentenced to death than whites, or that black killers of white victims are much more likely than any other killers to be sentenced to death. White support for the 100-to-1 law plummets when they learn of its racially skewed effects (Bobo and Johnson 2004).

2. The U.S. Sentencing Commission (2007) revised its crack and cocaine guidelines in 2007. Twenty years earlier the Commission, then differently constituted, made guideline sentences for crack offenses even more severe than the legislation required; those earlier provisions were repealed. Those changes, a *New York Times* article reported, merely nibble at the edges because the federal statute continued in force unaltered: "The sentencing commission's striking move on Tuesday, meant to address the wildly disproportionate punishments for crack and powder cocaine will have only a minor impact. Unless Congress acts, many thousands of defendants will continue to face vastly different sentences for possessing and selling different types of the same thing" (Liptak 2007b).

3. The test, available since 1998, is offered by Project Implicit (2008), which describes itself as combining "basic research and educational outreach in a

virtual laboratory at which visitors can examine their own hidden biases." The test can be taken at implicit.harvard.edu.

4. Horton did not call himself Willie, but William. Bush's campaign advisor Lee Atwater chose to use "Willie," which was more in keeping with the southern white practice of Atwater's childhood of "referring to black men with overstated familiarity" (Mendelberg 2001, 142; Jamieson 1992).

5. Two of those in Kennebunkport later told a reporter, off the record, that Bush never hesitated about adopting Atwood's proposal. He expressed concern that it might backfire, but that was all. "As far as I could tell, he had no qualms about it," one staff member recalled. "It was just the facts of life. He realized that as far behind as he was it was the only way to win" (Schieffer and Gates, 1989, 360).

CHAPTER 5

1. Rendition is the practice of seizing people without arrest warrants or other judicial oversight and sending them for questioning to places such as Syria, Saudi Arabia, and Egypt, which are known to use torture in interrogations. In two well-documented cases Mahar Arar, a Canadian, and Khaled Masri, a German, were detained by U.S. agents, flown to secret prisons in Syria and Afghanistan, tortured, interrogated, and eventually released when their captors realized they were innocent (Austen 2006; Landler 2007). The Canadian and German governments investigated and verified the victims' claims; the U.S. government has refused to admit wrongdoing, to apologize, or to pay damages. U.S. courts have refused to allow the men to file suit against the U.S. government, even though in Arar's case the rendition occurred when he was changing planes in an American airport.

The August 2002 U.S. Department of Justice "torture memo" advised that interrogation methods do not count as torture unless they are "equivalent in intensity to the pain accompanying serious physical injury, such as organ failure, impairment of bodily function, or even death" (Allen and Priest 2004, A3; Goldsmith 2007). That memo was withdrawn but was replaced by secret legal opinions that permitted use of the same or similar methods (Shane, Johnston, and Risen 2007). "This government does not torture people," said President Bush in October 2007 (Stolberg 2007), a claim that was possible (despite admission of water-boarding) only on the basis that the secret opinions did not define water-boarding and similarly inhumane practices as torture.

2. CERD lacks authority to enforce compliance with its recommendations. The United States ratified the treaty subject to a number of understandings and recommendations, including that ratification would not require changes in U.S. law and that private lawsuits may not be based on treaty provisions (Fellner 2009, 259).

3. Stan C. Proband, personal communication, December 27, 2007.

4. Readily available statistical data cited in this chapter, such as imprisonment rates, are based on U.S. Bureau of Justice Statistics reports, available at the Bureau's website (www.ojp.usdoj.gov/bjs/).

Chapter 6

1. "The approach taken in California has not been dramatically more effective at controlling crime than other states' efforts.... [California's law] is not considerably more effective at crime reduction than alternative methods that are narrower in scope" (E. Y. Chen 2008, 362, 365). Doob and Webster (2003) have in any case demonstrated fundamental problems with her analysis.

REFERENCES

Alexander, Michelle. 2010. *The New Jim Crow: Mass Incarceration in the Age of Colorblindedness*. New York: New Press.

Allen, Mike, and Dana Priest. 2004. "Memo on Torture Draws Focus to Bush." *Washington Post*, June 9, A3.

American Friends Service Committee. 1971. *Struggle for Justice*. New York: Hill & Wang.

American Law Institute. 1962. *Model Penal Code. Proposed Official Draft*. Philadelphia: American Law Institute.

———. 2007. *Model Penal Code: Sentencing*. Tentative draft no. 1 (April 9, 2007). Philadelphia: American Law Institute.

Anderson, David C. 1995. *Crime and the Politics of Hysteria: How the Willie Horton Story Changed American Justice*. New York: Random House.

Appleton, Catherine, and Bent Grøver. 2007. "The Pros and Cons of Life without Parole." *British Journal of Criminology* 47(4):597–615.

Apel, Robert, and Daniel Nagin. Forthcoming. "Deterrence." In *The Oxford Handbook of Crime and Criminal Justice*, edited by Michael Tonry. New York: Oxford University Press.

Associated Press. 1991. "Gravely Ill, Atwater Offers Apology." *New York Times*, January 13, section 1, part 1, p. 16.

———. 1995. "25 Years for a Slice of Pizza." *New York Times*, March 5, section 1, p. 21.

Austen, Ian. 2006. "Canadians Fault U.S. for Its Role in Torture Case." *New York Times*, September 19, A1.

Austin, James, John Clark, Patricia Hardyman, and D. Alan Henry. 2000. *Three Strikes and You're Out—The Implementation and Impact of Strike Laws*.

Final Report submitted to the U.S. National Institute of Justice. Washington, D.C.: National Institute of Justice, U.S. Department of Justice.

Baldus, David C., George G. Woodworth, and Charles A. Pulaski, Jr. 1990. *Equal Justice and the Death Penalty: A Legal and Empirical Analysis*. Boston: Northeastern University Press.

Beckett, Katherine. 1995. "Media Depictions of Drug Abuse: The Impacts of Official Sources." *Research in Political Sociology* 7:161–82.

———. 1997. *Making Crime Pay*. New York: Oxford University Press.

Beckett, Katherine, Kris Nyrop, and Lori Pfingst. 2006. "Race, Drugs, and Policing: Understanding Disparities in Drug Delivery Arrests." *Criminology* 44(1):105–37.

Beckett, Katherine, Kris Nyrop, Lori Pfingst, and Melissa Bowell. 2005. "Drug Use, Drug Possession Arrests, and the Question of Race." *Social Problems* 52(3):419–41.

Beckett, Katherine, and Theodore Sasson. 2004. *The Politics of Injustice*. 2nd ed. Beverly Hills: Sage.

Beha, James A., II. 1977. "'And Nobody Can Get You Out': The Impact of a Mandatory Prison Sentence for the Illegal Carrying of a Firearm on the Use of Firearms and on the Administration of Criminal Justice in Boston." *Boston University Law Review* 57:96–146 (part 1), 289–333 (part 2).

Bell, Daniel, ed. 1963. *The Radical Right*. Revised edition, expanded and updated. Garden City, N.Y.: Doubleday.

Benedetto, Richard. 2005. "GOP: 'We Were Wrong' to Play Racial Politics." *USA Today*, July 14. http://www.usatoday.com/news/washington/2005-07-14-GOP-racial-politics_x.htm (accessed July 26, 2010).

Bennett, William J., John J. DiIulio, and John P. Walters. 1996. *Body Count: Moral Poverty…and How to Win America's War against Crime and Drugs*. New York: Simon and Schuster.

Black, Earl, and Merle Black. 2002. *The Rise of Southern Republicans*. Cambridge, Mass.: Harvard University Press.

Blair, Irene V., Kristine M. Chapleau, and Charles M. Judd. 2005. "The Use of Afrocentric Features as Cues for Judgment in the Presence of Diagnostic Information." *European Journal of Social Psychology* 35:59–68.

Blair, Irene V., Charles M. Judd, and Kristine M. Chapleau. 2004. "The Influence of Afrocentric Facial Features in Criminal Sentencing." *Psychological Science* 15(10):674–79.

Blair, Irene V., Charles M. Judd, and Jennifer L. Fallman. 2004. "The Automaticity of Race and Afrocentric Facial Features in Social Judgments." *Journal of Personality and Social Psychology* 87(6):763–78.

Blair, Irene V., Charles M. Judd, Melody S. Sadler, and Christopher Jenkins. 2002. "The Role of Afrocentric Features in Person Perception: Judging by Features and Categories." *Journal of Personality and Social Psychology* 83(1):5–25.

Blasi, Gary, and John T. Jost. 2006. "System Justification Theory and Research: Implications for Law, Legal Advocacy, and Social Justice." *California Law Review* 94:1119–68.

Blow, Charles. 2009. "Welcome to the 'Club.'" *New York Times*, July 24, A23.

Blumstein, Alfred. 1982. "On Racial Disproportionality of the United States' Prison Populations." *Journal of Criminal Law and Criminology* 73:1259–81.

———. 1993. "Racial Disproportionality of U.S. Prison Populations Revisited." *University of Colorado Law Review* 64:743–60.

———. 1995. "Prisons." In *Crime*, edited by James Q. Wilson and Joan Petersilia. San Francisco: ICS.

Blumstein, Alfred, and Allen Beck. 1999. "Population Growth in U.S. Prisons, 1980–1996." In *Prisons*, edited by Michael Tonry and Joan Petersilia. Vol. 26 of *Crime and Justice: A Review of Research*, edited by Michael Tonry. Chicago: University of Chicago Press.

Blumstein, Alfred, Jacqueline Cohen, Susan Martin, and Michael Tonry, eds. 1983. *Research on Sentencing: The Search for Reform.* Washington, D.C.: National Academy Press.

Blumstein, Alfred, Jacqueline Cohen, and Daniel Nagin, eds. 1978. *Deterrence and Incapacitation: Estimating the Effects of Criminal Sanctions on Crime Rates.* Washington, D.C.: National Academy of Sciences.

Blumstein, Alfred, Jacqueline Cohen, Jeffrey Roth, and Christy Visher, eds. 1986. *Criminal Careers and "Career Criminals."* Washington, D.C.: National Academy Press.

Blumstein, Alfred, and Joel Wallman. 2006. "The Crime Drop and Beyond." *Annual Review of Laws and Social Sciences* 2:125–46.

Bobo, Lawrence, and Devon Johnson. 2004. "A Taste for Punishment: Black and White Americans' Views on the Death Penalty and the War on Drugs." *Du Bois Review* 1:151–80.

Bobo, Lawrence D., and Victor Thompson. 2006. "Unfair by Design: The War on Drugs, Race, and the Legitimacy of the Criminal Justice System." *Social Research* 73(2):445–72.

Bobo, Lawrence D., and Victor Thompson. 2010. In *Doing Race: 21 Essays for the 21st Century*, edited by Hazel R. Markus and Paula Moya. New York: Norton.

Bonczar, Thomas P. 2003. *Prevalence of Imprisonment in the U.S. Population, 1974–2001*. Washington, D.C.: Bureau of Justice Statistics, U.S. Department of Justice.

Bonczar, Thomas P. 2010. *National Corrections Reporting Program: Sentence Length of State Prisoners, by Offense, Admission Type, Sex, and Race,* Washington, D.C.: Bureau of Justice Statistics, U.S. Department of Justice. http://bjs.ojp.usdoj.gov/index.cfm?ty=pbdetail&iid=2056 (accessed August 6, 2010).

Boyd, James. 1970. "Nixon's Southern Strategy: 'It's All in the Charts.'" *New York Times*, May 17, 25, 105–11.

Bureau of Justice Statistics. 1980. "Profile of Jail Inmates 1978." Washington, D.C.: U.S. Government Printing Office.

——. 1984. "The 1983 Jail Census." Washington, D.C.: Bureau of Justice Statistics, U.S. Department of Justice.

——. 1990. "Profile of Jail Inmates 1978." Washington, D.C.: Bureau of Justice Statistics, U.S. Department of Justice.

——. 1996. "Prison and Jail Inmates, 1995." Washington, D.C.: Bureau of Justice Statistics, U.S. Department of Justice.

——. 2003. "Prevalence of Imprisonment in the U.S. Population, 1974–2001." Washington, D.C.: Bureau of Justice Statistics, U.S. Department of Justice.

——. 2006. "Prisoners in 2004." Washington, D.C.: Bureau of Justice Statistics, U.S. Department of Justice.

——. 2007a. "Prison and Jail Inmates at Mid-Year 2006." Washington, D.C.: Bureau of Justice Statistics, U.S. Department of Justice.

——. 2007b. *Sourcebook of Criminal Justice Statistics.* www.albany.edu/sourcebook/ (accessed September 18, 2007).

——. 2010. "National Corrections Reporting Program." http://bjs.ojp.usdoj.gov/index.cfm?ty=dcdetail&iid=268.

——. Various years-a. *Prisoners* [various years 1980–2005]. Washington, D.C.: Bureau of Justice Statistics, U.S. Department of Justice.

——. Various years-b. "Jail Inmates in [various years 1983–1989]." Washington, D.C.: Bureau of Justice Statistics, U.S. Department of Justice.

——. Various years-c. "Prison and Jail Inmates at Mid-Year [various years]." Washington, D.C.: Bureau of Justice Statistics, U.S. Department of Justice.

——. Various years-d. *Sourcebook of Criminal Justice Statistics* [various years 1980–2010]. Washington, D.C.: Bureau of Justice Statistics, U.S. Department of Justice.

——. Various years-e. Crime Victimization Survey: Criminal Victimization in the United States. Bureau of Justice Statistics, U.S. Department of Justice.

Cahalan, Margaret W. 1986. *Historical Correction Statistics in the United States, 1850–1984.* Washington, D.C.: Bureau of Justice Statistics, U.S. Department of Justice.

California Department of Corrections and Rehabilitation. 2008. *California Prisoners and Parolees—2007.* Sacramento: California Department of Corrections and Rehabilitation, Offender Information Services Branch.

Canadian Sentencing Commission. 1987. *Sentencing Reform: A Canadian Approach.* Ottawa: Canadian Government Publishing Centre.

Canedy, Dana. 2001. "Sentence of Life without Parole for Boy, 14, in Murder of Girl, 6." *New York Times*, March 10, A1.

Carlson, Kenneth. 1982. *Mandatory Sentencing: The Experience of Two States.* National Institute of Justice, U.S. Department of Justice. Washington, D.C.: U.S. Government Printing Office.

Carter, Dan T. 1996. *From George Wallace to Newt Gingrich: Race in the Conservative Counterrevolution, 1963–1994.* Baton Rouge: Louisiana State University Press.

Caulkins, Jonathan P. 2001. "How Large Should the Strike Zone Be in 'Three Strikes and You're Out' Sentencing Laws?" *Journal of Quantitative Criminology* 17:227–48.

Caulkins, Jonathan P., and Mark A. R. Kleiman. Forthcoming. "Drugs and Crime." In *The Oxford Handbook of Crime and Criminal Justice.* New York: Oxford University Press.

Caulkins, Jonathan P., and Peter Reuter. 1998. "What Price Data Tell Us about Drug Markets." *Journal of Drug Issues* 28(3):593–612.

Caulkins, Jonathan P., and Peter Reuter. 2010. "How Drug Enforcement Affects Drug Prices." In *Crime and Justice: A Review of Research*, vol. 39, edited by Michael Tonry. Chicago: University of Chicago Press.

Center for Constitutional Rights. 2009. *Racial Disparity in NYPD Stops-and-Frisks.* New York: Center for Constitutional Rights. www.CCRJustice.org.

Chen, Elsa Y. 2000. "'Three Strikes and You're Out' and 'Truth in Sentencing': Lessons in Policy Implementation and Impacts." Ph.D. dissertation, Department of Political Science, University of California at Los Angeles.

———. 2008. "Impacts of 'Three Strikes and You're Out' on Crime Trends in California and throughout the United States." *Journal of Contemporary Criminal Justice* 24:345–70.

Chen, Emmeline S., and Tom R. Tyler. 2002. "Cloaking Power: Legitimizing Myths and the Psychology of the Advantaged." In *The Use and Abuse of Power: Multiple Perspectives on the Causes of Corruption*, edited by Annette Y. Lee-Chai and John A. Bargh. New York: Psychology Press.

Clear, Todd. 2007. *Imprisoning Communities: How Mass Incarceration Makes Disadvantaged Neighborhoods Worse*. New York: Oxford University Press.

——— . 2008. "Communities with High Incarceration Rates." In *Crime and Justice: A Review of Research*, vol. 37, edited by Michael Tonry. Chicago: University of Chicago Press.

Coase, Ronald. 1978. "Economics and Contiguous Disciplines." *Journal of Legal Studies* 7:210–11.

Cohen, Thomas H., and Tracey Kyckhelhahn. 2010. "Felony Defendants in Large Urban Counties, 2006." Washington, D.C.: Bureau of Justice Statistics, U.S. Department of Justice.

Cohn, S., S. Barkan, and W. Halteman. 1991. "Public Attitudes toward Criminals: Racial Consensus or Racial Conflict." *Social Problems* 38:287–96.

Committee on Civil Rights. 1947. *To Secure These Rights*. Washington, D.C.: U.S. Government Printing Office.

Committee on the Elimination of Racial Disparity. 2008. *Consideration of Reports Submitted by State Parties under Article 9 of the Convention: Concluding Observations, United States of America* CERD/C/USA/CO/6. New York: United Nations.

Cook, Philip J. 1980. "Research in Criminal Deterrence: Laying the Groundwork for the Second Decade." In *Crime and Justice: An Annual Review of Research*, vol. 2, edited by Norval Morris and Michael Tonry. Chicago: University of Chicago Press.

——— . 2007. *Paying the Tab: The Costs and Benefits of Alcohol Control*. Princeton: Princeton University Press.

Courtwright, David T. 1982. *Dark Paradise: Opiate Addiction in America before 1940*. Cambridge, Mass.: Harvard University Press.

Curry, Theodore R. 1996. "Conservative Protestantism and the Perceived Wrongfulness of Crimes: A Research Note." *Criminology* 34:453–64.

Dasgupta, Nilanjana, Mahzarin Banaji, and Robert Abelson. 1999. "Group Entitavity and Group Perception: Associations between Physical Features and Psychological Judgment." *Journal of Personality and Social Psychology* 77(5):991–1003.

Davis, Allison, John Dollard, and American Youth Commission. 1940. *Children of Bondage: The Personality Development of Negro Youth in the Urban South*. Washington, D.C.: American Council on Education.

Davis, David Brion. 1960. "Some Themes of Counter-subversion: An Analysis of Anti-Masonic, Anti-Catholic, and Anti-Mormon Literature." *Mississippi Valley Historical Review* 47(2):205–24.

Death Penalty Information Center. 2010. "National Statistics on the Death Penalty and Race; Death Row Populations by Race." http://www.deathpenaltyinfo.org/race-death-row-inmates-executed-1976#inmaterace (accessed July 29, 2010).

Dills, Angela K., Jeffrey A. Miron, and Garrett Summers. 2008. "What Do Economists Know about Crime?" Working Paper No. 13759. Cambridge, Mass.: National Bureau of Economic Research.

Dixon, Travis, and Keith Maddox. 2005. "Skin Tone, Crime News, and Social Reality Judgments: Priming the Stereotype of the Dark and Dangerous Black Criminal." *Journal of Applied Social Psychology* 35(8):1555–70.

Doob, Anthony, and Cheryl Webster. 2003. "Sentence Severity and Crime: Accepting the Null Hypothesis." In *Crime and Justice: A Review of Research*, vol. 30, edited by Michael Tonry. Chicago: University of Chicago Press.

Du Bois, W. E. B. 1988 [1899] . "The Negro Criminal." In *The Economics of Race and Crime*, edited by Samuel L. Myers and Margaret C. Simms. New Brunswick, N.J.: Transaction Books.

Dworkin, Ronald. 1977. *Taking Rights Seriously*. Cambridge, Mass.: Harvard University Press.

———. 1986. *Law's Empire*. Cambridge, Mass.: Belknap Press.

Eberhardt, Jennifer L., Paul G. Davies, Valerie J. Purdie-Vaughns, and Sheri Lynn Johnson. 2006. "Looking Deathworthy: Perceived Stereotypicality of Black Defendants Predicts Capital-Sentencing Outcomes." *Psychological Science* 17(5):383–86.

Eberhardt, Jennifer L., Phillip Atiba Goff, Valerie J. Purdie, and Paul G. Davies. 2004. "Seeing Black: Race, Crime and Visual Processing." *Journal of Personality and Social Psychology* 87(6):876–93.

Edsall, Thomas, and Mary Edsall. 1991. *Chain Reaction: The Impact of Race, Rights, and Taxes on American Politics*. New York: Norton.

Ehlers, Scott, Vincent Schiraldi, and Jason Ziedenberg. 2004. *Still Striking Out: Ten Years of California's Three Strikes*. San Francisco: Justice Policy Institute.

Ehrlich, Isaac. 1996. "Crime, Punishment, and the Market for Offenses." *Journal of Economic Perspectives* 10(1):43–67.

Elffers, Henk, and Jan de Keijser. 2006. "Different Perspectives, Different Gaps: Does the Public Demand a More Responsive Judge?" Leiden: Netherlands Institute for the Study of Crime and Law Enforcement.

Engel, Robin Shepard, and Jennifer M. Calnon. 2004. "Examining the Influence of Drivers' Characteristics during Traffic Stops with Police: Results from a National Survey." *Justice Quarterly* 21(1):49–90.

Entman, Robert. 1992. "Blacks in the News: Television, Modern Racism, and Cultural Change." *Journalism Quarterly* 69(2):341–61.

Erikson, Kai T. 1966. *Wayward Puritans: A Study in the Sociology of Deviance.* New York: Wiley.

Fagan, Jeffrey, and Richard B. Freeman. 1999. "Crime and Work." In *Crime and Justice: A Review of Research*, vol. 25, edited by Michael Tonry. Chicago: University of Chicago Press.

Federal Bureau of Investigation. 2005. *Crime in the United States, 2004.* Washington, D.C.: U.S. Department of Justice.

———. Various years. *Crime in the United States* [various years 1995–2006]. Washington, D.C.: U.S. Department of Justice.

Feld, Barry C. 1999. *Bad Kids Race and the Transformation of the Juvenile Court.*
New York: Oxford University Press.

Fellner, Jamie. 2009. "Race, Drugs, and Law Enforcement in the United States." *Stanford Law and Policy Review* 20:257–91.

Festinger, Leonard. 1957. *A Theory of Cognitive Dissonance.* Palo Alto, Calif.: Stanford University Press.

Flamm, Michael W. 2005. *Law and Order: Street Crime, Civil Unrest, and the Crisis of Liberalism in the Sixties.* New York: Columbia University Press.

Fletcher, George. 1978. *Rethinking Criminal Law.* Boston: Little, Brown.

Frase, Richard. 2009. "What Explains Persistent Racial Disproportionality in Minnesota's Prison and Jail Populations?" In *Crime and Justice: A Review of Research*, vol. 38, edited by Michael Tonry. Chicago: University of Chicago Press.

Garland, David. 2001. *The Culture of Control: Crime and Social Order in Contemporary Society.* Chicago: University of Chicago Press.

———. 2005. "Penal Excess and Surplus Meaning: Public Torture Lynchings in 20th Century America." *Law and Society Review* 39:793–833.

Gest, Ted. 2001. *Crime and Politics: Big Government's Erratic Campaign for Law and Order.* New York: Oxford University Press.

Gilbert, Martin. 1992. *Churchill: A Life.* New York: Henry Holt.

Gilliam, F. D., and S. Iyengar. 2000. "Prime Suspects: The Influence of Local Television News on the Viewing Public." *American Journal of Political Science* 44:560–73.

Gilliard, Darrell K., and Allen J. Beck. 1996. *Prison and Jail Inmates, 1995.* Washington, D.C.: Bureau of Justice Statistics, U.S. Department of Justice.

Goldsmith, Jack. 2007. *The Terror Presidency: Law and Judgment Inside the Bush Administration.* New York: Norton.

Green, John C. 2007. *The Faith Factor: How Religion Influences American Elections*. Westport, Conn.: Praeger.

Greenwald, Anthony, and Linda Hamilton Krieger. 2006. "Implicit Bias: Scientific Foundations." *California Law Review* 94:945–67.

Gusfield, Joseph. 1963. *Symbolic Crusade: Status Politics and the American Temperance Movement*. Urbana: University of Illinois Press.

Hafer, Carolyn L., and Laurent Bègue. 2005. "Experimental Research on Just-World Theory: Problems, Developments, and Future Challenges." *Psychological Bulletin* 131(1):128–67.

Hagedorn, John. 1998. "The Business of Drug Dealing in Milwaukee." Wisconsin Policy Research Institute. www.csdp.org/research/drugdeal.pdf.

Hamilton, Alexander, James Madison, and John Jay. 2006 [1818]. *The Federalist*. Edited by George Stade. New York: Barnes and Noble Classics.

Harrington, Michael P., and Cassia Spohn. 2007. "Defining Sentence Type: Further Evidence against Use of the Total Incarceration Variable." *Journal of Research in Crime and Delinquency* 44(1):36–63.

Hegel, G. W. F. 1991. *Elements of the Philosophy of Right*. Edited by Allen W. Wood. Translated by H. B. Nisbet. Cambridge: Cambridge University Press.

Herbert, Bob. 2005. "Impossible, Ridiculous, Repugnant." *New York Times*, October 6, p. A37.

Hochschild, Jennifer L., and Vesla Weaver. 2007. "The Skin Color Paradox and the American Racial Order." *Social Forces* 86(2):643–70.

Hofstadter, Richard. 1965. *The Paranoid Style in American Politics and Other Essays*. Chicago: University of Chicago Press.

Home Office. 1990. *Crime, Justice, and Protecting the Public*. London: Home Office.

Hood, Roger, and Carolyn Hoyle. 2008. *The Death Penalty: A Worldwide Perspective*. 4th ed. Oxford: Oxford University Press.

Hood, Roger, and Carolyn Hoyle. 2009. "Abolishing the Death Penalty Worldwide: the Impact of a New Dynamic." In *Crime and Justice: A Review of Research*, vol. 38, edited by Michael Tonry. Chicago: University of Chicago Press.

Human Rights Watch. 2008. *Targeting Blacks: Drug Law Enforcement and Race in the United States*. New York: Human Rights Watch.

———. 2009. *Decades of Disparity: Drug Arrests and Race in the United States*. New York: Human Rights Watch.

Hurwitz, J., and M. Peffley. 1997. "Public Perceptions of Race and Crime: The Influence of Racial Stereotypes." *American Journal of Political Science* 47(2):375–401.

International Centre for Prison Studies. 2007. "World Prison Population List." 7th ed. London: Kings College London.

———. 2009. *World Prison Brief*. Kings College London. www.kcl.ac.uk/ depsta/law/research/icps/worldbrief/wpb_stats.php (accessed November 14, 2009).

———. 2010. *World Prison Brief*. Kings College London. www.kcl.ac.uk/ depsta/law/research/icps/worldbrief/wpb_stats.php (accessed July 20, 2010).

Jamieson, Kathleen Hall. 1992. *Dirty Politics: Deception, Distraction, and Democracy*. Oxford: Oxford University Press.

Johnson, Devon. 2008. "Racial Prejudice, Perceived Injustice, and the Black-White Gap in Punitive Attitudes." *Journal of Criminal Justice* 36:198–206.

Johnson, Kevin R. 2010. "How Racial Profiling in America Became the Law of the Land." *Georgetown Law Review* 98(4):1005–77.

Joint Committee on New York Drug Law Evaluation. 1978. *The Nation's Toughest Drug Law: Evaluating the New York Experience*. A Project of the Association of the Bar of the City of New York and the Drug Abuse Council, Inc. Washington, D.C.: U.S. Government Printing Office.

Jolls, Christine, and Cass R. Sunstein. 2006. "The Law of Implicit Bias." *California Law Review* 94:969–96.

Jones, Trina. 2000. "Shades of Brown: The Law of Skin Color." *Duke Law Journal* 49:1487–557.

Justice Policy Institute. 2004. "Three Strikes and You're Out: An Examination of the Impact of Three Strikes Laws 10 Years after Their Enactment." San Francisco: Justice Policy Institute.

Kennedy, Sheila. 2007. *God and Country: America in Red and Blue*. Waco, Texas: Baylor University Press.

King, Ryan S. 2008. *Disparity by Geography: The War on Drugs in America's Cities*. Washington. D.C.: The Sentencing Project.

Kovandzic, Tomislav, John Sloan, and Lynne Vieraitis. 2002. "Unintended Consequences of Politically Popular Sentencing Policy: The Homicide Promoting Effects of 'Three Strikes' in U.S. Cities (1980–1999)." *Criminology and Public Policy* 1(3):399–424.

Kovandzic, Tomislav, John Sloan, and Lynne Vieraitis. 2004. "Striking Out as Crime Reduction Policy: The Impact of 'Three Strikes Laws' on Crime Rates in U.S. Cities." *Justice Quarterly* 21(2):207–45.

Kyckelhahn, Tracey, and Thomas H. Cohen. 2008. *Felony Defendants in Large Urban Counties, 2004*. NCJ 221152. Washington, D.C.: Bureau of Justice Statistics, U.S. Department of Justice.

Lamis, Alexander P., ed. 1999. *Southern Politics in the 1990s*. Baton Rouge: Louisiana State University Press.

Landler, Mark. 2007. "German Court Confronts U.S. on Abduction." *New York Times*, February 1, A1.

Langan, Patrick. 1985. "Racism on Trial: New Evidence to Explain the Racial Composition of Prisons in the United States." *Journal of Criminal Law and Criminology* 76:666–83.

Lappi-Seppälä, Tapio. 2008. "Trust, Welfare, and Political Culture: Explaining Differences in National Penal Policies." In *Crime and Justice: A Review of Research*, vol. 37, edited by Michael Tonry. Chicago: University of Chicago Press.

Lauritsen, Janet L. 2003. "How Families and Communities Influence Youth Victimization." OJJDP Juvenile Justice Bulletin. Washington, D.C.: U.S. Department of Justice, Office of Juvenile Justice and Delinquency Prevention.

Layman, Geoffrey. 2001. *The Great Divide: Religious and Cultural Conflict in American Party Politics*. New York: Columbia University Press.

Legislative Analyst's Office, California Legislature. 2005. *A Primer: Three Strikes—The Impact after More Than a Decade*. Sacramento: Legislative Analysts' Office.

Levinson, Justin D. 2007. "Forgotten Racial Equality: Implicit Bias, Decisionmaking, and Misremembering." *Duke Law Journal* 57(1):345–424.

Levitt, Steven, and Sudhir A. Venkatesh. 2000. "An Economic Analysis of a Drug Selling Gang's Finances." *Quarterly Journal of Economics* 115(3):755–89.

Lieberson, Stanley. 1980. *A Piece of the Pie: Blacks and White Immigrants since 1880*. Berkeley: University of California Press.

Lijphart, Arend. 1999. *Patterns of Democracy: Government Forms and Performance in Thirty-six Countries*. New Haven: Yale University Press.

Liptak, Adam. 2007a. "Lifers as Teenagers, Now Seeking Second Chance." *New York Times*, October 17, A1.

———. 2007b. "Whittling Away, but Leaving a Gap." *New York Times*, December 17, A21.

Loftin, Colin, Milton Heumann, and David McDowall. 1983. "Mandatory Sentencing and Firearms Violence: Evaluating an Alternative to Gun Control." *Law and Society Review* 17:287–318.

Loftin, Colin, and David McDowall. 1984. "The Deterrent Effects of the Florida Felony Firearm Law." *Journal of Criminal Law and Criminology* 75:250–59.

Loury, Glenn C. 2002. *The Anatomy of Racial Inequality*. Cambridge, Mass.: Harvard University Press.

———. 2007. "Racial Stigma, Mass Incarceration and American Values." Tanner Lectures in Human Values, Stanford University, April 4 and 5. www.econ. brown.edu/fac/Glenn_Loury/louryhomepage/.

———. 2008. "Race, Incarceration, and American Values." In Glenn Loury, Pamela S. Karlan, Tommie Shelby, and Loïc Wacquant, *Race, Incarceration, and American Values*. Cambridge, Mass.: MIT Press.

Loury, Glenn, with Pamela S. Karlan, Tommie Shelby, and Loïc Wacquant. 2008. *Race, Incarceration, and American Values*. Cambridge, Mass.: MIT Press.

Lowndes, Joseph E. 2008. *From the New Deal to the New Right: Race and the Southern Origins of Modern Conservatism*. New Haven: Yale University Press.

Maag, Christopher. 2007. "Short but Troubled Life Ended in Shooting and Suicide." *New York Times*, October 12, A21.

MacCoun, Robert, and Karin D. Martin. 2009. "Drugs." In *Handbook on Crime and Public Policy*, edited by Michael Tonry. New York: Oxford University Press.

MacKenzie, Wayne, Don Stemen, and Derek Coursen. 2009. "Prosecution and Racial Justice: Using Data to Advance Fairness in Criminal Prosecution." New York: Vera Institute of Justice.

Maddox, Keith B., and Stephanie A. Gray. 2002. "Cognitive Representations of Black Americans: Re-exploring the Role of Skin Tone." *Personality and Social Psychology Bulletin*. 28:250–59.

Males, Mike, and Dan Macallair. 1999. "Striking Out: The Failure of California's Three Strikes and You're Out Law." *Stanford Law and Policy Review* 11:65–81.

Marvell, Thomas B., and Carlisle E. Moody. 2001. "The Lethal Effects of Three Strikes Laws." *Journal of Legal Studies* 30:89–106.

Massey, Douglas S. 2007. *Categorically Unequal: The American Stratification System*. New York: Russell Sage Foundation.

Massey, Douglas S., and Nancy Denton. 1993. *American Apartheid: Segregation and the Making of the Underclass*. Cambridge, Mass.: Harvard University Press.

Massing, Michael. 1998. *The Fix*. New York: Simon and Schuster.

Mauer, Marc. 2007. "Racial Impact Statements as a Means of Reducing Unwarranted Sentencing Disparities." *Ohio State Journal of Criminal Law* 5:19–46.

McDonald, Douglas C., and Kenneth C. Carlson. 1993. *Sentencing in the Federal Courts: Does Race Matter?* Washington, D.C.: Bureau of Justice Statistics, U.S. Department of Justice.

McDowall, David, Colin Loftin, and Brian Wiersema. 1992. "A Comparative Study of the Preventive Effects of Mandatory Sentencing Laws for Gun Crimes." *Journal of Criminal Law and Criminology* 83:378–94.

McNulty, Thomas, and Paul E. Bellair. 2003. "Explaining Racial and Ethnic Differences in Serious Adolescent Violent Behavior." *Criminology* 41:709–48.

Mendelberg, Tali. 2001. *The Race Card: Campaign Strategy, Implicit Messages, and the Norm of Equality*. Princeton: Princeton University Press.

Miller, Marc L., and Ronald F. Wright. 2008. "The Black Box." *Iowa Law Review* 94:125–96.

Moody, Carlisle E., Thomas B. Marvell, and Robert J. Kaminski. 2003. "Unintended Consequences: Three-Strikes Laws and the Murders of Police Officers." Cambridge, Mass.: National Bureau of Economic Research.

Moynihan, Daniel Patrick. 1965. *The Negro Family: The Case for National Action*. Washington, D.C.: Office of Policy Planning and Research, U.S. Department of Labor.

———. 1993. "Iatrogenic Government: Social Policy and Drug Research." *American Scholar* 62(3):351–62.

Mullet, Charles F. 1966. *Fundamental Law and the American Revolution, 1710–1776*. New York: Octagon.

Murakawa, Naomi. 2005. "Electing to Punish: Congress, Race, and the American Criminal Justice State." Ph.D. dissertation, Princeton University, Department of Political Science.

Murray, Joseph, and David P. Farrington. 2008. "Effects of Parental Imprisonment in Children." In *Crime and Justice: A Review of Research*, vol. 37, edited by Michael Tonry. Chicago: University of Chicago Press.

Musto, David. 1999. *The American Disease: The Origins of Narcotic Control*. 3rd ed. New York: Oxford University Press.

Musto, David F., and Pamela Korsmeyer. 2002. *The Quest for Drug Control: Politics and Federal Policy in a Period of Increasing Substance Abuse, 1963–1981*. New Haven: Yale University Press.

Myers, Gustavus. 1943. *History of Bigotry in the United States*. New York: Random House.

Myrdal, Gunnar. 1944. *An American Dilemma: The Negro Problem and Modern Democracy*. New York: Harper and Brothers.

Nagata, Judith. 2001. "Beyond Theology: Toward an Anthropology of 'Fundamentalism.'" *American Anthropologist* 103:481–98.

Nagin, Daniel S. 1978. "General Deterrence: A Review of the Empirical Evidence." In *Deterrence and Incapacitation*, edited by Alfred Blumstein, Jacqueline Cohen, and Daniel Nagin. Washington, D.C.: National Academy Press.

———. 1998. "Criminal Deterrence Research at the Outset of the Twenty-first Century." In *Crime and Justice: A Review of Research*, vol. 23, edited by Michael Tonry. Chicago: University of Chicago Press.

Nagin, Daniel, Francis T. Cullen, and Cheryl Lero Jonson. 2009. "Imprisonment and Reoffending." In *Crime and Justice: A Review of Research*, vol. 38, edited by Michael Tonry. Chicago: University of Chicago Press.

National Commission on Marihuana and Drug Abuse. 1972. *Marihuana: A Signal of Misunderstanding*. Washington, D.C.: U.S. Government Printing Office.

Nellis, Ashley, and Ryan S. King. 2009. *No Exit: The Expanding Use of Life Sentences in America*. Washington, D.C.: The Sentencing Project.

New York Times. 1964. "GOP Moderates Score Goldwater." July 5, 31.

Newburn, Tim. 2007. " 'Tough on Crime': Penal Policy in England and Wales." In *Crime, Punishment, and Politics in Comparative Perspective*, edited by Michael Tonry. Vol. 36 of *Crime and Justice: A Review of Research*, edited by Michael Tonry. Chicago: University of Chicago Press.

Norris, Pippa, and Ronald Inglehart. 2004. *Sacred and Secular: Religion and Politics Worldwide*. New York: Cambridge University Press.

Office of Applied Studies. Various years. *National Survey on Drug Use and Health* [various years 2001–8]. Rockville, Md.: Substance Abuse and Mental Health Services Administration.

———. 2010. *Results from the 2008 National Survey on Drug Use and Health: National Findings*. Rockville, Md.: Substance Abuse and Mental Health Services Administration. http://www.oas.samhsa.gov/NSDUH/2K8NSDUH/tabs/toc.htm (accessed September 26, 2010).

Office of National Drug Control Policy. 2008. *The Price and Purity of Illicit Drugs 1981–2007*. Report submitted by the Institute for Defense Analysis. Washington, D.C.: Executive Office of the President.

———. 2009. *ADAM II: 2008 Annual Report*. Washington, D.C.: Executive Office of the President.

Pager, Devah. 2007. *Marked: Race, Crime, and Finding Work in an Era of Mass Incarceration*. Chicago: University of Chicago Press.

Peffley, Mark, and Jon Hurwitz. 2010. *Justice in America: The Separate Realities of Blacks and Whites*. Cambridge: Cambridge University Press.

Phillips, Kevin P. 1969. *The Emerging Republican Majority*. New Rochelle, N.Y.: Arlington.

———. 1991. *The Politics of Rich and Poor: Wealth and the American Electorate in the Reagan Aftermath*. New York: HarperCollins.

Pierce, Glen L., and William J. Bowers. 1981. "The Bartley-Fox Gun Law's Short-Term Impact on Crime in Boston." *Annals of the American Academy of Political and Social Science* 455:120–37.

Pizzi, William T., Irene V. Blair, and Charles M. Judd. 2005. "Discrimination in Sentencing on the Basis of Afrocentric Features." *Michigan Journal of Race and Law* 10:327–53.

Plant, E. Ashby, B. Michelle Peruch, and David A. Butz. 2005. "Eliminating Automatic Racial Bias: Making Race Non-diagnostic for Responses to Criminal Suspects." *Journal of Experimental Social Psychology* 41:141–56.

Pratt, Travis C., Francis T. Cullen, Kristie R. Blevins, Leah E. Daigle, and Tamara D. Madensen. 2006. "The Empirical Status of Deterrence Theory: A Meta-analysis." In *Taking Stock: The Status of Criminological Theory*, edited by Francis T. Cullen, John Paul Wright, and Kristie R. Blevins. New Brunswick, N.J.: Transaction.

Project Implicit. 2008. "General Information." www.projectimplicit.net/generalinfo/php.

Provine, Doris Marie. 2007. *Unequal under Law: Race in the War on Drugs.* Chicago: University of Chicago Press.

Rachlinski, Jeffrey J., Sheri Lynn Johnson, Andrew J. Wistrich, and Chris Guthrie. 2009. "Does Unconscious Racial Bias Affect Trial Judges?" *Notre Dame Law Review* 84(3):1195–246.

Raphael, Steven, Harry Holzer, and Michael Stoll. 2006. "How Do Crime and Incarceration Affect the Employment Prospects of Less Educated Black Men?" In *Black Males Left Behind*, edited by Ronald Mincy. Washington, D.C.: The Urban Institute.

Reeves, Thomas C. 1982. *The Life and Times of Joe McCarthy: A Biography.* New York: Stein and Day.

Reeves, Jimmie L., and Richard Campbell. 1994. *Cracked Coverage: Television News, the Antic-cocaine Crusade, and the Reagan Legacy.* Durham, N.C.: Duke University Press.

Reiss, Albert J., Jr., and Jeffrey Roth, eds. 1993. *Understanding and Preventing Violence.* Washington, D.C.: National Academy Press.

Reuter, Peter, Robert MacCoun, and Peter Murphy. 1990. *Money from Crime: A Study of the Economics of Drug Dealing in Washington, D.C.* Santa Monica, Calif.: RAND.

Roberts, Julian V., Loretta J. Stalans, David Indermaur, and Mike Hough. 2003. *Penal Populism and Public Opinion.* New York: Oxford University Press.

Roberts, Julian, and Andrew von Hirsch, eds. 2010. *Previous Convictions at Sentencing: Theoretical and Applied Perspectives*. Oxford: Hart.

Roediger, David R. 2008. *How Race Survived U.S. History*. London: Verso.

Rosenmerkel, Sean, Matthew Durose, and Donald Farole. 2009. "Felony Sentences in State Courts, 2006—Statistical Tables." Washington, D.C.: Bureau of Justice Statistics, U.S. Department of Justice. http://bjs.ojp.usdoj.gov/content/pub/pdf/fssc06st.pdf (accessed August 6, 2010).

Rossman, David, Paul Froyd, Glen Pierce, John McDevitt, and William Bowers. 1979. *The Impact of the Mandatory Gun Law in Massachusetts*. Report to the National Institute of Law Enforcement and Criminal Justice. Washington, D.C.: U.S. Government Printing Office.

Rubin, Paul. H. 2009. "Don't Scrap the Death Penalty." *Criminology and Public Policy* 8(4):853–59.

Sabol, William J., Todd D. Minton, and Paige M. Harrison. 2007. "Prison and Jail Inmates at Midyear 2006." Washington, D.C.: Bureau of Justice Statistics, U.S. Department of Justice.

Sabol, William J., Heather C. West, and Matthew Cooper. 2009. "Prisoners in 2008" (revised April 1, 2010). Washington, D.C.: Bureau of Justice Statistics, U.S. Department of Justice.

Schieffer, Bob, and Gary Paul Gates. 1989. *The Acting President*. New York: Dutton.

Schiraldi, Vincent, and Tara-Jen Ambrosio. 1997. "Striking Out: The Crime Control Impact of 'Three-Strikes' Laws." San Francisco: Justice Policy Institute.

Schlesinger, James R, Harold Brown, Tillie K. Fowler, Charles A. Horner, and James A. Blackwell. 2004. "Final Report of the Independent Panel to Review DoD Detention Operations." Washington, D.C.: Department of Defense.

Shane, Scott, David Johnston, and James Risen. 2007. "Secret U.S. Endorsement of Severe Interrogations." *New York Times*, October 4, A1.

Shane-Dubow, Sandra, Alice P. Brown, and Erik P. Olsen. 1985. *Sentencing Reform in the United States: History, Content and Effect*. Washington D.C.: U.S. Government Printing Office.

Shelby, Tommie. 2008. "Commentary." In Glenn Loury, with Pamela S. Karlan, Tommie Shelby, and Loïc Wacquant, *Race, Incarceration, and American Values*. Cambridge, Mass.: MIT Press.

Shepherd, Joanna M. 2002. "Fear of the First Strike: The Full Deterrent Effect of California's Two- and Three-Strikes Legislation." *Journal of Legal Studies* 31:159–201.

Singer, Richard. 1979. *Just Deserts: Sentencing Based on Equality and Desert*. Lexington, Mass.: Ballinger.

Smith, Michael E., and Walter Dickey. 1999. *Reforming Sentencing and Corrections for Just Punishment and Public Safety.* Washington, D.C.: National Institute of Justice, U.S. Department of Justice.

Snell, Tracy L. 2009. *Capital Punishment, 2008—Statistical Tables.* Washington, D.C.: Bureau of Justice Statistics, U.S. Department of Justice. http://bjs.ojp. usdoj.gov/index.cfm?ty=pbdetail&iid=1757 (accessed August 6, 2010).

Snyder, Howard, and Melissa Sicklund. 2006. *Juvenile Offenders and Victims: 2006 National Reports.* Washington, D.C.: Office of Juvenile Justice and Delinquency Prevention, U.S. Department of Justice.

Snyder, Richard. T. 2001. *The Protestant Ethic and the Spirit of Punishment.* Grand Rapids, Mich.: Eerdmans.

Spohn, Cassia. 2000. "Thirty Years of Sentencing Reform: The Quest for a Racially Neutral Sentencing Process." In *Criminal Justice 2000*, vol. 3, edited by National Institute of Justice. Washington, D.C.: National Institute of Justice, U.S. Department of Justice.

——— . 2002. *How Do Judges Decide? The Search for Fairness and Justice in Punishment.* Thousand Oaks, Calif.: Sage.

——— . Forthcoming. "Race, Ethnicity, and Criminal Justice." In *The Oxford Handbook of Crime and Criminal Justice,* edited by Michael Tonry. New York: Oxford University Press.

Stolberg, Sheryl Gay. 2007. "Bush Defends Interrogations, Saying Methods Aren't Torture." *New York Times,* October 6, A1.

Stolzenberg, Lisa, and Stewart J. D'Alessio. 1997. "'Three Strikes and You're Out': The Impact of California's New Mandatory Sentencing Law on Serious Crime Rates." *Crime and Delinquency* 43(4):457–69.

Stout, David. 2007. "Harry Dent, an Architect of Nixon 'Southern Strategy,' Dies at 77." *New York Times,* October 2, B7.

Stutman, Robert. 2008. "Interview with Robert Stutman." Public Broadcasting Service website for the *Frontline* show "Drug Wars." www.pbs.org/wgbh/ pages/frontline/shows/drugs/interviews/stutman.html (accessed December 8, 2008).

Thernstrom, Stephan, and Abigail Thernstrom. 1997. *America in Black and White: One Nation, Indivisible.* New York: Simon and Schuster.

Tonry, Michael. 1995. *Malign Neglect: Race, Crime, and Punishment in America.* New York: Oxford University Press.

——— . 1996. *Sentencing Matters.* New York: Oxford University Press.

——— . 2004. *Thinking about Crime: Sense and Sensibility in American Penal Culture.* New York: Oxford University Press.

————. 2005. "Obsolescence and Immanence in Penal Theory and Policy." *Columbia Law Review* 105:1233–75.

————. 2007. "Determinants of Penal Policies." In *Crime, Punishment, and Politics in Comparative Perspective*, edited by Michael Tonry. Vol. 36 of *Crime and Justice: A Review of Research*, edited by Michael Tonry. Chicago: University of Chicago Press.

————. 2008a. "Crime and Human Rights: How Political Paranoia, Religious Fundamentalism, and Constitutional Obsolescence Combined to Devastate Black America." ASC 2007 Presidential Address. *Criminology* 46:1–33.

————. 2008b. "Learning from the Limitations of Deterrence Research." In *Crime and Justice: A Review of Research*, vol. 37, edited by Michael Tonry. Chicago: University of Chicago Press.

————. 2009. "The Mostly Unintended Effects of Mandatory Penalties: Two Centuries of Consistent Findings." In *Crime and Justice: A Review of Research*, vol. 38, edited by Michael Tonry. Chicago: University of Chicago Press.

————. 2010. "The Questionable Relevance of Previous Convictions to Punishments for Later Crimes." In *Previous Convictions at Sentencing: Theoretical and Applied Perspectives*, edited by Julian Roberts and Andrew von Hirsch. Oxford: Hart.

Tonry, Michael, and Anthony N. Doob, eds. 2004. *Youth Crime and Youth Justice: Comparative and Cross-national Perspectives*. Vol. 36 of *Crime and Justice: A Review of Research*, edited by Michael Tonry. Chicago: University of Chicago Press.

Tonry, Michael, and Matthew Melewski. 2008. "The Malign Effects of Drug and Crime Control Policies on Black Americans." In *Crime and Justice: A Review of Research*, vol. 37, edited by Michael Tonry. Chicago: University of Chicago Press.

Törnudd, Patrik. 1993. *Fifteen Years of Declining Prisoner Rates*. Research Communication no. 8. Helsinki: National Research Institute of Legal Policy.

Tyler, Tom. 2006. *Why People Obey the Law*. Princeton: Princeton University Press.

Uggen, Christopher, Jeff Manza, and Melissa Thomson. 2006. "Citizenship, Democracy, and the Civic Reintegration of Criminal Offenders." Annals of the American Academy of Political and Social Science 605(1):281–310.

Unnever, James D. 2008. "Two Worlds Far Apart: Black-White Differences in Beliefs about Why African-American Men Are Disproportionately Imprisoned." *Criminology* 46(2):511–38.

Unnever, James D., Francis T. Cullen, and Brandon K. Applegate. 2005. "Turning the Other Cheek: Reassessing the Impact of Religion on Punitive Ideology." *Justice Quarterly* 22:304–39.

Unnever, James, Francis T. Cullen, and James D. Jones. 2008. "Public Support for Attacking the 'Root Causes' of Crime: The Impact of Egalitarian and Racial Beliefs." *Sociological Focus* 41(1):1–33.

Unnever, James D., Francis T. Cullen, and Cheryl N. Lero Jonson. 2008. "Race, Racism, and Support for Capital Punishment." In *Crime and Justice: A Review of Research*, vol. 37, edited by Michael Tonry. Chicago: University of Chicago Press.

U.S. Department of Commerce. 2002. *Statistical Abstract of the United States: 2003*. Washington, D.C.: U.S. Government Printing Office.

———. 2006. *Statistical Abstract of the United States: 2007*. Washington, D.C.: U.S. Government Printing Office.

———. 2007. *Statistical Abstract of the United States: 2008*. Washington, D.C.: U.S. Government Printing Office.

———. 2010. *Statistical Abstract of the United States: 2010*. Washington, D.C.: Bernan Press.

U.S. Sentencing Commission. 1995. *1995 Special Report to the Congress: Cocaine and Federal Sentencing Policy*. Washington, D.C.: U.S. Sentencing Commission.

———. 2007. *Cocaine and Federal Sentencing Policy*. Washington, D.C.: U.S. Sentencing Commission.

———. 2009. *2008 Sourcebook of Federal Sentencing Statistics*. Washington, D.C.: U.S. Sentencing Commission.

van Zyl Smit, Dirk. 2002. *Taking Life Imprisonment Seriously in National and International Law*. The Hague: Kluwer Law International.

von Hirsch, Andrew, Anthony E. Bottoms, Elizabeth Burney, and Per-Olof H. Wikström. 1999. *Criminal Deterrence and Sentence Severity: An Analysis of Recent Research*. Oxford: Hart.

Wacquant, Loïc. 2002a. "From Slavery to Mass Incarceration." *New Left Review* 13 (Jan.–Feb.): 41–60.

———. 2002b. "Deadly Symbiosis: Rethinking Race and Imprisonment in Twenty-first-century America." *Boston Review* 27 (April/May): 41–60.

———. 2008. "Commentary." In Glenn Loury, with Pamela S. Karlan, Tommie Shelby, and Loïc Wacquant, *Race, Incarceration, and American Values*. Cambridge, Mass.: MIT Press.

Wald, Kenneth D., and Allison Calhoun-Brown. 2007. *Religion and Politics in the United States*. 5th ed. Lanham, Md.: Rowman and Littlefield.

Walker, Samuel, Cassia Spohn, and Miriam DeLone. 2006. *The Color of Justice: Race, Ethnicity, and Crime in America.* 4th ed. Belmont, Calif.: Wadsworth.

Walmsley, Roy. 2007. *World Prison Population List.* 7th ed. London: International Centre for Prison Studies.

Weaver, Vesla Mae. 2007. "Frontlash: Race and the Development of Punitive Crime Policy." *Studies in American Political Development* 21 (fall): 230–65.

Webster, Cheryl, and Anthony Doob. 2007. "Punitive Trends and Stable Imprisonment Rates in Canada." In *Crime and Justice: A Review of Research*, vol. 36, edited by Michael Tonry. Chicago: University of Chicago Press.

Western, Bruce. 2006. *Punishment and Inequality in America.* New York: Russell Sage Foundation.

Whitebread, Charles H., II, and Richard J. Bonnie. 1974. *A Marihuana Conviction: The History of Marihuana Prohibition in the United States.* Charlottesville: University Press of Virginia.

Whitford, Andrew B., and Jeff Yates. 2009. *Presidential Rhetoric and the Public Agenda: Constructing the War on Drugs.* Baltimore: Johns Hopkins University Press.

Whitman, James Q. 2003. *Harsh Justice: Criminal Punishment and the Widening Divide between America and Europe.* New York: Oxford University Press.

Wickham, Dewayne. 2008. "Bill Clinton Admits 'Regret' on Crack Cocaine Sentencing." *USA Today*, March 4.

Wilson, James Q. 1990. "Drugs and Crime." In *Drugs and Crime*, edited by Michael Tonry and James Q. Wilson. Vol. 13 of *Crime and Justice: A Review of Research*, edited by Michael Tonry and Norval Morris. Chicago: University of Chicago Press.

Wilson, William Julius. 1978. *The Declining Significance of Race: Blacks and American Institutions.* Chicago: University of Chicago Press.

——— . 1987. *The Truly Disadvantaged: The Inner City, the Underclass, and Public Policy.* Chicago: University of Chicago Press.

Wolfe, Tom. 1987. *The Bonfire of the Vanities.* New York: Bantam.

Wood, Gordon S. 1969. *The Creation of the American Republic: 1776–1787.* Chapel Hill: University of North Carolina Press.

Woodberry, Robert D., and Christian S. Smith. 1998. "Fundamentalism et al.: Conservative Protestants in America." *Annual Review of Sociology* 24:25–56.

Yankelovich, Daniel. 1991. *Coming to Public Judgment: Making Democracy Work in a Complex World.* Syracuse, N.Y.: Syracuse University Press.

Zimring, Franklin E., Gordon Hawkins, and Sam Kamin. 2001. *Punishment and Democracy: Three Strikes and You're Out in California.* New York: Oxford University Press.

INDEX